D1525505

The Desiring Modes of Being Black

Literature and Critical Theory

Jean-Paul Rocchi

ROWMAN & LITTLEFIELD
INTERNATIONAL
London • New York

Published by Rowman & Littlefield International, Ltd.
Unit A, Whitacre Mews, 26-34 Stannary Street, London SE11 4AB
www.rowmaninternational.com

Rowman & Littlefield International, Ltd., is an affiliate of
Rowman & Littlefield
4501 Forbes Boulevard, Suite 200, Lanham, Maryland 20706, USA
With additional offices in Boulder, New York, Toronto (Canada), and London (UK)
www.rowman.com

British Library Cataloguing in Publication Information
A catalogue record for this book is available from the British Library

ISBN: HB 978-1-78348-398-3
ISBN: PB 978-1-78348-399-0

Library of Congress Cataloging-in-Publication Data Available

Names: Rocchi, Jean-Paul, author.
Title: The desiring modes of being Black : literature and critical theory / Jean-Paul Rocchi.
Description: Lanham, Md. : Rowman & Littlefield International, 2018. | Series: Global critical Caribbean thought | Includes bibliographical references and index.
Identifiers: LCCN 2018008874 (print) | ISBN 9781783484003 (electronic) | ISBN 9781783483983 (cloth) | ISBN 9781783483990 (paper)
Subjects: LCSH: American literature--African American authors--History and criticism--Theory, etc. | Identity (Philosophical concept) in literature. | African Americans--Intellectual life. | Literature and society--United States--History.
Classification: LCC PS153.N5 (ebook) | LCC PS153.N5 R585 2018(print) | DDC 810.9/896073--dc23
LC record available at https://lccn.loc.gov/2018008874

The Desiring Modes of Being Black

Global Critical Caribbean Thought

Series Editors

Lewis R. Gordon, Professor of Philosophy, UCONN-Storrs, and Honorary Professor, Rhodes University, South Africa

Jane Anna Gordon, Associate Professor of Political Science, UCONN-Storrs

Nelson Maldonado-Torres, Associate Professor of Latino and Caribbean Studies, Rutgers, School of Arts and Sciences

This series, published in partnership with the Caribbean Philosophical Association, turns the lens on the unfolding nature and potential future shape of the globe by taking concepts and ideas that while originating out of very specific contexts share features that lend them transnational utility. Works in the series engage with figures including Frantz Fanon, CLR James, Paulo Freire, Aime Cesaire, Edouard Glissant and Walter Rodney, and concepts such as coloniality, creolization, decoloniality, double consciousness and la facultdad.

Titles in the Series

"I want to be an honest man and a good writer."
—James Baldwin, "Autobiographical Notes" (1952),
Notes of A Native Son (1955)

Contents

Foreword

The Caribbean Philosophical Association's book series Global Critical Caribbean Thought here offers a volume that reaches from the Caribbean and Europe through ideas from Frantz Fanon to alienated Europe and West Asia through those from Sigmund Freud to North America through others from W. E. B. Du Bois and James Baldwin back to Africa in a symbiosis of themes in the writings of Rozena Maart. Many others, including Paget Henry and I, accompany the author, Jean-Paul Rocchi, on this journey, where text as object meets existential lived-reality in black.

A philosophy of freedom, philosophy of existence is also a meditation on desire. Black existentialism, then, is also an expression of black desire. For Rocchi, it is, as the title of this book attests, among the desiring modes of being black.

The text—indeed, *every text*—calls forth. Seduced, "I" identify. In identifying, "I" exemplify identification. The whole act, flowing with ambiguity and ambivalence, brings "me," in which also lurks "us," back to the self. The desired desire, through moments of desiring, reaches out in a boomerang effect of arriving, at times snapping, back. Such is the story of the Euromodern self, which, as Bartolomé de las Casas, Enrique Dussel, and so many from the Global South have argued, is a conquering self, the one who "is" by virtue of what and who "he" conquers.

What, however, is realized by the conquered, the colonized, since the conqueror couldn't have emerged prior to what "he" produced? "His" link, despite "his" efforts to be without the dominated, is symbiotic. Through "them," "he" *is*.

From the dark among the dominated, there is an identifying utterance: "We are black."

Such a statement from such utterers is a speech act, Rocchi avers, of a desired identity in an act of identification. It is a desiring mode, so to speak. Not all blacks seek or accept this. Some, as so many from Du Bois to Richard Wright to Fanon have argued, remain stratified in the object status of "blacks." This lower-case stasis is locked under the act, the construction, of another's control. There is no "I" or "me." There is only "it," metaphorically sometimes spoken of as "he," "she," or "they." Only spoken of or about, there is no inside from which to reach to the world of existence.

"We are black" offers a challenge. In desiring what, at least from the perspective of double consciousness—to see oneself as seen through the eyes of the negating standpoint—is undesirable, this black brings desire to the undesired through investments of the self. An agent of history is born.

The Euromodern world, after all, produced blacks through a moment of desire and repulsion similar to Mary Shelley's Modern Prometheus, who fled after looking into the eyes of the creature he created. This world, creators of that kind avowed, is legitimate only when creatures of such misdeeds disappear. The blacks, then, find themselves indigenous to a world in which they are rejected. They suffer a loss, for there is no place to which to return in which they were both black and belonged. Where else is there to turn but to the question of becoming a question—where else but the possibility of a future in which black turns to Black? Where else is that but an effort to move from Euromodernity to a world in which Afro-modernity could emerge—in setting afoot a new humanity—without being an imitation of the former?

To create without connection to that which is created is a fantasy of Euromodernity. Colonial subjects, after all, are people thrown into a Manichean world of opposing contraries. Universally separated, interaction becomes an imposed impossibility. Yet, as a repressed term, it haunts its separation. Desired distance intensifies intimacy. Desired non-relations are in colonialism and its racist rationalizations at the price of what relations signify. A human world, marked by interactivity, intersubjectivity, is one in which the self cannot be self-maintained. Its condition of possibility is, in a word, sticky.

As the impulse to wash oneself clean of stickiness, often through resources of licking one's fingers clean, should make apparent, the sugar that clings to the moment of self-emergence is sexual. Sex, after all, is a meeting, a crossing of the Manichaean divide, of the self and the other. Erasing the other while maintaining the self requires a non-other beneath that other. A new, analogical other of self-to-self as self-to-other emerges as a narcissistic fantasy. The production of the racialized non-self, then, is also a sexual phenomenon. It is, to reiterate, sticky.

Rocchi homes in on this sticky intimacy through an intimate prophet of its implication. James Baldwin, offering his body of thought through thought of his body, racially sexualized and sexually racialized, sings the leitmotif of this blue melody. Black desire is to come out, so to speak, from the shadows of repressed terms.

Repressed or, as is now fashionable, dissociated terms are also frustrated ones. They cut. Where the self could only be masculine, this fissure occasions horror. Castration in one form, threats through circumcision in others, each frightening possibility recoils the masculine, imagined virile self into a potential victim.

There are at least two themes that dominate African American literature, the black side of this swan song, which we could at this point call one of the textual hauntings of Euromodernity—identity and liberation: Who or what are we? Can and will we ever be "free"? These are intimate poles, for who we are depends on where we are going and where we are going often depends on who or what we are.

We cannot inaugurate this journey of identity and liberation through avoiding our intimacies, Rocchi declares. His point is simultaneously theoretical and lived. Corsica and Guadeloupe, two homelands for Rocchi outside France, yet simultaneously governed from "within" French "civilization," meet in his flesh, words, and writing.

A living bearer of Corsican and Guadeloupian Creole standing up against imperial English and French, layers of creolization, as Jane Anna Gordon would say, meet in what flows through these pages without closure. Global critical Caribbean thought is, after all, not locked in the Caribbean alone, where in 1492 Euromodernity began. It reaches forth from Amerindian blood and words through those whom empires forced together, through the lash, chains, and currency, from across the globe into what was resisted, denied, and transformed into living culture despite efforts of their erasure.

The Desiring Modes of Being Black is a creature of these worlds without the pathos of imitation. In these pages, there is the offspring of creativity beyond mirrors. There is *possibility* in *modes*. It is properly *critical* in that it speaks to the crisis of thinking under and through such circumstances. A crisis is, as its etymology attests, a decision to be made where the desire is to avoid having to choose.

Choices need not be closed, however. You have opened this book, dear reader. Turn the page. Continue, I ask you, through to its end, which, as my words should by now make evident, will offer possibilities of new beginnings.

—Lewis R. Gordon

Acknowledgments

With the exception of the introduction and chapter 2, the chapters of this book are revised and completed versions of journal articles or book chapters formerly published in French and in English. The introduction is a revised version of "La *dés*-écriture de l'identité: race, sexualité et littérature africaine américaine" to be published in the forthcoming volume *À la recherche d'identités sexuelles* (Éditions Le Manuscrit) edited by Gilbert Elbaz. It was translated by William Hamlett. Chapter 2, "The Making of a Man: A Modernist Etiology of American Masculinities—Trauma, Testimony, Resistance" is a translation by Olivier Borre of "*Faire un homme.* Etiologie moderniste des masculinités américaines: trauma, témoignage, résistance" to be published in the forthcoming issue of *Revue Française d'Etudes Américaines* on black modernism edited by Claudine Raynaud and Frédéric Sylvanise.

Chapter 1, "The Other Bites the Dust: Toward an Epistemology of Identity," was initially published in 2006 under the title "'The Other Bites the Dust.' La mort de l'Autre: vers une épistémologie de l'identité," in *L'Objet identité: épistémologie et transversalité*, edited by Jean-Paul Rocchi, *Cahiers Charles V*, no. 40:9–46. It was translated by Joelle Theubet.

Chapter 3, "Dying Metaphors and Deadly Fantasies: Freud, Baldwin, and the Meta-Psychoanalysis of Race," was initially published in 2006 under the title "Dying Metaphors and Deadly Fantasies—Freud, Baldwin, and Race as Intimacy," in *Historicizing Anti-Semitism*, edited by Lewis R. Gordon, Ramon Grosfoguel, and Eric Mielants, *Human Architecture. Journal of the Sociology of Self-Knowledge* 7, no. 2:159–78. Chapter 3 also includes portions of "Literature and the Meta-Psychoanalysis of Race (After and with Fanon)," published in *Palimpsest: A Journal on Women, Gender, and the Black International* 1, no. 1 (2012): 52–67, which is itself a translation by Joelle Theubet of "Littérature et métapsychanalyse de la race (Après et avec Fanon)," published in *Vers une pensée politique postcoloniale. A partir de Frantz Fanon*, edited by Sonia Dayan-Herzbrun, *Tumultes* 31 (2008): 125–44.

Chapter 4, "Desire as 'E mag e nation': South African Black Consciousness and Post-Identity in Rozena Maart's 'No Rosa, No District Six,'" was initially published in 2006 under the title "'Walls as words as weapons as womb as woooooow'; Fente murale, fente t/sex(u)[elle], fondu identitaire jouir/écrire ou la postidentité dans 'No Rosa, no District Six' de Rozena Maart," in *Images de soi dans les sociétés postcoloniales, Actes du colloque de l'Université des Antilles et de la Guyane*, edited by Patricia Donatien-Yssa, Paris, Éditions Le Manuscrit: 179–215. It was translated by Joelle Theubet and published in 2014 as "Intersecting Identities and Epistemologies in Rozena Maart's 'No Rosa, No District Six,'" in *Postcoloniality-Decoloniality-Black Critique: Joints and Fissures*, edited by Sabine Broeck and Carsten Junker, Frankfurt, Campus Verlag, 369–88.

Chapter 5, "'The Substance of Things Hoped For': Melvin Dixon's *Vanishing Rooms*; or Racism Intimately," was initially published in 2006 under the title "'*The Evidence of Things Not Seen, The Substance of Things Hoped For*'; *Vanishing Rooms* de Melvin Dixon ou le racisme intimement," in *L'Objet identité: épistémologie et transversalité*, edited by Jean-Paul Rocchi, *Cahiers Charles V*, no. 40:291–308. It was translated by Joelle Theubet.

Chapter 6, "Writing as I Lay Dying: AIDS Literature and the H(a)unting of Blackness," was initially published in 2008 under the title "'Writing as I Lay Dying': AIDS Literature and the Death of Identity," in *Genre(s)*, edited by Frédéric Regard, *Études Anglaises* 61, no. 2:350–58.

Chapter 7, "The Word's Image: Self-Portrait as a Conscious Lie," was initially published in *Black Europe: Subjects, Struggles, and Shifting Perceptions*, edited by Jean-Paul Rocchi and Frédéric Sylvanise, *Palimpsest: A Journal on Women, Gender, and the Black International* 4, no. 2 (2015): 225–34.

For their trust, I wish to express my heartfelt thanks and appreciation to the editors of the Global Critical Caribbean Thought series, Lewis R. Gordon, Jane Anna Gordon, and Nelson Maldonado-Torres. I am also grateful for the wonderful work done by the translators Joelle Theubet, William Hamlett, and Olivier Borre and for the commitment of the editorial team at Rowman & Littlefield International, which provided very helpful reviews of the book manuscript and wise pieces of advice for its revision and completion.

I address special thanks to my friends Athéna Efstathiou-Lavabre, Frédérique Lab, Catherine Mazodier, and Claire Sanderson, who have proofread several portions of this book.

Parts of this book have been presented at conferences organized by international academic associations such as those of the Caribbean Philosophical Association (CPA), the Collegium for African American Research (CAAR), *Callaloo*, and the Association Française d'Études Américaines (AFEA), and in many workshops and seminars in different locations including the Université Paris-Sorbonne, the École Normale Supérieure (Ulm), the University of Birmingham (UK), the Université François Rabelais-Tours, the Université des Antilles, the Du Bois Institute at Harvard University, the University of California at Berkeley, Temple University, the University of Virginia, Rutgers University, the University of Connecticut, the University of Kwa-Zulu Natal, the University of Witwatersrand, Oxford University, the Université Paul Valéry-Montpellier 3, the Université de Lille, the Fondation Frantz Fanon, and the Institut des Amériques. My work has greatly benefitted from colleagues' insights on these occasions. But I am especially indebted to my colleagues at the Université Paris-Diderot, the Université Paris-Est Marne-la-Vallée, and the Université Paris-Est for the fruitful exchanges we have had for many years.

For our ongoing critical conversation which in many respects is reflected in this book, special thanks go to Myron M. Beasley, Sabine Broeck, Vincent Broqua, Olivier Brossard, Cécile Coquet-Mokoko, Anne Crémieux, Emmanuelle Delanoë-Brun, William Dow, Sarah Fila-Bakabadio, Arlette Frund, Abigail Lang, Silyane Larcher, Hélène Le Dantec-Lowry, Xavier Lemoine, Guillaume Marche, Monica Michlin, Alexandra Poulain, Claudine Raynaud, Robert Reid-Pharr, Marlon B. Ross, Antje Schuhmann, Frédéric Sylvanise, and Cyril Vettorato, and to Lewis R. Gordon, Rozena Maart, and the doctoral candidates and junior researchers working with me: Carline Blanc, Yannick Blec, Elisa Cecchinato, Georges Faye, Mélanie Grué, Yohann Lucas, Lucile Pouthier, Kate Russell, and Eglantine Zatout.

For the unconditional support they have provided and the inexhaustible source of inspiration they are to me, I thank my family and especially Marie-Jeanne Marne, Ghjuvanteramu Rocchi, François Rocchi, Charlotte Rocchi, Yves Lansou, Gabriel Lansou, and Lisa Lansou.

It is the warmth of friendship, brotherhood, and sisterhood that has given impetus and movement to this book. I thus say thank you to Josette Albertini, Paule-Marie Albertini and Jean-Luc Prelle, Sarah André, Nanou Anselme-Raffalli, Jean-Michel and Laetitia Bariseau, Myron M. Beasley, Julia Bodin, Maria Canonici and Gilles Guerrini, Anne Crémieux and Sophie Vasset, Laura Crocitti, Dominique Cros-Pophillat, Jean-André Delfini, Jean Ducos, Hervé Dufourcq, Athéna Efstathiou-Lavabre and Yoann Lavabre, Daniel Ferreira, Véronique Fivian, Lewis and Jane Gordon, Philippe Gros, Frédérique Lab and Ghislaine Souriac, Annie Laffillé, Silyane Larcher, Xavier Lemoine and Philippe Le, Catherine Liddicott and Roger Woodhouse, David Linx, Kristell Lozac'hmeur and Arnaud Dupont, Rozena Maart and Juan Solis, Catherine Marcangeli and Steve Sheperd, Marie Marchetti, Catherine Mazodier, Monica Michlin, Peggy Pacini and Dominique Lemaire, Capucine Poulain and Ludovic Belchior, Jean-Francois Poli, Claire Sanderson, Antje Schuhmann, Emmanuelle Sisco and Antoine Paoli, Fabrice Sisco, Frédéric

Sylvanise, Michael Walsh, and my fellow singers at the Chœur d'Adultes de Vincennes.

The Desiring Modes of Being Black: Literature and Critical Theory is published with the financial support of the Research Center LISAA (*LIttérature SAvoirs et Arts*) of the Université Paris-Est Marne-la-Vallée.

Introduction

The Desiring Black Subject as Reading Method

WRITING "I" OR THE TRACE OF THE SELF

Some ten years before, having returned to the New Latin Quarter, I was struck, meandering among bookshelves, by the cover photo of Giovanni's Room *(1955). Blond hair, set as if balanced upon the seated body of a naked man, set himself upon an unmade bed. The sheets' folds, in a flustered mess, extended the dip of his spine along the vanishing line, to the right, and out the window of the room. That was all I saw—the folds and hollows of emotion—and, like David, an American exile taking refuge in France and who, at the beginning of the novel, could not see his reflection turn black with the falling night through the window, I needed a second text by Baldwin to see the black show through and to hear, in this blackness, the African American voice. I abandoned Oscar Wilde and left for America. This is how it began.*

What does it mean to mark the founding moment of research? It provides a frame and a direction—an idealization that strives to prove the researcher's quality, the condition that makes the proof possible, the scientificity of its methodology as recognized by his/her peers. It may seem paradoxical that a founding moment of research be autobiographical, that an autobiographical character be found in research where subjectivity has no place. For all this, research that seeks to show that intellectual works on identity are not limited to a boundless quest for the self, and that they also make the error of postulating a definition of difference, can hardly exclude the subjectivity of the subject and its writing, beginning with his/her very own.

The paradox is not paradoxical if one excludes—forgets, perhaps—that every founding moment is chosen and exists among others.

1

It is therefore knowingly that I hold other founding biographical moments out of frame.

It is no longer out of ignorance—an ignorance that would determine the choice—that I place Baldwin, and, after him, Dixon, Hemphill, or Saint, before my own lived experience, their homosexuality before the race that they un-wrote, but because this inversion of before and after reinvents identity as a space to write.

This inaugural moment has worth in that it is immediate and frames, in that it is representation. The conscious choice that underlies representation does not efface what is outside of its frame, which, in return, could not possibly be wholly explained. All it does is open a space, to make a place for reinvention and for research.

This text was supposed to appear at the beginning of the summary of my Habilitation thesis, defended in November 2007 at Paris-Diderot University. A useless addition, I deleted it. But I retained its essence in a theorization that better complied with the context. Even if self-citation borders on self-satisfaction, it is a lesser evil compared to that of being unheard and misunderstood. I cite myself, therefore: "When put into perspective, the autobiographical dimension is not to be excluded. It does not absorb the distance between the subject and its object. It appears in the bond that links the lack that structures the two: to write 'I' produces a place for the object. The lack coming to lack, desire becomes race, and, instead of being conceived of as desire, [race] generates crisis and chaos. This is the fundamental philosophical contribution of black consciousness to knowledge that, in engulfing its 'I,' its desire, its affectivity, rises over an object that has become idealized, the fantasy of its own total rationalization, without lack, and, with it, the excluded possibility of its progress: that it can fail. This is the major contribution of gay, lesbian, and queer studies. It is the force of literature and our position."[1]

There is great danger in mixing up genres, the text, and its study. This danger renders the critic's empathy for the literary text suspicious, liable to go beyond rationality through sentiment and emotion or beyond identity through identification. To take oneself for the writer whom one seeks to understand. This narcissism would abolish critical distance, as a search for the Self and not for science, for the particular and not the universal: the researcher is called to dissipate such suspicions, and particularly when his/her identity is manifestly shared with his/her object of study. This is often the case for studies of blacks on blacks, women on women, or LGBTQ people on LGBTQ people. Such studies must demonstrate that they are not undertaken for the wrong reason. The wrong reason is their self-interest, the right reason would be their interest, in itself.

Accordingly, it would be appropriate in all circumstances to eliminate one's own traces while talking about another's text so that identification does not become identity, so that empathy is not confused with disguised narcissism, that love of Self that seems like lovelessness toward others, haunting the so-called minority literatures, too outspoken, and contemporary autofiction, too self-centered.

Yet evacuating the Self while talking about the text of an other amounts to signing it in his/her place. Just as positivist science emptied the subject and its philosophy, critical discourse speaks the text from a non-place, inhabited only by non-subjectivity, without body or consciousness. As if writing and saying "I" were not the reflexive trace of the Self that is already no longer *my*self. As if writing "I am homosexual" signed the epistemological catastrophe, the failure of rationality, irrelevance, supplement, surplus, as true as it may be that lesbian, gay, and queer studies could easily go without an umpteenth coming-out, the literature of the same name would very well take another one, in the same way that, in the past, African American feminist literature was able to compensate for historiography.

The "I," or the trace of the self, is of interest here less for its permanence than for what is at play in its disappearance: the feint by which one could escape from reality and oneself. To repudiate the subjectivity of the critical subject, his/her history, his/her affects, to not consider from where, he/she speaks, to whom he/she is speaking and to what end, amounts to depoliticizing the situation of enunciation, nullifying the possibility for the speaker to position him-/herself and to define his/her space. It is to make of positioning a posture and a pretense. And, as such, useless.

This feint proceeds from the bad faith that also leads to the idealization of critical discourse in and of itself—narcissistic as well—to intellectual colonization, to the reification of the subjects one observes and analyzes, to the perversion by which the literary text becomes the imagined reflection of a reality from which we might escape. It is also this transcendence that kills the other in the text without having to answer to it, since it sets the rules.

For better or worse, the reasoning is the same: it postulates that identification and identity are differentiated *a priori*. In this disjunction the fascination for literature that exerts force upon critical discourse is born: putting all variation in identity in tension, in masks, in subjectivities that the reader can project, carry, invent for him-/herself. This freedom that criticism approaches in order to comprehend, it strives to renounce so as to not remain within the fiction and to be able to return to critical reason. Renunciation and loss are the condition of its identity. It emerges through distance, a created and regulated distance between free and plural identification and identity—consolidated and fixed.

The basis of my work is to observe how literature lends movement to identity and to listen to its question: What do our identifications with the text say about our identities? Why does literature make it possible to think of identity as fiction, even if, outside the relationship to the text, identity presents itself as the perfect example of the subject's truth?

If identity is the truth of the subject to the point of wedding its subjectivity and commanding his/her identifications, it is because modernity conceives of the subject as interiority, a circumscribed space that cannot allow itself to overflow.

There are two phenomena that participate in this partition of space into interiority and exteriority: race and sex. They maintain an analogous relationship. The science of the nineteenth century saw a comparable menace to civilization in race mixing and in homosexuality. Their relationship is also metaphorical: the castration of the black American equates a feminization— like, in the anti-Semitic Europe of the beginning of the twentieth century, the circumcision of the Jew. But the analogous and metaphorical relation between race and sex is an optical illusion because it postulates a difference while it is actually race and sex, together, that create it. If there is a relation between a term and its analogous or metaphorical double, it is not because there is difference between them, but because there is space for it to be there. The difference between what is interior and exterior, between what is the Self and the Other. This is the space of modern subjectivity, and it is race and sex that, together, form its boundaries.

African American literature represents a chance to explore this space, its *un*-writing: that of identity, that of the theories of the subject and, particularly, Freudian psychoanalysis, of which the construction of gender and sexualities contains the memory of race. It is a very American story. One of space. Between black identity and American identification, between race and sex, between consciousness and desire. Seen as an itinerary of the century, this space can be divided into three movements: exclusion, inclusion, and disappearance.

These words summon three African American scenes. W. E. B. Du Bois begins *The Souls of Black Folk*, published in 1903, with a scene of exclusion borrowed from his own childhood. In the hills of New England, a young girl his age refuses to take his visiting card because he is black. The recollection closes on the image of prison with walls like shadows, under the azure sky, out of reach for the prisoner, which confines him from his promised, yet withheld, liberty. The image is exemplary of the aesthetic of the African American perspective. It does not content itself with hollowing out race, the visible phenomenon of skin color, the sense and the value given to it, but it also makes visible what one does not want to see, so that it can be contemplated in all its horror. From this childhood scene, Du Bois puts forward his spatial algebra of racism: the second-zone citizen, inside a space of proclaimed freedom and equality, contradicts it. Once expelled, he no longer contradicts it. He reinforces it. From his fringe, he gives space its border.

Besides being an important part of a lived experience and a feeling that founds his consciousness, as they would found those of Baldwin and Fanon, racism, for Du Bois, is a problem. It is to be the problem, to absorb it, to incarnate it to the point of engulfing the space that allows it to be posed. Text and writing re-establish this space that racist reality refuses. Through his concept of double consciousness, Du Bois makes of the black an American who must be recognized, without whom the very historical and political space of Americanness becomes an aberration. This double consciousness puts pressure on the space of Americanness without fundamentally calling it into question. Borrowing from Anglo-Saxon white masculinity and marked by puritanism, black identity, according to Du Bois, integrates emotion only insofar as it is rationalized, framed, and mastered—a divorce whose political and aesthetic effects would be felt throughout the century in the Harlem Renaissance, in the emergence of feminine voices, in the writings of desire of the extreme contemporary, which reject the fracture between consciousness and desire. The divorce is overcome with James Baldwin. A half-century later, the walls of Du Bois's prison are those, in flames, of the American house: Baldwin asks, who would want to be integrated with it? The azure obscures the castrated bodies of blacks that burn and haunt the erotic dreams of their executioners. With Baldwin, racism is no longer a problem that rationality can resolve. It is of the order of fantasy and of puritanical, masochistic pleasure, sadistic pleasure erected into a system. Not a perversion or an inversion of the law like Sade's systemic transgression of constraints, but law and civilization themselves—a permanent nightmare for a reality. Transcribed, it becomes a prefiguration of Toni Morrison, a text that blurs because it goes beyond its own space. It is beautiful in its sustained effort to call on love to approach hate, in its attempt to safeguard the idea of a good sovereign while at the same time eroding all illusion about it.

Baldwin does not seek to find recognition for the black in the American space but to demonstrate that white Americanness is a phantasmatic idealization that the black, by racist and sexual violence, is forced to support. It is in substituting desire for the division of space, in racism and in segregation, that he sees a way out of the nightmare. By reconciling consciousness and desire in an ethic of inclusion, Baldwin attempts to perfect the double consciousness of Du Bois, marked by failure because black and white, as they are not on the same level, could not possibly become respective and relative Others for one another. Desire, where race and sex take shape, where reason and emotion contain themselves mutually, is the common and unifying space where Baldwin intends to return them to in the end. This desire is eminently political because from it, the subject determines space and identity, and not the inverse, as in Du Bois.

Then the space runs out, atrophies, like a sick body that empties itself, and makes identity look like a fetish. AIDS closes the century on a space born with double consciousness, transformed by desiring consciousness and that, with dying consciousness, disappears. This is the unheard-of situation in which sickness and death struck an entire generation of writers and artists at the beginning of their forties, in which their quality as witnesses was linked precisely to the fact that they did not have the time to be, in which identity reached its catastrophe, its nudity, the duration, but also a duration that does not last, that would not last, because it was outside time, like the subject that dies is outside a humanity, which he/she haunts without it seeing or remembering him/her. It is an apocalypse with neither mystery nor transcendence. By the inevitable character that it is accorded and the indifference it inspires, this eclipse of humanity recalls others and inscribes it in a history of the damned of the earth and of perverted peoples, the subjugated, the colonized, the gassed, the raped. Beyond territorial quarrels and memorial competitions, this history opens itself to the possibility of solidarities, the necessary utopia that transforms difference into dissidence and refounds the humanistic project in plurality. It also raises the essential question of the nature of the link to the Other, what ties, bonds, strangles, and then is cut: Why are certain people unworthy to live and unworthy to be remembered?

Literature translates this question into its own language: How to represent that which disappears, that which is disappearing, and along with it, he/she who writes it? Whether the authors are French or American, the writings of AIDS confront the origin and the end of the central metaphor of effacement, which linguistically reproduces the reoccurrence of the future perfect; a permanent tension between two terms, two poles, which without being an in-between space, since the space disappears, impedes the ability to think about duality, identity, and difference. Even the identity of such texts suffers from this. They join literary genres without truly becoming a literature of testimony, neither fiction, nor truly poetry. It is writing searching for its place. Writing, as Duras says in a contemporary text of the same name (1993), about the death of a young English pilot.

If writing, panic-stricken, searches for its place, identity seems to intervene to find it. Death is its compost, negative space, the non-place that makes it possible as long as writing refuses to give in to it and resists it until the end. As resistance to death, it is often figured in France by the writer, the quintessence of French identity. In *L'Accompagnement* (1994) by René de Ceccatty, the dying writer is surrounded by his friends, other writers; his books are at his bedside and the book that Ceccatty wrote will continue to accompany him. American writings on AIDS also have their cultural specificity. They contain accents of confession, the traces of the regeneration of innocence, and above all the resurgence of the racist metaphors of the black. They are summoned from a history of race and sex in which fear of race mixing and the appeal of guilty desire are inscribed upon peoples' faces. It is this history that analogously connects race mixing and contamination by HIV. It is this history that recalls the image of the black to make him die in the place of the white voice. *Borrowed Time: An AIDS Memoir* (1988a) by Paul Monette is inhabited by such a sacrifice where identity presents its ultimate resistance: kill the black to stay white.

For African American literature, AIDS comes to reflect upon its own negation. Through its aesthetic of perspective, African American literature and its particular form of realism question less the perception of reality than its modes of receptivity and the projection of a fantasy that doubles and supplants it. In this perspective, what is at stake is not only the representation of that which disappears but also what space, as it disappears, reveals about itself: that it never existed. There is no refuge. How to face this ultimate failure: literature, this space that black consciousness gave itself to remedy its lack in the world, appears to be an optical illusion. What remains?

The poetry and prose of Essex Hemphill and Assotto Saint resonate with these questions. The fiction of Melvin Dixon as well, and particularly his novel *Vanishing Rooms* (1991), constructs itself around the collapse of the last refuge, love shared like exchanging blows, and that, for a moment, reunited the black Jesse and the white Metro, raped and killed under the insults, those he whispered in the moment of ecstasy so that Jesse would hit him, so that he could get pleasure out of him. The novel is built and collapses on this refuge, which closes in upon itself. It is reflected, outside the text, in the AIDS to which the author succumbs while writing. On the inside, it is invisible because the narrated story is anterior to its discovery. But he passes on his power of contamination to the novel in which all the voices end up sounding alike.

In this way, all the spaces close. It is the space of desire, the algebra of the relationship, that disappears. It is the hole in black consciousness, the parable without lesson of the history of a relationship: to negotiate for Du Bois, to imagine for Baldwin, and impossible for Dixon. This impossibility stirs up homosexual solitude as well. This solitude is not the disenchantment of the century, the need for consolation that Stig Dagerman does not succeed in fulfilling and that pushes him to invalidate all the reasons to live in the methodic justification of his upcoming suicide (1952/1981). It is a more terrible solitude, without melancholy, because it suggests that there was nothing to lose in the first place. It is devastating like an alienation, always conscious like a combat. It brings Dixon closer, beyond racial identity, to another American author of the same generation, the photographer David Wojnarowicz. Taken together, their solitude leads them to no longer conceive of identity in terms of space and relationships but as a superior value drawn from their lived experience, solitude, raised higher through death. Caring companionship is the value by which identity can remain without resisting death or abdicating life.

This is a representation of my work on identity. The opening text is a metaphor, and its mirror-image in miniature, whose literary style, with psychoanalytical and auto-ethnographic overtones, blossoms in the concluding chapter of this book, "The Word's Image: Self-Portrait as a Conscious Lie," in which I theorize the link between my artistic production as a collagist and my academic research. In this analytical narrative I finally comment upon several collages hanging on the walls of my studio flat in Paris that I observe in turn and that I weave into the transatlantic journey spanning the twentieth century that led my family from Guadeloupe to Cameroon and to France and Corsica. Somehow, both texts—the opening metaphorization meant to vanish but returning eventually and chapter 7 with collages acquiring form and color only through imagination—stand together for the intellectual and affective journey *The Desiring Modes of Being Black: Literature and Critical Theory* intends to encapsulate in content and composition. Circular in its structure, this collection refrains from falling prey to a teleological perspective, a petrifying threat looming over any work on identity but rather favors the upsurge of desire and of knowledge-as-lack within the analysis and the rationalization it stems from.

A critique of theory through literature that celebrates the diversity of black being, this book explores how literature may contribute to unearth theoretical blind spots or shortcomings while reasserting the legitimacy of emotional turbulence in the controlled realm of reason that rationality claims to establish. This approach operates a critical shift by notably examining psychoanalytical texts from the literary viewpoint of black desiring subjectivities and experiences, starting with mine as the opening text, while chapter 7 can then be read as a *mise-en-scène*, unwinding the initial "writing 'I' or the trace of the Self" while revealing the "behind-the-scene" of the other chapters. The speaking "I" here is first and foremost that of the reader around whom the book's main outlook revolves and, more particularly, his/her ability to cope with his/her identifications to the text, thus giving central stage to textuality itself. Meanwhile, *The Desiring Modes of Being Black* also aims at paving the way for a black-and-queer-inspired psychoanalysis—which in the present-day academic landscape has the favor of neither black theorists nor queer critics. In this combination of psychoanalysis and the politics of literary interpretation of black texts, and while confronting twentieth-century political and ideological discourses on identity, what is at stake is determining how contemporary African American and black literature and queer texts come to defy and possibly challenge the racial and sexual postulates of subjectivity theories such as psychoanalysis and, in a broader sense, any disciplinary perspective or theoretical system that claims to define race, gender, and sexualities. More than a simple thread, this intends to be a strong positioning unifying the chapters with the studied texts and topics. Beyond particular focuses they also share common themes such as traumatic experiences; the tension between the fantasy and a racialized, sexualized, and gendered social reality; the confrontation between individual memory and the writing of collective history; the cultivation of a sense of Self, through transference and introjection in the midst of a community; the body as a space of intimacy subject to pathogenic physical and psychological violence; and, in response to the overwhelming presence of death, the desiring subjective modes of writing. More precisely, the reifying dynamics of racial metaphors and their sexualization are looked upon in chapter 3 ("Dying Metaphors and Deadly Fantasies: Freud, Baldwin, and the Meta-Psychoanalysis of Race") and in chapter 5 ("'The Substance of Things Hoped For': Melvin Dixon's *Vanishing Rooms*; or Racism Intimately") but also in chapter 6 ("Writing as I Lay Dying: AIDS Literature and the H(a)unting of Blackness"). Intimacy as a place of permanent transformation through desire and playing on the spatiotemporal categorization of structures of signification, epistemological frameworks, and community allegiances is an issue running through chapter 5, chapter 4 ("Desire as 'E mag e nation': South African Black Consciousness and Post-Identity in Rozena Maart's 'No Rosa, No District Six'"), and chapter 7. Both chapter 2 ("The Making of a Man: A Modernist Etiology of American Masculinities—Trauma, Testimony, Resistance") and chapter 4 explore gendered identity formation in racialized contexts from the child's viewpoint. What these correspondences and echoes draw is the general pattern of a research work whose publication spans a twelve-year period. It is best described by the figure of the Moebius strip, which also defies a strict chronological order. The strip of identity would be made of, on one side, literature, and on the other, theories of subjectivity and more specifically, psychoanalysis. On the edges that join and separate both sides there would be the relationship between literature and theory further analyzed in chapter 1 ("The Other Bites the Dust: Toward an Epistemology of Identity") and chapter 3: how cultural identities, be they racial, gender-related, and/or sexual, are being theorized and how literature—itself a space where these theorizations are applied—can in turn be used to challenge and dismantle these constructs.

Obviously, the point of this anthology is therefore not to propose a definite and final answer to the questions of desire and being in black literary and theoretical texts, but rather through the selection, re-writing, and re-composition of essays—most of which were initially published in French and kept their original critical apparatus—to present the picture of a reflection in progress. A progress with circumvolutions but *progressing still*.

As I say about my students' work, mine is a *work in progress*. It is also the result of an accompaniment of which Baldwin marked the start and whose intellectual genealogy I would like now to retrace.

BALDWIN'S UN-WRITING OF IDENTITY AND
THE GENEALOGY OF THE METHOD

This research is inscribed in a double perspective. It concerns African American literature of the twentieth century. In this sense, it is nano-disciplinary and diachronic. But its particular object being identity and its racial, sexual, and gendered dimensions, it is also transversal and synchronistic. This work illustrates the attempt to move beyond the artificial divide between the consolidation of a field and an inter-/transdisciplinarity often seen as a distortion of the object and the discipline. The inherent complexity of the object identity imposed, over the course of research, the necessity of turning to the crossing of perspectives that do not belong to the same fields of knowledge *a priori*. As the opening chapter, "The Other Bites the Dust: Toward an Epistemology of Identity," demonstrates while actualizing the passage from interdisciplinarity to transdisciplinarity,[2] the object identity is labile to the point that it dislocates at their joints the theoretical frames in which one insets it. As such, textuality, theories of the subject and of subjectivity, including the powerful and influential Freudian theory of psychoanalysis, do not dominate the culturalist and sociological substrate of race and sexualities. The fractal and rhizomatic dimension of this object is reflected within it and requires that these theoretical frames be reimagined. It is accordingly less the object identity in literature that is being sought than identity insofar as it is literature.

The work of James Baldwin, where the sociologist rivals the philosopher and the author, is my master-text. Emotion works in it to unravel meaning, rationalized stability of identities, and outside the text, confronts the reader directly with his/her own postures. The primary vector of this personal face-off with politics, including the politics of the text, is the artist and, particularly, the writer. His/her task is to perpetually recycle culture so that it does not remain the unalienable truth of some, and it is to him/her that identity appears as a necessary illusion for the cohesion of the social body. He/she dissipates the mirage of supposedly natural identities and exposes the cultural laws that define them to criticism. In doing this, identity comes to light as choice more than heritage. The condition and the preservation of this liberty, dangerous for the group, depends upon multiple and free identification. Its accomplishment and its incapacitation are respectively represented in the same year in two major pieces: the essay "Notes of a Native Son" (1955) and the novel *Giovanni's Room* (1955). As in the rest of the work—which deploys an ethic of inclusion—Americanness, homosexuality, and black identity are indissociable, which is also encapsulated by the conclusion of Baldwin's last essay: "Each . . . contains the other" (Baldwin, 1985: 829). Americanness, homosexuality, and black identity cannot be separated according to the demarcation that Baldwinian criticism has long established in its forms of writing.

The work of the memorialist and the engaged intellectual, putting down African American consciousness in essays, would reserve for novels and short stories a necessarily less political homoerotic or homosexual sensibility. Beyond the constraints of epistemology that, besides, lead to underestimating the signifying power of emotion in the political thought of W. E. B. Du Bois or excluding Frantz Fanon from the European philosophical canon, this partition of consciousness between reason and emotion, rationality and affect, social and political writing, and writing of the imagination hints already at the fractures in the modern subjectivity and the unthinkable aspects of identity corollary to them, among which that of conceiving and feeling race as the imagined desire of the subject. Baldwin proposes an archeology of this philosophical, cultural, and social aberration, and he does so indistinctly in his essays and fiction. As the principal part of the corpus that is constantly returned to, they also provide a source for a critical methodology for their own analysis and that of other texts, principally African American ones.

The work of James Baldwin is an American discourse on the method. His teaching consists in unlearning to look at skin color, which is not in itself evidence of anything. It is also an anti-rational enterprise that aims to reconcile consciousness and desire and, from this ideal subjectivity, call into question identities and the role in their elaboration by negativity (the black for the white, homosexuality for heterosexuality, the feminine for the masculine) and their respective blind spots (race for sexualities and genders and vice versa), a perspective that is critically examined in chapter 1 where it crisscrosses that of the subject-researcher's subjectivity. Central in the historical, cultural, and literary problematic of Americanness, race and sexuality each construct their oppositional duality while simultaneously being, one for the other, the "lack-to-think" that encloses them as categories. The explanation and surpassing of the opposition black/white is, for example, to seek in sexuality. Baldwin unseals these categories and puts them back in motion in a writing where they are only posed as opposites in order to put one another into question. This comprehension and anatomy of race is unique in the century. It borrows from Hegelian logic and the double consciousness of Du Bois in which a new African American is refined through the synthesis of the opposition between the black and the American. Baldwin, however, instills this fusion with a homoeroticism that renders their *a priori* position unstable. Black consciousness is not determined, for Baldwin, in its relationship to white consciousness but in its relationship to desire. With Frantz Fanon, for whom *la conscience nègre* is self-sufficient and justifies the rejection of the Hegelian dialectic, Baldwin shares, in his etiology of race, the predominant importance of the sexual dimension. Yet he does not make the same use of it. In Fanon, it is above all a reflection of racism as social pathology inherited from colonialism. Race and sexuality are thus in a relation of metaphorization and, if they interpenetrate, they belong to differentiated categories of thought. In Baldwin, race and sexuality contain one another. Together, they contribute to each other's respective construction and eventually appear as separate. The exploration of America, its cultural matrix, is a genealogical retracing toward its primordial division, its ideological justifications, and its political motivations. Beyond black consciousness and African American identities, Baldwin's perspective, doubly attached to race and to homosexuality, opens a breach in the modern conception of the subject's subjectivity, notably in the Freudian theory that, for fear of it overshadowing its own discourse on sexuality, withholds race out and out.

Singular on the level of the history of ideas, the Baldwinian approach remains equally, and in many respects, avant-garde on the level of contemporary criticism. In the United States, lesbian, gay, and queer studies, like African American and black studies, remain to some extent prisoners of a political and disciplinary logic that leads to reductionism of the object and sometimes to scientific dead ends showing that the culturalist and sociological frames are insufficient on their own. By its polymorphic nature, our object requires a multiplication of viewpoints and a variety of methodological tools. Besides, existing as a mental reality and developing through lack, the lacuna, the fault, and negativity, this object poses itself as empirically elusive and unthinkable. In this perspective, the literary prism remains, for us, the most adequate. This is not to claim that the literary prism should be less determinant in the construction of the reality that it intends to observe— as testify the texts that contribute to the development of a national consciousness and the critical reading analyzing the evolution and form of such a prism—but rather treated as a field of knowledge and creation founded on imagination and calling, for it is one that seems most pertinent.

From here, what is to be called literature and African American literature? How can it provide a method to study identity? Unlearning to look, as James Baldwin teaches, is a beginning and an attempt to respond. What justifies the appellation of African American literature is a view of America, its history, and its culture, from a unique point of view, which is radically different from those of the black postcolonial literatures. It is neither exterior, as African Americans were among the first to construct the country, nor interior, because, within it, they are denied their humanity. This point of view, continued until the beginning of the twenty-first century, is that of the hole, of absence, of invisibility, and of erasure. There is neither materiality nor another space than that of the imagination, where, from Equiano to Morrison, from Baldwin to Dixon, an aesthetic of optics is drawn. In it, America reveals itself to be a fantasy of which race, a murderous and insane idealization, is the basis. A fantasy that African American literature seizes and appropriates for its own sake. To make it palpable, so that it can be looked at directly, in the text with all its horror, often converted into beauty, and not through

American reality in which, over the centuries, slavery, segregation, and racism construct an imagined parallel world, an oblique perception, and a truncated consciousness. Unlearning to look at skin color to see in it the fantasy of race is the primary matter of African American literature and what its form transmits. Observing it in the depths of its sexual mysteries and listening to it recount a history of America and of its identity is, besides, Baldwin's primary concern.

Unable to cover the work in a comprehensive perspective, which is always illusory, and before learning to unlearn, my first works on Baldwin privileged the thematic method. The formal networking of themes showing itself to be taken in what Levi-Strauss called a "packet of relations," the perspective was structural while the critical reading of ideological presuppositions in the speeches and texts was inspired by post-structuralism, essentially through Foucault and Derrida.

I then leaned toward discursive and semiotic strategies that the essayist and author follows in order to blur the relation between perception and meaning, the analysis situating itself half-way between black phenomenology, as the veil of Du Bois and the masks of Fanon incarnate it, and the constructivism of American gay and queer theoreticians in their critique of a naturalized masculinity (Rocchi, 2001b). In Baldwin, the signifier that dehumanizes the black, his veil and his mask, is the screen of black skin upon which the white projects, inversely, his own image, where white skin, masculinity, and heterosexuality are associated, as illustrates the short story "Going to Meet the Man," the object-study of chapter 2. A doubling of this screen, the Baldwinian text offers up what the cultural and political environment forbids: allowing the gaze to pierce, re-establishing it in the circulation of drives that tie to the black gaze and make it lose its reifying power. Transformed by the gaze, what circulates on the surface of the text and between the different protagonists that he evokes is emotion. Whether it is the Du Bois of *The Souls of Black Folk*, understanding in the valleys of New England what the appearance of the black subject means, or the Fanon of *Black Skin, White Masks* interpellated, from the moment he arrived in metropolitan France, by the simple and devastating words of a child—"Look at the nigger! . . . Mommy, look at the nigger!" (91)—consciousness grasps itself in the gaze of the Other through emotion. While in Du Bois it is a source of alienation that, if not mastered, can betray weakness and depravity, for Fanon it is a possibility of un-alienation as long as it allows one to foil the deceptive rationalization of antiblack racism. Baldwin chooses to make it circulate freely, and because it abolishes difference, it is also the vehicle of his identitary revolution. Combined with indifferentiation, the circulation of emotion and of the gaze would find itself half a century later in the writings of the generation of writers and poets that Baldwin influenced, and notably Essex Hemphill, Assotto Saint, and Melvin Dixon. In my study of the image and language

(Rocchi, 2001b), what appeared clearly, at that stage, was that emotion accompanying the emergence of self-consciousness was of a homosexual order, assumed and signified by a text that, besides, analyzes it as culturally repressed in American society. If the importance of emotion in the thought, writing, and the Baldwinian thematic nexus had been identified, at the time I did not fully appreciate the degree of divorce between rationality and emotion, consciousness and desire, in the *epistemes* of the subject and of identity. Only approached through the American cultural frame and the motif of race and sexuality, such a fracture would work from the inside of a great number of theoretical systems with hermetically closed categories and concepts that, in such a state, would be inapplicable to the text from which one must draw one's hermeneutical tools.

I take the same retrospective lesson from the analysis of the relations that James Baldwin maintained with American black nationalism (Rocchi, 2004a). Social and cultural anthropology were paramount to understand the different senses of black identity in Senghor or Césaire, to specify the uniqueness of the African American situation and its political forms. Besides being tempted by the dogma of black essence, movements of liberation, like the Nation of Islam or the Black Panthers, and, before them, to a lesser degree, that of Martin Luther King Jr., were haunted by the perversion for which Baldwin blamed *Native Son* (1940) by Richard Wright in "Many Thousands Gone" (1951): remaining determined by the gaze of whites and reproducing the partitive logic on social, racial, and sexual levels. It was the double figure of the androgyne and the person of mixed race that allowed the overcoming of essentialism, of social categorization, and a black nationalism constructed in reaction to that of the whole American nation. Baldwin's mixed race or racial hybrid, of course, echoes with the synthesis completing the double consciousness in Du Bois but, in the image of the circulating gaze, this racial synthesis is not an arrested movement. Race, and the hybrid with it, are conceived as a continuum, as indicates "the darker brother," one of the recurrent expressions that Baldwin uses to refer to the African American. Additionally, racial hybridity doubles itself with androgyny, which does not necessarily align with the mental bisexuality established by Freud, because, for Baldwin, masculinity and femininity contain themselves mutually, as well as the black race and the white race. Although he uses them himself, the terms "mixed race," "hybrid," and "androgyne" are actually improper. They all effectively refer to a movement in an open space where the idea of identity itself, coming from difference, is inconceivable.

Baldwin's hybrid is syncretic, and it is this syncretism of identity in Baldwin that would be confronted with the image of the mixed-race person in Freud. There, it metaphorizes fantasy through the conception that racial duality serves as conceptual and ideological structure for the binary construction of gender and sexualities. Read through that of Baldwin, the Freudian text appears to place psychoanalysis not only in a racial perspective, which criticism has demonstrated, but in a modern conception of the subject according to which the renunciation of the homoerotic and homosexual possibility founds white consciousness as well. This is the main argument of chapter 3.

By refining one's method, and without changing objects, the study as it advances sees transformation in perspective, more psychoanalytical and philosophical, while never ceasing to be literary, the safeguard against the theoretical imprisonment that it claims to shake up and fears for itself. I have already laid the foundation of a philosophical reflection that would be led by black experience (2001c). It would seek to understand how Baldwin could free himself, by the text and by his imagination, from the spatio-temporal frame and its dichotomies before/after, interior/exterior, with which the permanence of identity is measured. Baldwin claims this freedom by uprooting the origin from place and from the past to anchor it in desire. Today is better perceived the impact of this gesture that, in the light of more recent works, takes on its whole dimension just as much on the literary level as the philosophical level. Indeed, if the theme of the origin runs through African American literature, it does so in a double and determinate relation to space, as a place and as a condition of existence. The displacement from Africa to America, in the slave trade, from the South to the North of the United States during slavery, or the "passing," which refers to the movement from one community to the other in the time of segregation, only makes sense in terms of survival. Displacement is a question of life or death, often physical, sometimes mental, always political, as chapter 4 reminds us. Dissociating the place of the conditions of existence runs the risk of reduction, to which I have not always escaped myself in some places. Thus, when Anthony Appiah in *In My Father's House* (1992) closes Du Bois in an essentialism tainted with biological and anthropological racism that would rely upon a mythification of Africa as an origin, he obliterates the historical context of segregation and minimizes that of the revolutionary that the myth would nourish in the pan-Africanism of Du Bois to which, besides, a powerful African Americanist critical orthodoxy prefers to substitute Du Bois as the voice of American interracial reconciliation. Similarly, reading slave stories only through the prism of the autobiographical pact of Philippe Lejeune, or in a *stricto sensu* textualist perspective, deforms the text that, as Frederick Douglass explains in his autobiography, and Gates in *Figures in Black* (the first part of his literary theory), becomes the possibility of the existence of a slave who is deprived of it, and, accordingly, of his origin too. In his critical study of African American literature, *Ride Out the Wilderness: Geography and Identity in Afro-American Literature* (1987), Melvin Dixon detailed the importance of this ambivalence of space. The "wilderness," the "underground," the "mountaintop" are the privileged places and textual metaphors of African American regeneration. It is also this effort to reconcile space, understood as the place and conditions of existence, that is translated by attempts to sub-stract the black diaspora from territorial borders and national cultures. How-ever, if the black Atlantic, defined as a structure of cultural and affective production, does not disassociate the two levels of place and conditions of existence, it still remains a closed space, precisely because it is structured. From here, the before, the after, the interior, the exterior, and the possibility of over-signification of origin resurge, beyond the immanence of existence that, quite contrarily and as demonstrated in chapter 4, Rozena Maart re-asserts. In other terms, even Gilroy's reading, as fractal and uncentered as it may be, does not escape from the permanence of black identity, from a form of transcendence and essentialism that certain queer critics have identified, notably through masculinist and heterosexist symptoms. A critical counter-point, Rozena Maart's writing is a queer and feminist breach with the black masculinist nationalism of the new South Africa and with the mythification of the post-colonial moment as a radical break in which only demonstrably heterosexual South African men would be counted.

The analysis of the spatial problematic in African American and black literature and thought faces two pitfalls: closing the geographic space and underestimating the conditions of existence. Each of them binds space and black identity, perhaps more than they are in the texts, to an origin over-invested with sense. My becoming familiar with black existential philosophy, such as that established by Lewis R. Gordon (1995a, 1995b, 1999, 2006a, 2006b) and George Yancy (1998) in their reading of Douglass, Du Bois, and Fanon, among others, led me to reread Baldwin and the theme of the origin in this perspective. Applied to Baldwin, I name it with the expression "the desiring mode of being black" (Rocchi, 2007a). A modality of black existing, Baldwinian desire is a space that is always open, but it is also, always rein-vented in contact with another, an origin by which black identity liberates itself from closed categories and spaces that theoreticians inherit from histo-ry. At the same time, because intersubjectivity in Baldwin is represented within a racial context posing an inequality that interracial desire fundamen-tally contradicts, desire as a modality of black-existing is equally always political. As Robert Misrahi argues in *La Problématique du sujet aujourd'hui* [The Problematic of the Subject Today], the reconciliation between con-sciousness and desire leads to possibilities of theoretical and philosophical opening up, but also invites a rereading of the African American and black canon, beyond the aesthetics/politics dyad, the slitting up of social catego-ries, the artificial classification of literary genres, or fields of knowledge, from which the writing might be drawn. The emotion that circulates in the texts of Du Bois and of Fanon indicate, for example, that a desiring con-sciousness similar to that of Baldwin works upon the body of their political philosophy. What remains to be determined, in their case, is the degree of such an influence. It is at its highest in Baldwin, where consciousness and desire are identified.

The turn from a hermeneutic of black and homosexual identity to paying attention to the desiring black consciousness is operated by the same material: the text. It materializes the immaterial—race as imagined desire. It is in tight collaboration with the reader, who is required, in parallel, to change perspectives. The reading of this text, that of the desiring black consciousness, runs into the obsolescence of critical tools. When it points out the immersion of African American popular songs in the writing of Du Bois, the influence of jazz in the syncopated style of Ralph Ellison, the accents of the Southern dialect in the words of Zora Neale Hurston, the voice, in this way similar to the point of view, reconstructs the text as a surface, a colored skin. After all, what does one see in the text if not its blackness, its identity, what identifies it? The culturalist explanation, in the vein of Laurence Levine, does not entirely convince: it is not the color of the skin that is seen, but the manifestation of African American culture. But what about Twain, Faulkner, or Styron, who use the same strategies to make their blacks speak and to make them visible? This explanation does now allow us to account for the persistence of this enigma: African American literature seeks to transcend the color of the skin by the text where that color is invisible. Even in reading. It is thus, to reveal the desiring black consciousness, the reading of the text that must be changed.

As a psychology of depths, Freudian psychoanalysis has, through the invention of the unconscious, given this necessary volume to a conception of identity that never stops at the surface, at the visible. However, in its own genesis, the unresolved dilemma between the evocative force of literature and the power of the theoretical system causes race and sexuality to re-emerge as circumscribed frameworks. To unlearn to look at identity, it is also necessary, through the desiring black consciousness, to begin to un-write psychoanalysis, which is what chapter 3 proposes to do.

As an anti-system based on the emotion and the identification of the reader, the Baldwinian text does not deliver a psychoanalytical theory of race as such. But, like all literary works, it is a place of what Pierre Bayard calls an "activity of pre-theorization," a work by which elements of thought can be brought together and structured. These elements that, for example, literary analysis names themes, motifs, or narration are in Baldwin interracial rapport, sexuality, and the unconscious. Knowledge of human psychology and its depths, of which writers have an intuition that Freud would employ in his theory, doubles itself here with a felt knowledge of American puritanism, the constraints that it imposes upon sexuality and its racial manifestations. One of its strongest illustrations is in the novel *Giovanni's Room*, unappreciated by critics, but recently redeemed by its queer readers, and among the first of all the works that I have studied by the author. This analysis revealed that from the narration of David, a young white American who finds in France the deadly closet of his repressed homosexuality, emerges a black sign (Rocchi, 1999). I identified it as the semiotic residue of the litter-box that is David's unconscious where he conceals the evasions of his misled homosexual consciousness, what he calls a "cavern . . . in my mind" (14). This trash only took on African American meaning in the measure of the whole work, which describes the living spaces of African Americans at several places, and notably the Harlem ghetto, as the place of the social and mental repression of white America. The black sign of *Giovanni's Room*, for me, would be the "pre-theorization" and the basis of the "meta-psychoanalysis of race" sketched in chapter 3, an anti-theory drawn from applied black literature and not reproducing the divide between consciousness and desire that, by the permanence of race and the renunciation of homosexuality, work upon psychoanalysis (Rocchi, 2008a). As a phenomenon betraying the unconscious articulation of race and sexuality, I would just as well find this black sign in the analogy that Freud establishes between the person of mixed race and fantasy (Rocchi, 2004c) than in the racial and sexual fantasy that Freud projects from himself, through psychoanalysis (Rocchi, 2009).

Insignificant if not invisible when cut from the work, the black sign is, besides, a striking image of the blind spot that race remains for lesbian, gay, and queer theory when it renounces thinking about Freud within a comprehensive perspective of identity. In the form of racial and racist metaphors, it haunts even the white writings of the extreme contemporary in their representation of AIDS (Rocchi, 2008b), as we will see about Paul Monette, George Whitmore, and David Wojnarowicz.

I have referred to their African American and black homologues with the expression "post-identity," first used in reference to Rozena Maart (Rocchi, 2006a). The "post" signified the return to the political space of plurality. Violent, pornographic, eminently political, these queer voices furiously instill in their texts a voluntarily transgressive subjectivity by which all heritage is subordinated to a personal and chosen aesthetic, what would be formulated later as "race as an imagined desire." I considered this, in Essex Hemphill, Assotto Saint, and Dixon, a surpassing, a hollowing-out of race. Thus, in Dixon, particularly in his novel *Vanishing Rooms*, which is studied in chapter 5, the aesthetic organizes itself around these same empty spaces that make holes in the diegesis. Metaphor metamorphosed, it speaks, again and again, the unspeakable of slavery, the incommunicability, the existential anguish, the *no man's land* of interracial homosexual love and, in relief, carrying the text toward its own nothingness, the specter of AIDS of which the author dies while still writing (Rocchi, 2006b). By their apparent formal and political isomorphism, the queer perspective and the "post-identitary" prism led to an analogical reading of Dixon and of other contemporary authors, be they black or white. It almost sufficed to bring them together into the same space to make the interracial nightmare dissipate in the desire of literature. But, confronted with the gaze of the Other, the phantasmatic idealization of the object by the researcher evaporated. Interracial tension had not disappeared. It had, in fact, arrived at a new height with AIDS and its writings that, together, placed the surpassing of identity into view, which the title of Assotto Saint's poem "Wishing for Wings" evokes, and the violent return of race. In certain texts, race tended to disappear by the representation of a subjectivity beyond identity: a subjectivity filled by death. In others, on the contrary, resistance to death was the sign of its return.

This tension does not efface its interraciality but displaces it in a space where it empties itself of meaning, where racial categorization no longer stands, where there is no longer the possibility of a relationship because the space disappears, AIDS and death swallow it up. In the dying consciousness of death. Racial separation and the cultural revolution held on by a string that the metaphor took up again to inscribe both the black and the white again. Though space disappears with death, it creates another to inhabit race and close it with the text: the void. Where the black makes sense and death comes quickly, where American identity falls apart and finally survives via race. It is the story of disappearing possibility. An artistic, cultural, and literary revolution. It does not happen and aborts. This is the subject of chapter 6.

For African American literature, another side of this aesthetic of perspective that I have described about Baldwin opened up: not the phenomenon of race, its perception, and the inscription of an African American meaning that would invalidate it, but the absurd phenomenon of the dying body that, emptying out, hollows out and atrophies the space that it is in. The world is engulfed in the dying subject because he/she no longer has the material to generate his/her space. In itself, the metaphor of African American history. The literary and cultural revolution was born in this metaphor, in its potentiality to change spaces, contexts, and meanings: no longer to be in the space of history, the context of oppression, the identitary meaning, but to penetrate a higher dimension where the phenomenon is not a halted meaning for the subject because there is no longer meaning. In death. Race as an imagined death.

Among the African American authors of his generation, only Melvin Dixon, to my knowledge, comes near to this very Baldwinian concept. To the question of identity posed by the desiring black consciousness of Baldwin, Dixon responds: death. In *Vanishing Rooms*, the metaphor conjures up race and AIDS, consciousness reduced to identity, and desire ensnared in death. In doing this, it represents the alpha and the omega of disappearance: like whiteness, the metaphor is visible in that it has disappeared. It inflects itself by race and by AIDS that it makes disappear while simultaneously destroying itself. Only the text retains the trace. It is the phenomenon that, through the metaphor, challenges perception.

Determined by the quest for legitimization and territorial influence, the prism of queer criticism, whether it is Euro-American or African American, did not notice the invisibility of the text and what is revolutionary about it in the representation and conception of identities. African American readers thus make a cultural and political phenomenon of AIDS that subordinates, effectively, the aesthetic dimension while it is by form that race disappears and makes sense, culturally and politically. Other readings, like those of Susan Sontag and Ross Chambers, exclude the racial parameter or minimize it. Hermeneutics, in culture, attains its aporia here: race remains because, over-signified on one hand, it continues to exist though its space disappears, and, on the other hand, it is denied in itself. Beyond the critical discourse and culture, AIDS opens up on an epistemological catastrophe. It is the joining of desire and death, bringing sex back to its truth, failure, and it abolishes the relationship of the Other and oneself. It is the impossible difference from which one only exits by race.

In the American context, Melvin Dixon exits race through the story of AIDS that he un-writes and that becomes the metaphor for African American identity: *a priori* invisible and without meaning, made visible in order to make sense. Effectively, the novel evacuates AIDS by situating its diegesis in 1975, before the discovery of the HIV virus. The narrative construction analyzed in chapter 6, however, reflects it by a polyphony from which plurality disappears. The multiple and juxtaposed narrations melt progressively together into an indifferentiation similar to the intercellular process of the virus's progression: it penetrates the cell, modifies its DNA from the inside, and changes its identity. In the narrative structure, the voice and the style of each narrator lose their proper identity. Signified but submitted to form, the racial dimension is absorbed. I will find this attempt again in David Wojnarowicz, who is not African American, to represent the surpassing of identity by form and its abyss, a sort of writing of death that only exists through the suicide of its space: the American space of race. Marked by Rimbaud, Burroughs, and Genet, whose influence he claims, Wojnarowicz mediates the relation to the Other by a hallucinated vision of the subject who dies, and the space that disappears around him. His double identity of writer and photographer makes him enter into the aesthetic of the African American perspective: he is conscious of the racial dimension of American perception and resists it by the same means as black authors. Another proof that consciousness is not an affair of skin color, as long as the skin can die.

Wojnarowicz knows how we die. His writing is of an unbearable violence precisely because it supports the violence that it represents in an effort that we know is in vain, death, announced, being the very principle of writing. That this defining feature of a consciousness that is dying and writes itself characterizes a whole generation of writers and artists is an entirely new situation in the American context. It is its own *terra americana*, and it un-veils itself as what it is not: space without race.

In this, AIDS and its disappearing space are the metaphor of race in that it swallows up the American subject in history. After Baldwin, Dixon and Wojnarowicz come as writers of the desiring black consciousness. And they are beyond black and white. They write the desiring consciousness that dies. The others remain in their America, the pallid territory of their resistance to death, where the metaphors of the black rise up from the past. This return is particularly striking in the memoirs and poetry of Paul Monette. I have called them "the black h(a)unting of white AIDS literature," also one of the central themes of chapter 6. A double-focal specter, the black metaphor is terrifying because it inhabits the text to die in the place of the white voice. It haunts it because, through it, we see the return, in the miasma of American guilt, in the Gordian knot of race and sex, the attractive fear of miscegenation. And the infection of the extreme contemporary prolongs the memory of contamina-tion by race. Expiatory, the black metaphor intervenes to pose the question of the relationship to the other, simple and naked: What space for desire and death? Unresponsive, the text sublimates itself in the racism of a writing that remains beautiful. Intimate, they are the American insanity that Baldwin described so well.

To read for their possibility—to write finally.

Chapter One

The Other Bites the Dust

Toward an Epistemology of Identity

Why is it always the apartment buildings of Blacks that burn?

—*Libération*, August 27–28, 2005 [1]

Outside Brooklyn Law School yesterday, a man selling recordings of famous African Americans was upset at the failure to have prepared for the worst. The man, who said his name was Muhammad Ali, drew a damning conclusion about the failure to protect New Orleans. "Blacks ain't worth it," he said. "New Orleans is a hopeless case."

—David Gonzalez, "The Victims:
From Margins of Society to Center of the Tragedy,"
New York Times, September 2, 2005

This innocent country set you down in a ghetto in which, in fact, it intended that you should perish . . .You were born where you were born and faced the future you faced because you were black and for *no other reason*. The limits of your ambition were, thus, expected to be set for ever. You were born into a society which spelled out with brutal clarity, and in as many ways as possible, that you were a worthless human being. You were not expected to aspire to excellence: you were expected to make peace with mediocrity.

—James Baldwin, "My Dungeon Shook,"
in *Letter to My Nephew on the One Hundredth
Anniversary of the Emancipation*

If we—and now I mean the relatively conscious whites, and the relatively conscious blacks, who must, like lovers, insist on, or create, the consciousness of the others—do not falter in our duty now, we may be able, handful that we are, to end the racial nightmare, and achieve our country, and change the history of the world. If we do not dare everything, the fulfillment of that prophecy, re-created from the Bible in song by a slave, is upon us: *God gave Noah the rainbow sign, No more water, the fire next time!*

—James Baldwin, "Down at the Cross,
Letter from a Region in My Mind," in The Fire Next Time

If we were to parody Frantz Fanon, who wrote in *Peau noire, masques blancs* [Black Skin, White Masks], "The Negro is not. Anymore than the White man,"[2] we could immediately start with a well-meaning but dizzying sentence like "The Other is not, if it is not always as the Other of the Other"—a slightly disillusioned attempt to extract oneself from the logic of differentiation that entangles us and which nevertheless orders the combat against the hierarchies that it brings about. There is, in this "Other of the Other," a memory and an anticipation of the Same, that the chronos of the enunciation or the *topos* of the written word nevertheless renders different—a difference that, while certainly restrained, is also relative, interactive, inter-subjective. A difference that cannot be radical. And from which springs an initial reformulation of our postulate: it is not the Other who is not. It is yours; your Other does not exist.[3]

IN THE ABYSS OF THE OTHER

How, then, can be explained the popularity of the Other in our academic discourse, particularly when identity becomes the object of study? Elevated to the status of a protean concept, operating from one system to another, like a practical commodity readily substituted for sociological categories that are too simple, too subjective, or too complex, the Other has become a *prêt-à-penser*, or a ready-to-use concept, a theoretical box overflowing with always more specific tools—hybridity, *métissage*, racial/sexual/gender-related in-betweens, diaspora, interculturality, and more, which, as they multiply, make what they pretend to clarify even more opaque. In this abyss of the Other, where has the human subject gone? What eludes us in this obscurity?

The Other is not the same. Until recently relegated to the margins, it is today at the center of intense attention. And there is no doubt that the progressive but inevitable legitimization of gender, African American, ethnic, or LGBTQ studies—in France, often issuing from recently established disciplines like, in the case of African American research, American studies, which in its turn was originally a dissident colony of English studies—is at the same time the possibility of a political break-through, of scientific progress and of an epistemological rupture. Yet disciplinary history attests to the fact that yesterday's dissidences give birth to today's doxas, and the destiny of psychoanalysis is far from being the only example of this. A neurotic repetition, the incessant definition of the territories of knowledge is perhaps the price to be paid for attaining the recognition that, by thus supplanting the quest for truth, subordinates knowledge to the exigencies of the institution. Perhaps it also betrays the deeper meaning of the production of knowledge: once the dominant theory has been unmasked, the will for domination remains. As evident as that may be, this statement is no less true for all objects or fields of study, all disciplines, whether recognized or about to be, and including those that built their identity from an epistemological rupture that one had hoped would create a renewal in its wake.

Yet, and as an example of this, the notion of race has remained in many respects the blind spot of gender and sexuality studies while African American research on both sides of the Atlantic, mindful of its relatively fresh legitimacy, confines to its periphery the approaches that contravene its chosen hetero-patriarchal model.[4] And what can one say about post-colonial studies in which, as Houston A. Baker Jr. humorously charges, one still strives to demonstrate, through a sort of protest criticism whose political inefficiency and scientific inanity have long been proven, that a certain autochthonous work is every bit as good as *Jane Eyre* (Baker: 388)? It is on the strength of the term "post" that the precedence of the empire is preserved, on the obstinacy of science that reassembles what history believes to have dismantled. What should one think then of the stereotype present in the many works where the Other is advanced as the object of desire (hooks, 1992: 21–39) or exhibited as the favored victim of violence? Specular, the academic discourse in this instance redoubles the violence that it is supposed to study and thus paradoxically contributes to the creation of Otherness (Rocchi, 2005): by signifying a human subject whose experience of difference is above all empirical and relative by nature, the Other becomes, through the academic discourse, an ontological category. He/she passes through a human dimension that the researcher abandoned for himself/herself to that of an abstraction and theorization, proof of the researcher's value and professional identity.

POSITING IDENTITY—AND THE DIFFERENCE THAT MAKES

These frequent shifts toward the essence are a fundamental violence that often proceeds from an insufficient reflection on the location where the discourse issued, and on the nature of the perspective toward the object of study—in other words, from the absence of critical reflexivity. The undeclared effect or goal of this is to keep the scholar in the reassuring and illusory gap in which *he/she cannot be in the place* of his/her object of study. The idea here is precisely to not put oneself in the other's place, an untenable and falsely reflexive posture leading to ventriloquism and intellectual colonialism, but to imagine the *possibility* of being the other. It is the consciousness of this possibility, moreover, that serves as the foundation for a deontological imperative, as Alain Supiot and the *Conseil national du développement des sciences humaines et sociales* (National Council for the Development of Human and Social Sciences) remind us in their prospective assessment of French research:

> The ethical question [in the human sciences] comes, firstly, from what one studies about human beings who possess a certain autonomy, a certain liberty and responsibility, and that those who study them must also do so from the perspective of autonomy, responsibility and liberty. [5]

Whether they generate, in spite of their best intentions, new hierarchies, that they dull their subversive potential with sterile oppositional strategies, that they take from the so-called dominate/subaltern/marginal/black/ethnic/ Muslim/Jewish/lesbian/gay/transgender . . . subject his/her immanence, thus excluding reciprocity and responsibility, studies dedicated to identity as an object are often revealed as prisoners of an aporia: unconsciously repeating observed differentiation and hierarchies. A blindness whose persistence is such that one is tempted to render the ideologies, which supposedly breathed their last breath with the grand paradigms, accountable for it.

These methodological deviations are rooted in the primacy of duality and in the power of a thinking based on analogy (Rocchi, 2004c: 205–10). By distinguishing and identifying objects among themselves, the analogy does render the world meaningful and intelligible, but it initially induces a logic of identification and differentiation, which postulated the identity, the difference, and their value. Only an examination of the conditions of the production of these values and a criticism of the role played by the human subject— who defines and who is defined—can disengage them from their fixed state and underscore their relative and variable characters. And yet these mechanisms of identification and differentiation and their postulates are often taken as secondary. What matters is identity and difference in themselves and not the processes from which they result. A metalepsis that relieves oneself from the responsibility of the object identity, this lacuna produces difference even at the level of scientific discourse, but this Otherness caused by the discourse appears as an effect of the representation of the observed object. There is consequently no reason to suspect some sort of predetermination of which one would have inopportunely forgotten. The Other is not predetermined. He/she is. Period.

This bias is not only thematic and methodological but also ideological and political. Underestimating that Otherness is derived from a predetermination, that it is a social construction, of which one determines the meaning when measuring it against its effects through time, is in this capacity exemplary. This is one aspect of the theoretical and philosophical debate about the notion of race. In "'Race,' Writing and Culture," Tzvetan Todorov assimilates the nineteenth-century discourse on race and the twentieth-century idea of cultural difference, explaining that the contemporary ideology of cultural difference suffers from both excessive universalism and relativism, just as the ideology of race did a century earlier, relativist in its classification of human beings and universalist in its values, which it held to be true everywhere. This argument, in fact, serves in Todorov's article to conclude a partial rehabilitation of the philosophy of the Enlightenment whose humanism would not be always denatured by racism or sexism (1985: 372–74). A number of existential black and African American philosophers oppose this reading of history. Lewis R. Gordon thus recalls that in Hegel's *Philosophy of History*, the relationship between Europe and Africa, white and black, is an absolute opposition, on the order of being and nothingness (Gordon, 1997: 25–28). Clarence Sholé Johnson emphasizes, for his part, that the social construction of blacks as ontologically inferior individuals is a scientific project attested to by *L'Encyclopédie* and the *Encyclopedia Britannica* and which has been moreover disseminated across all disciplines (Johnson: 174–76). But in an even more significant fashion, and contrary to Todorov, for whom they are reduced to historical contingencies facilitating, it's true, his improbable connection between race and culture, Gordon and Johnson locate their analyses of the racial discourse in the existential consequences that they had for blacks. That is, in what the construction of the black-being-as-Other concretely signified for centuries and continues to signify: slavery, colonization, and oppression, from the viewpoint of what this human invention, with its social and utilitarian prerogatives, was able to allow in terms of European politico-economic hegemony and what it continues to incite in a neocolonial era.

It is then particularly dangerous—or at least politically oriented—to accommodate the two important dimensions represented by historicity and the existential reality of subjects in history. If they are true for a culturalist and conservative approach like Todorov's, the political stakes of this methodological difficulty are also true for a literary approach where, as Gordon criticizes in Gates's works, literary theory becomes the only criteria for the evaluation of a social phenomenon, thus depoliticizing it (Gordon, 1995: 102).

"POLITICS SIT ON EVERY SIDE OF EVERY TEXT"[6]

The motif of "tragic mulatto," which Werner Sollors dissects in his exemplary study *Neither Black, Nor White, Yet Both*, is a good illustration of the political dimension produced by methodological choices:

> The very fact that the term "Tragic Mulatto" has become part of the dominant vocabulary in American literary studies and cultural discourse raises the pos-

sibility that the stereotype not only has helped to criticize an ideology of the
past (notably that of active abolitionists in the age of slavery), but has also
served as a vehicle of the ideological wish for a wholesale rejection of the
representation of interracial life in literature . . . In other words, the term
"Tragic Mulatto" may have come to such prominence in criticism and in the
public realm not because it permits a better understanding of past ideologies,
but because it supports, in the guise of subversive-seeming ideological criticism, the ideology of racial dualism and the resistance to interracial life that
are still more prevalent in the United States than are calls for hybridity. (242)

Sollors concludes his analysis by arguing that the expression "tragic mulatto" and the discrediting of nineteenth-century literature dealing with interraciality serves today in the United States as an apologia for racial essentialism, the justification of a world in black and white where the in-between
("intermediary categories") would not have their place. From the first pages
of his work, whose approach is thematic, contextual, and more than just
formal (16), Sollors clearly defines his position, which is at the same time
ideological, methodological, and disciplinary: he suggests leaving behind
black-white binarism (15–18) by drawing on the literary representation of
racial mixing, a motif rather disdained by ethnic and gender studies even
when they intend to knock national literatures off their pedestal (10).

In this way, the American literary critic appears to subscribe to the critical
and ideological current of interculturality or of cultural hybridization, the
theoretical avatar of multiculturalism. Eric Sundquist's *To Wake the Nations*,
which deals with the interpenetration of African American and Euro-
American cultures and texts, is one of the most eloquent examples of this,
using the approach of "New Historicism." This current opposes—though
weakly in truth—now-classic research work in cultural anthropology (like
Levine's *Black Culture and Black Consciousness*) or in literary theory
(Gates's *The Signifying Monkey*), which are more attached to transcribing
and fixing an African American identity that, without being authentic—a trap
into which no one falls any longer—would be in the very least defined and
autonomous. In "Caliban's Triple Play," Houston A. Baker Jr. is not so easily
duped and reproaches Gates for giving birth to an African American textuality based on the duality and rationalism of the Enlightenment, the very ideas
that he meant to forcefully refute (Baker, 1985: 383).

The same observation could be made regarding Sollors's project whose
postulates should be reconsidered. Reading the above quotation, several implicit truths do indeed raise questions. According to the American critic,
there is a caesura between the ideologies of the past and those of the present.
And yet, without even claiming that they have a transhistoric value, can it be
sustained that the ideologies lack connections, particularly those of race in
the United States, denying them the parts of genesis or history they share? It
is in fact quite difficult to comprehend, not to mention combat, the ideology

of dualism/contemporary racial separatism by isolating it from the ideologies linked to slavery and segregation. To erase the past in order to declare that yes, decidedly, racial mixing is better than separatism, one being, moreover, an empirical reality while the other emerges more precisely from an ideology ("the ideology of racial dualism and the resistance to interracial life" [242]), which actually reveals itself as an aporia. In contrast to Todorov, who synthesized two different centuries to identify race and culture, Sollors obtains the same result by discriminating between a before and an after onto which he retrospectively superposes a hierarchy and values—positive for racial mixing, pejorative for dualism/racial separatism. But this is akin to an act of faith by which one replaces the critique of hierarchies by the belief in values, as if it were sufficient to reject *a priori* the ideological character of an idea such as hybridity to render as obsolete the original duality of which it is the trace, if not the variation. By virtue of which reading of the world or of history would American "interracial life," a vague and undetermined ensemble, be a more articulate counter-example of racial binarism than the illustration of this division? It is only in the context of race as a psychic and cultural reality, in which the insignificance of skin color becomes meaningful, that the notion of mixed race makes sense. In this respect, racial hybridity and dualism cannot be conceived as separable identities.

Furthermore, in this discourse with anti-ideological pretensions, what becomes of the autonomy, the choice, the liberty, the subjectivization of the human subjects that he studies? What of their individual and personal reinscription in history? What about those who oscillate between black and white, like Joe Christmas in William Faulkner's *Light in August*? What about those who choose to reject the heritage of slavery, like Kabnis in Jean Toomer's *Cane*? What about those who choose to pass as white, like Rena in Chestnutt's *The House behind the Cedars* or the female characters in Nella Larson's novels? What about those who, like Malcolm X, proclaim themselves black and not mixed race? By wanting to abolish difference, it seems that Sollors in fact gives new impetus to differentiation in that he artificially opposes the ideology of race and racial mixing, perceived here through the exclusive angle of a social phenomenon denuded of any ideological characteristics. Playing on the paradigms of race and culture, the differentiation that Todorov proposes, for its part, stems from a confusion between these two categories and, in so doing, minimizes, on the one hand, the creation of the black-being-as-the-absolute-Other, while on the other hand, embellishing the racial rapport as well as its subsequent historical atrocities with relativism. The meaning of this discourse comes out of the same logic: to make abstraction of the historical and social invention of the subject and of his/her possible re-subjectivizations *in situ*. A form of essentialism in itself.

One thus reinforces the constancy of the Janusian couple identity/difference and makes the double prevail over the transversal, the space where the

subject can invent himself/herself in spite of the determination and the sig-
nifications that one had elaborated for him/her. When one considers the
object identity, it is always an essentialist approach to duality that creates
difference. Even when one concentrates on the so-called intermediary categories, the critical perspective on this *in-between* remains veiled in order to
glimpse only the suffering caused by the rending apart, the bitter negotiation
that the "in-between" would require, weakly verifying, thanks to an authentic
syllogism, the hypothetical permanence of identities through time. The perspective on the geographical, cultural, racial, sexual, or gendered "in-between" does not take into consideration the choice, the liberty of identification, the polymorphous desire, the (re)inventions of subjectivities even
though identity, at the center of determinisms and of history, is above all an
affair of repositioning. In "(Re)Conceptualizing Blackness and Making Race
Obsolete," Clarence Sholé Johnson writes about it in these terms:

> Far from discounting blackness and whiteness as descriptors of pigmentation,
> however, my view recognizes such uses of the terms. But it goes beyond them
> in suggesting a political use as well. The political use is one in which black-
> ness is subversive of the status quo, viz. whiteness. Given this use, there is no
> incongruity in the idea of a person being pigmentationally white and political-
> ly black, or of a person being pigmentationally black and politically white. All
> it means to say that a person is politically black is that the person is anti-status
> quo; that she or he is ideologically committed to de-centering whiteness; that
> she or he is oppositional or counterhegemonic. (180)

IDENTITY AS AN OBJECT: CAN IDENTITY BE EXTERIOR TO ONESELF?

It is thus the same type of reasoning that underlies the anti-essentialist as well
as the essentialist conceptions of identity.[7] These postures are even more
misleading as their apparent differences, of object or of context, mask their
profound similarity: at times one invokes materiality to oppose difference
and *métissage*, at times ideality to justify a necessary alterity. It was the case
in the late 1990s with some French psychoanalytic experts who loudly castigated "the engendering of the same by the same," of the so-called symbolic
order of the difference of the sexes, that would be caused by the PACS—the
French civil contract allowing the union of gay and lesbian couples.[8] It is in
the name of these same transcendences, the Good, the True, the Just, upon
which the volatile ideologies rely, that one speaks and quiets the subject.

Though strengthened by their specific comparative contexts, their shared
objects and their crossed disciplines, the methodological innovations in the
matters of the human sciences do not appear as the best safeguard against
ideological deviations and partisan readings. Comparison is not reason, one

would immediately be tempted to object, but the obstacle is not that comparison is not reasonable, but the way in which it is being reasoned. Here, again, positing identity as an object is a political affair.

Consider the following transatlantic perspective: the comparative study of the politics of identity in the United States and in France. Whether privileging a communitarian conception of ethnic-racial identities or subordinating them to the supra-identity of Republican citizenship, the cultural data particular to both the United States and to France cannot be ignored. In the meantime cultural particularities cannot withstand the universalism of ideology. For example, what values can one still confer to the American visibility and the French invisibility of minorities when one repositions these distinct phenomena in the perspective of transnational existential realities like racism, the failure of so-called politics of integration, or a common differentialist ideology? Furthermore, the subject-researcher cannot be in the same way both exterior to his/her own culture and to the non-native culture to which he/she compares it—an undesirable solution in the first place. If one considers one's own culture as exterior to oneself, one risks underestimating in fact its influence on the construction of one's viewpoint and, aided by the participating observation, conveniently making the non-native object a screen behind which to hide the indigenous object.

It is up to the subject-researcher to define, individually and collectively, his/her methods by confronting the epistemological difficulties raised by these methods, and he/she must do this whether he/she uses post-modern relativism or a more traditional anchorage in the discipline as, in the wake of Peter Novick, Marie-Jeanne Rossignol proposes for research in social sciences:

> The researchers who do not accept the most extreme conclusions of Derrida's disciples are not all victims of the objectivist and disciplinary illusion: they are conscious of constructing their object, of being themselves its messenger when they establish a problem and organize a demonstration, of values and of prejudices, and finally, of being subjective individuals. [9]

Allowing a glimpse beyond cultures, methodologies, and ideologies, the fundamental question of the responsibility of the subject-researcher, the exteriority of the object in relationship to the subject appears from that point on as central to understanding the persistent nature of a logic of differentiation in the scientific discourse. If, as it has just been done, one can bring different contexts closer together and attempt to isolate what between them constitutes a common identity, the sameness of certain characteristics, evaluated in time and in space (as in the example of the experience of racism), this is precisely because, in this case, the French and American contexts could be considered as exterior to us. Even though it does not go without raising several epistemological difficulties, this nevertheless remains possible because culture is fundamentally data and determination exterior to the subject. This is also true for the discourses on race and sex, which fall under the category of object and which, singularly and collectively, can be understood by research in literature, cultural studies, and psychoanalysis. Now that the comparativist approach has been described, I will evoke the connection between apparently distinct objects, the disciplinary intersections and the ways by which one can respond to them.

RACE—THE OBSCURE OBJECT OF [ ]

Once one has positioned race and sex as objects, which the putting into discourse hopes to render exterior, what becomes of their conscious reality for the subject? Of his/her idea of it? We know that since Freud, Fanon, or Baldwin, each thinker completing the ideas of the others, that race and sex— and not the discourses dedicated to them—do not correspond to any other immediate conscious information. The former, biologically insignificant, cannot empirically be singled out; the latter, often subject to repression, is scarcely more empirical, except when rendered manifest by sexual differentiation, the social gender.

Both therefore represent a "limitation of thought," to use the expression of Gilles Varet in *Racisme et philosophie* [Racism and Philosophy]:

> [Race] does not fall into the category of object. Despite what I want or do, *the idea remains indelibly etched in my very consciousness.* It has left its enduring trace on me, although I do not really know where to locate it. And though it has definitively escaped my grasp, it calls on me to confess from whence I came. More than this, it pushes me forward in a direction that I no longer know how to decipher. In short, it ceaselessly requires from inside my active acquiescence, or this conscious recognition, whose urgency my intelligence would like to push aside, by forcing it back outside of me, among all the exterior processes, among all the world's determinisms. [10]

A psychic and cultural reality, as Frantz Fanon showed us, with which sex merges at the fundamental points of intersection represented by origin and generation, as Baldwin demonstrated, race escapes us. If race is, then it is in spite of an imperfect correspondence to self-consciousness. How can it then be considered as sameness, repetition of the *idem*, when the subject cannot even immediately experience it? Could it be that it is not methodologies and ideologies, but rather this impossible ipseity of race for the subject-researcher, added to the often repressed notion of sex, that is the cause of the logic of differentiation in critical discourses? Is it because the subject-researcher can apprehend in himself/herself neither the race nor the sex that he/she talks

about and so creates identity, at first as sameness, and consequently measured against of difference, thus exteriorizing the elusive into the form of a
discourse that is necessarily and by default reifying? More than a limitation,
this is more accurately the failure of thought. Crystallized here by race and
sex, it is the "challenge [posed by] Western thought to philosophy as a
discourse and a tradition,"[11] as Foucault presented it at the College de France
during his March 24, 1982, lecture that was transcribed in *L'Herméneutique
du sujet* [The Hermeneutics of the Subject]:

> How can what is given as the object of knowledge (*savoir*) connected to the
> mastery of *tekhnê*, at the same time be the site where the truth of the subject
> we are appears, or is experienced and fulfilled with difficulty. How can the
> world, which is given as the object of knowledge (*connaissance*) on the basis
> of the mastery of *tekhnê*, at the same time be where the "self" as ethical subject
> of truth appears and is experienced? If this really is the problem of Western
> philosophy—how can the world be the object of knowledge (*connaissance*)
> and at the same time the place of the subject's test; how can there be a subject
> of knowledge (*connaissance*) which takes the world as object through a *tekhnê*
> and a subject of self-experience which takes this same world, but in a radically
> different form of the place of its test?[12]

Without totally grasping the meaning of race and sex as manifestations of
the "self," the subject-researcher may be able, however, to think of them or at
least render them thinkable:

> It is perhaps essential to the very nature of race that it cannot be seen head-on,
> but only through a rapport of laterality. One would then reach this important
> conclusion that race is not a thing, a block, a principle, an essence, but a
> relationship: because it is not denying a reality to make of that reality a "rela-
> tional reality." And in this way also race becomes once again "thinkable."[13]

From the perspective of laterality, of the relational reality or of the rapport, more obvious for sex than for race, these two manifestations would
therefore become thinkable. This supports the importance of methodological
innovations such as the comparativist approach, shared objects or crossed
disciplines, as mentioned earlier.

Yet, in the same way that, according to Lacan's formula, "there is no
sexual relationship," it seems that there is no fully realized racial relationships in the scientific discourses on identity, and particularly for those of us,
whether American or European, in African American studies. In the translation toward the Other, necessary for comprehending race in itself, something
has stalled.

THE SUBJECT, SUBJECTIVITY, AND
THE IMPOSSIBLE RELATIONSHIP

To the essentialist, shifting already referred to in American research corresponds a European propensity for denial. Whether we call it repression as psychoanalysis does, or bad faith, fleeing from what one is, as Sartre calls it, this refusal of responsibility not only translates into a difficulty in curbing in one's own ranks what one calls "white supremacy in the United States and what one more willingly designates here using the term "institutionalized racism"[14] but also has repercussions in the scientific arena.[15]

If, faced with the unbalanced numerical and hierarchical representativity of so-called visible minorities at the university, one cannot invoke *prima facie* the individual responsibility of the subject-researcher because the university system—like every other established collective structure—has an effect of diluting this responsibility, and even though there is no correlation of the cause and effect between what comes from a social injustice overflowing the limits of French universities and the epistemological obstacles of a field of research such as African American studies, the lack of responsibility induced by the environment nevertheless reinforces the denial, making the world as object of knowledge into a radically different place for testing of the self, as Foucault suggests. How do I understand what I am running from there, precisely where my knowledge makes my fleeing possible in the first place? A vestige of this denial and lack of responsibility in chosen scientific orientations, African American research in Europe struggles at times—despite its multidisciplinary character and its openness toward the exterior—to give itself certain objects such as white and European identities or the subjective relationship of the subject-researcher to the idea of race. What it invokes and convokes for him/her. A perspective which is not encouraged by the suspicion of disciplinary dispersion, the blade of the "heteronomy of objects" falling that much more easily when the field concerned is marginal or in the process of legitimization. This state of facts, though less true today than before, continues to reinforce, however, the conception of the field as an over-rationalized and controlled space in which the subject-researcher also participates, at times unwillingly, enjoined to privilege objective knowledge and to challenge any perceptible subjectivity in the choice of a different object.

Taken as a manifestation of the self, race is therefore first grasped in the Other—the black or white American object—but is not fully realized by the necessary return toward the self. This absence of reflexivity is also symptomatic of a French cultural difficulty that was recently illustrated by the media's questioning of the "competition of memory" (*concurrence mémorielle*) between blacks and Jews, slavery and the holocaust. If, in this case, the French media have more readily leaned toward the "black malaise,"[16] this is in stark contrast to what they did four years earlier when the vote in the *Assemblée Nationale* for the Taubira-Delannon law, which recognized the slave trade and slavery of blacks as a crime against humanity, and whose resulting polemic saw the mobilization of defenders of the "French republican model" who, by convoking the frightening specter of English communitarianism, of affirmative action and Judeo/African American tensions, sought to evade, in even the most progressive spheres, French historic and political responsibilities. An errant and non-reflexive comparative approach, the perspective on the Anglo-American object served in this respect to protect the supposed coherence of the French subject.

One is thus in the presence of the incompleteness of the racial relationship—incompleteness in the double acceptation of the term: at the psychological level, where it goes back to the sentiment of unaccomplishment, and at the epistemological level where it designates, in a hypothetico-deductive system, the undecidable character of certain propositions. Of course, this is all nothing but hypothesis, as it is in the course of the present analysis as well, because we touch upon the absolute and the undecidable: the subjectivity of the subject.

To attempt to comprehend the impossible racial relationship, one can envision inviting history and psychoanalysis to the table with philosophy, as Foucault did in the chapter he dedicated to the human sciences in closing *Les Mots et les choses* [The Order of Things]. How can denial, lack of responsibility, the relationship impeded by the self-reflexivity of race, as they are manifested in the Other, not be the correlate and the stigmata of a long occultation of the history of slavery and colonization, buried national traumas from which, nourished by the work of historians, African American research—and it is here its indisputable contribution to scientific progress—allowed Europe to begin to be released?[17]

At the very heart of the knowledge that he/she collectively produces, the subject-researcher, considered individually, may continue in effect to struggle with a paralyzing culpability. This is because one anticipates ones own sentiment of culpability. While in Europe, this culpability manifests itself by a refusal of white conscious reality, however important it may be in grounding the thesis that race is nothing but relationship and positioning—an even more distinct prohibition as it is based on an objectivist conception of the knowledge from which the subjectivity of the subject is excluded—this same guilt is performed in the United States through the practice of the "confessional," the public confession of a sentiment of culpability that Houston Baker Jr. scoffs at when white academics are concerned (Baker, 1985: 387–89).[18] Where comparison is both reason and irrationality.

CULPABILITY AND CATASTROPHE

Affecting the production of knowledge and the ethics that it requires, the historical roots of culpability gain in vigor upon contact with another form of guilt, and one inherent to scientific activity—the culpability tied to the desire for knowledge and its resulting transgression of the forbidden, as Maud Mannoni analyzes in *La Théorie comme fiction* [Theory as Fiction]:

> Knowledge has a rapport with desire, and also with the unmasking of the cause of this desire. But in the mastery of knowledge, just as in the control of desire, something escapes the subject. This part goes back to that which, in the desire for knowledge, can spring up like an interdiction of knowledge . . . It corresponds also to the impossibility of rendering an account of what inhabits us, what reveals the position to the impossible constitution, in all beings, of their limits. The subject can only then hold himself/herself up as desiring knowledge by transgressing a knowledge of mastery, i.e., by engaging himself/herself in an infinite quest of an unknown . . . In his/her relationship to the Other, the subject's desire is therefore a permanent contradiction. [19]

Critical of the Freudian doxa, of the notion of the analyst as "a specialist, that is, someone who places himself/herself in the service of an impersonal knowledge,"[20] Mannoni provides in this passage an introduction to a work in which, in support of psychoanalysts like the English doctor Winnicott or Harold Searles, the American author of *L'Effort pour rendre l'autre fou* [Collected Papers on Schizophrenia and Related Subjects], she supports the thesis that the analyst must let himself/herself be questioned by the madness of the Other—in this case of his/her analysand. And to pursue this line of thought, she explains that "theory can also become a pure instrument of knowledge, a sort of foil, that exempts the subject from any modification at the level of the being."[21] The similitude in the subject/object relationship for the analyst and the subject-researcher—that is, must the latter also allow himself/herself to be interrogated by his/her object of study, the race in the Other, as the former does by the madness of the Other?—allows us to address the question of the subject-researcher's desire for knowledge.

Because why would the desire to know make the subject-researcher feel guilty, if it is not due to the possibility of revealing himself/herself to himself/herself as a place of "the unknown" ("*non-su*"), a fragile being delivered to an indetermination? This is precisely what prevents him/her from "the knowledge of mastery" ("*le savoir de maîtrise*") by which he/she exists and exercises the profession of a "specialist." Foucault says the same when he affirms that the techniques and practices of the subject in relationship to himself/herself (the subject as "desiring to know" in Mannoni) are anterior to the rule, to the law ("the knowledge of mastery" in Mannoni), even when they impose themselves on him/her (Foucault, 2001: 109).

Understood as pure and impersonal understanding (*connaissance*), knowledge (*savoir*) becomes henceforth the adequate means to bypass the interdiction of the realization that something always escapes the subject and the subject-researcher.

Knowing the race of the Other defers the catastrophe that comes from the consciousness that race is not apprehended in me. It is knowledge that renders the impossible racial relationship, already mentioned in relation to the subjectivity of the subject, impossible—an epistemological abyss, if there is one—and, at the philosophical level, it also creates the Hegelian cleavage between self-consciousness and the desire that it induces.

Indeed, Mannoni's reading of Freud is also an implicit criticism of a predominant Hegelianism that holds that self-consciousness is only accomplished through desire, the desire to be recognized by the Other. The knowledge of mastery that Mannoni identifies—in other terms, the pure and impersonal knowledge, or what I call the reifying scientific discourse—is proof of a consciousness of Self that is never fully realized because the desire to be recognized by the Other cannot pre-exist self-consciousness unless the desire and the Other had been previously postulated. But would that be possible without the self-consciousness to which they are precisely supposed to give access? Lambasting Jean-Paul Sartre and his *Orphée Noir* [Black Orpheus] for being guilty of presenting "black consciousness" as a step toward the universality of class, Fanon had already rejected this illogicality, but by contenting himself with inversing the terms, which fatally led him to transfer the logic of differentiation from the racial level to that of sexuality and gender (Rocchi, 2001c: 152).

> Black consciousness is immanent in itself. I am not a potentiality of something, I am fully what I am. I do not have to look for the universal. There's no room for probability inside me. My black consciousness does not claim to be a loss. It is. It merges with itself. (Fanon, 1952: 123)

Here again is the cleavage between consciousness and desire. A rupture that, along with Fanon, demands that the production of knowledge respond to the unanswerable question that reflects the impossible racial rapport: Who am I?

In response to this charged question, which, in the service of the reflexivity of the subject, would permit us to bypass determinisms and differentiations, one always substitutes the same reply: the Other. An Other evicted from oneself and who does not exist, prevented from leaving the superior position in which he has been placed. Transcendent.

WITH U: L'AMO(U)R DE L'AUTRE

Flight, denial, lack of responsibility of the subject; intellectual aporia, alienation of scientific discourse, domination by the knowledge of mastery. How
could these flaws of the subject and these failings of thought, from whence
philosophy as an exercise, an attempt, and a venture puts itself in motion,
unravel themselves at the altar of the Other in a catastrophe without alpha or
omega as they emerged from absolute rupture between the subject and the
truth? It is from this point of Cartesian rupture that Robert Misrahi and
Michel Foucault conceive of the failure of a failure that could have become a
salvation. The former does so in a historic epistemology of contemporary
philosophy where the Other, through the cleavage between consciousness
and desire, is erected in transcendence; the latter in an epistemological ar-
chaeology of ancient philosophy where the care of the Self (*"le souci de
soi"*), the *epimeleia heautou*, would open the heretofore forgotten path of
reflexivity. In *La Problématique du sujet aujourd'hui*, Misrahi establishes
the following assessment:

> Thus from Kierkegaard to Ricœur, and from Heidegger to Levinas, the philos-
> ophy of the same is contested to leave room for the philosophy of the Other,
> who is not necessarily the other man but Otherness as Being and Infinite . . .
> Because the only possible basis of sense and value, the human subject, was
> challenged in fact by these doctrines to make room for what they call the
> being; they all put themselves in paradoxical situation of philosophies working
> towards their own destruction by using the recourse to an unknowable being,
> who is, however, supposed to give these philosophies foundation and justify
> them. In this voluntary philosophical shipwreck it is the subject himself/herself
> who risks being engulfed. [22]

For Misrahi, the cause of this shipwreck is the distinction between consciousness and desire operated by classical theories of the subject, a differentiation that prevents them from *"realizing this fundamental and integrated
unity*: only a consciousness that is desire is able to constitute itself as a
subject and to understand this act of constitution that is simultaneously existential and gnoseological, ethical and reflexive."[23] This conception of the
subject involves all "qualitative content of the founding activity and the
personal identity"[24] and requires the establishment "in an integral description
of desire, the triple relationship of affectivity to liberty, to consciousness, and
to the other."[25] Affectivity, the amputation of which, as previously seen, is
harmful for the subject and the object being studied, is also the base of the
regrounding of studies on identity: How is the Other *really* embodied in us?
How does he/she change us? We, who study him/her?

Without a doubt, European blacks, when they are in this field, search for
themselves in the African American object. Doubtless women, lesbians,

gays, and transgender individuals see themselves in studies on gender and sexuality. Without a doubt. But the others, what are they searching for when they look at them, what do they see when they see themselves looking at them? Their image, the very image of the Other, or the image of the same changed by the other? Before we put ourselves in the service of pure intellection, where does our interest in the other, in the "real life" that Sollors spoke of, come from? As Varet claims, there is indeed a sort of "excitement or sexual trembling" (*"quelque émoi ou frémissement sexuel"* [278]) in the discovery of race, in the fictive, veritable, but always *lived* experience of meeting of the other, of a brother or a lover, who touched us, perhaps even changed us. What remains of this? Why should nothing rest of it? Should one worry about it? Science is perhaps not without consciousness, but it does not remain armed with a consciousness that is deliberately forgetful of the care of the Self.[26]

This is also Foucault's line of questioning in *L'Hérméneutique du sujet*, in which "the dynamic muddle, the mutual call of the *gnôthi seauton* and the *epimeleia heautou* ('know thyself' and the care of the self)" (67) that traverses Greek, Hellenistic, and Roman thought echoes the reconciliation of desire and consciousness that Misrahi advocates. Both texts respond with a reflection on the reflexivities that constitute the subject, the history of their challenges, and their different practices:

> Throughout the period we call Antiquity, and in quite different modalities, the philosophical question of "how to have access to truth" and the practice of spirituality (of the necessary transformations in the very being of the subject which will allow access to the truth), these two questions, these two themes, were never separate . . . Now, leaping over several centuries, we can say that we enter the modern age (I mean, the history of truth enters its modern period) when it is assumed that what gives access to the truth, the condition for the subject's access to the truth is knowledge (*connaissance*) and knowledge alone.[27]

Before the modern period, it was necessary to know oneself in order to know, and to do this one had to care for oneself. In Antiquity, the care of the Self "is formed and can only be formed in reference to the Other."[28] The movement toward the Other does not make of the Other a transcendence because "this other who is the master"[29] must first of all care that I care about myself. As Socrates did for Alcibiades, and in contrast to his lovers, who only wanted his body (58), the Other affects me by caring about me. Socrates becomes a master through Alcibiades, whom he cares about, and who, thus transfigured, can know himself, can know, in order to *in fine* care about others and the city-state. It is this political aim that maintains this "other who is the master" in the immanence of a world where one experiences oneself and where we can experience the world together in order to change it.

What comes out of this textual and philosophical relationship is that there can only be a reconciled subject through a reflexivity that is *not experienced by the Other but experienced via the Other*. The Other can only mediate this reflexivity if he/she is immanent, placed in a humanity that *can be experienced* and for which no theory postulating the truth as exterior and superior to the subject can be relevant—whether this theory is Foucault's perspective of the Same or Misrahi's interpretation of the Other.

What does experiencing what the Other experiences mean for the impossible racial relationship? What is signified by this intention, this desire, and this lack, which one cannot realize, satisfy, and fulfill without resorting to domination, recognition, and difference? Precisely, that outside of desire and consciousness—together and concomitant—there is no racial relationship. That is not to say that the relationship is empirically impossible—it is even its condition for existing—but rather that, as soon as the Other is theorized as an *a priori*, even before being experienced, the relationship becomes false, unjust, the generator of injustice because it is disjointed, cut off from the world. It is an interrupted relationship from the moment it is pronounced, rather than a *"manque-à-dire,"* or a lack of saying, that affects us and, by affecting us, allows us to be. Say the Other and it is already too late. It is necessary to experience the Other.

SUBJECT TO WORRY

A poorly negotiated reflexivity makes the subject-researcher run the risk of denaturing his/her object and distorting his/her own subjectivity. But as Foucault allows us to see concerning the Socratic method of reflexivity, a poorly negotiated reflexivity also seems to be the symptom and the cause of a cæsura between the subject-researcher and the world, of the disconnection between research, scientific progress, political action, and social transformation. There is no doubt that one cannot care about others when one does not care about oneself, and even more so when the so-called care of the Self only has meaning through the Other and for others. This crisis is not new, as Misrahi likes to remind us by referring to Husserl, the thinker of the crisis "before being the thinker of the subject of knowledge."[30]

Superior to the modification of methodologies, would political action be the ultimate proof of research, the long dreamed of release from the crisis? We may begin to doubt this when we remember that, across the Atlantic, and even though they were born out of social movements, feminist, gay and lesbian, and African American studies, for example, allowed themselves to gangrene in a closed identity logic, a logic from which, in France, these fields are not exempt. Would social transformation be the result of the narcissistic promise that our epistemological ruptures will make an impression on the world? This would be to naively continue to believe, on the ruins of our schools of stone or of thought and the cadavers of our tutelary masters, in a finality of knowledge that the hate of the Other, ceaselessly recurring, viscerally proves wrong. Moreover, isn't it through doctrines to reject, obstacles to overcome, and ruptures to provoke that the thought is being conceived—an experience that the master-thinker, who is prepared to be exposed to public contempt by his/her disciple, knows to be necessary?

And as a result, here again, political action and social transformation as a means of experiencing the Other cannot prove anything. And for good reason. In this case, they are not really a way of experiencing the Other, because the inversion of the rapport between theory and experience always allows for the undermining of the disjunction. Serving here as an end and not a finality, political action effectively closes research in on itself by furnishing it with the responses that the latter must not obtain from the world or from itself, should it continue to ethically interrogate the world. One can hardly wish for a hierarchy to distribute political action, social transformation, and research, each in relation to the other. But their interdependence is also a consequence of reflexivity, of the subject-researcher's methods of subjectivity and of the *de facto* social subject that the subject-researcher remains. Research is its own social field. Its spaces of diffusion and expression, beginning with the structures of education,[31] are first place of its testing in terms of political action and social transformation, as Lewis R. Gordon explains.

Far from being able to hide behind the impasses of philosophy, the perverse misuses of the human sciences, the weight of history, the isolation of research vis-à-vis social fields, our responsibility is in fact total. Ethics is not only in the method, nor only in politics. It is the only acceptable transcendence because it is subjective; ethics as an oxymoron. And the subject alone is accountable. His/her research is a totality ingrained in the always deferred response of the Other as both subject and subject to worry regarding the method of comprehending the Other and acting in the world. The dialogue with the Other is without end and must exist in relation to a third term: oneself, the person one becomes through this experience.

TRIANGULATION AND TOTALITY: THE OTHER AND NOTHINGNESS

Such is the state of the Other in the research on identities: so that the Other is neither transcendence nor misinterpretation, it is necessary to bring him/her out of the laterality, the rapport, the comparative approach, the "inter" and to immerse oneself with him/her in the triangulation. At the intersection of two objects, two disciplines, two methods, the eye—that gleams upon contact with them and leaves open the field of vision that it separates between them. *Trans*disciplinarity[32] rather than "inter."

Trans for passage, change, disquiet, depersonalization, alienation. The experience of the other. The reflexivity of a subject who alters himself/herself in the apprehension of his/her object. This alone is the condition for preventing the object identity from becoming an imposture, a denigration of the human sciences at the center of which, moreover, it places itself, in an epistemological configuration that requires interrogation, just as it requires of "the relationship between the thought and the formalization . . . the modes of being, of work of language" (Foucault: 1966).[33] Return of the subject to the disciplines that founded it as positive knowledge, an object to unveil in order to recognize oneself. Transdisciplinarity.

At the risk, it is true, of "disdaining the necessity of taking into consideration the pertinence of the tool to the object, of the semantic lability of the terms to which one has recourse, of the variety and the difference of viewpoints," as Marc Chénetier writes in his defense of the "nano-disciplinarity." At the risk of "dissolving the notions that are operational [in the discipline solicited by the researcher], of taking from them any efficacy by abduction or importation, reimplantation on unfavorable terrain."[34]

At the risk also of not trying to think, to reinvent, thus ceding to the transcendence of the *tekhnê* and to its delusory power.

No zero risk.

Let us take, then, the risk of upsetting the territorialities of knowledge: to allow LGBTQ studies a glimpse of the experience of race; to echo their questions about the psychoanalytical gap between desire and identification; to interrogate, aided by the African Americanist contribution, the racial metaphors of the Freudian unconscious; to confront fixed identities and the essentialist errings of African Americanist research with free identifications generated by the practices of homosexuality; to deafen Western philosophy with the critical concert of black voices. To play at being "debunkers," at Baker's Calibans, on the literary landscape as well where even the most attentive formalists become intoxicated by so much beauty that they no longer hear the Other who cries out from the very text. And yet it is the same eye that sees itself there, the same voice that one listens to, hers, his, ours, where experiencing the Other is not stealing his/her place, nor anchoring him/her in it, since language offers an infinite variety of referents and interpretations in "the vastness of its *a priori*"[35] (Derrida). What Baker calls the linguistic, phonetic, and poetic territory where Caliban leads his guerrilla war and plays his triple play (Baker, 1985: 394).

Because it is only a game.

Experiencing what the Other experiences is a game. Destined to failure, like race, and elusive, like sex whose pleasure is without logic (Bersani, 1986: 40–41).

Failures that art and literature alone can capture and that they put, in a sort of *mise en abyme*, in the experience of the Other that I can only experience through myself. It is the death of the Other that creates this impossible reflexivity, and for it to retain its human dimension we must try to learn, despite our fear and despite everything, to die alone. Because that is how one dies.

AND BEYOND (ADDENDUM): "THE DEATH OF THE SAME OTHERS & THE DISCIPLINE OF *JOUISSANCE*"

The following text prolongs the reflexion initiated with "The Death of the Other: Toward an Epistemology of Identity" on the critical examination of knowledge production and the epistemological and political consequences of a vexed relation to otherness, particularly when the subject-researcher's re-flexiveness is at stake. It was presented five years after the first publication of the article at the annual conference of the Caribbean Philosophical Association, "Shifting the Geography of Reason VII: The University, Public Education, and the Transformation of Society," Rutgers University, New Brunswick, New Jersey, September 29–October 1, 2011.

Both texts are the basis for a larger project, currently in progress, on social environments, such as prison and academia, functioning as spaces of rectification. The aim is to observe and comprehend the racist and racializing dynamics of these spaces for their political and subjective outcome—to (re)inscribe in the black subject the destiny of non-being through his/her impossible (re)construction as a desiring subject. How he/she is submitted to objectively superior forces determining from the outside the articulation be-tween space and being so that freedom, agency, one's relation to the world and others remain constantly conceivable while totally inaccessible—an end-lessly regenerated frustration. More subtle and perverse than plain segrega-tion and discrimination, racist and racializing rectification will thus be stud-ied for the power and efficiency they draw from the psycho-affective perver-sion of their social justification: from the reform and social adaptability of the subject to the disciplining curbing of his/her fantasies as connecting projections of a desiring subjectivity; from social transformation and progress to the maintaining of a social order; from race as an imagined desire, as James Baldwin conceived it, to the consolidation of an ethno-racially predetermined social order whereby the stifling of the imaginative and desiring force of race eventually bars the subject from self-actualization.

A transitional text between epistemological speculation and sociopolitical critique, "The Death of the Same Others & the Discipline of *Jouissance*" focuses on the academic systemic recourse to public and private humiliation as a technique of power that both sustains the hierarchical organization of institutions and the mapping of disciplines while exposing subjects from minority-groups to the endless repetition of the traumatizing experiences through which they have lived outside of academia. Such a perversion of knowledge and its pervasive reality cannot be exclusively explained in rational terms. The ongoing reshuffling of a sadistic drive, timely tamed and whose effects are racializing, also needs to be taken into account for a complete diagnosis and a thorough analysis whose sketch is included here.

The overall theoretical background of this part is primarily composed of the intersecting points of Frantz Fanon's work on black consciousness and queer theory. Among them one may situate the common intertwining of theory and praxis along a shared critique of binarisms, the interest for the body viewed as a space for change, the analogous conception of sociogeny and performativity, or the kinship between linguistic subjectivization of queer individuals and the Fanonian reading of colonial language. Within this theoretical web of which the relation between body and body consciousness is the organizing center, this study intends to articulate more specifically the reification of black bodies as described by Fanon in *Peau noire, masques blancs* (1952) with Sara Ahmed's analysis of objects and orientations in *Queer Phenomenology* (2006). The point is to examine the physical and intellectual presence of black, non-white, and non-French scholars within, respectively, the material space of French universities and the immaterial mapping of social sciences still resisting transdisciplinarity and transatlantic perspectives. This particular phenomenon and the way it is institutionally and politically handled (i.e., made in/existent and/or in/visible) can be regarded as a contemporary manifestation of "*l'esprit colon*" (the colonial spirit)—a pervasive undercurrent in social sciences and academic institutions, at its peak during the French Third Republic, as Olivier Le Cour Grandmaison argues in *La République impériale: politique et racisme d'état* [The Imperial Republic: Politics and State Racism] (2009).

While marginally allowing black scholarship—works addressing issues related to black cultures and philosophies, race relations and racism as pursued in African American and diasporic studies, Africana cultures and philosophies, postcolonial critique and cultural studies, all blatantly minor fields of the French academic landscape—the academic body locks itself in what Lewis R. Gordon has called "disciplinary decadence" (2006b), a foreclosure of disciplines whose hierarchization recalls the French colonial genealogy of subordination. What may first appear as an analogy (between academic and disciplinary hierarchization on the one hand and colonial subordination on the other) seems more of a causality brought to light by the presence of black scholars and the existence of black scholarship. They impede the *working* fantasy of a superior self-sameness unless their presence and work re-shape the shadowy Imperial Republic by remaining in the background or at the periphery. If one may argue that dichotomy in the colonial context and Manicheism in decolonization, which Fanon describes in "De la violence," the opening chapter of *Les Damnés de la terre* [The Wretched of the Earth] (1961), have been passed on to (post)colonial contemporary France, one should also stress that what is at stake is no longer the preservation of immutable Western essences—a dream now shattered—but the rescue operation of the forlorn empire as a continuously unfulfilled quest. This, in practice, means that beyond the sheer and too overt exclusion of black scholars and black scholarship, what is in fact sought for is the regulation of their presence and potential influence, with the systemic control of academic contact zones which otherwise might contribute to the creolization of knowledges. In the mapping of social sciences this translates into the marked reluctance that inter-/transdisciplinary and transatlantic approaches still inspire. Here is thus required a specific technology of discipline which articulates racialization and sexual phantasmatics and whose syntax cannot be fathomed without a queer and psychoanalytic analysis of perversion—the perversion of the power/knowledge dyad. While trying to show the centrality and contemporaneousness of Fanon's thought, as testified by the un-disciplinary use of Ahmed, Gordon, and Le Cour Grandmaison, who are all readers of Fanon, the present study therefore aims at analyzing what is coined here as "the discipline of *jouissance*"—the technology organizing the distribution of power and the circulation of blacks either as castrated and subservient disciples or as powerless objects of others' *jouissance*.

A pleasurable and limitless quest for the forlorn thing, *jouissance* has been described by Lacan as a transgression beyond signification. It nevertheless inhabits the institutional matrix of power and knowledge under the guise of humiliation, as Michel de Certeau explains in "L'institution de la pourriture: Luder" (1987). Humiliation is the reverse side of a Napoleonic meritocracy that still extends from the bottom to the top of the French educational system. It gives a shape to *jouissance* and meets at the same time one of its requirements—the injunction of submission and self-destruction that translates into the learned and self-imposed bracketing of subjective specificity for the sake of a national grand narrative that celebrates self-sameness through unity. It is this political mythology that supports the mapping of social sciences and the petrification of knowledges in disciplines. Not only is humiliation learned and self-imposed, it is also passed on vertically (through the hierarchical structure) and horizontally (through peers). In the case of black, non-white, non-French scholars, it gets even stronger since their scholarship may contravene academic self-celebration. Moreover, they incarnate the historical defeat of the anti-humanistic colonial project whose prolongation as the imperial fantasy of superior self-sameness is also contradicted by their physical presence. An antiblack violence, humiliation aims here at securing the academic fantasy of a space where blacks and black scholarship are led to embody the limit of what is scientifically acceptable while shaping white and French superiority. As scholars are taught to know their place both intellectually (through assessments) and physically (through their circulation in the national academic space), other Others are also taught not to trespass limits. As far as French *banlieues* are concerned these limits are material. But all of them partake of the visible phenomenon that supports the absolute *jouissance* of the Imperial Republic—a fantasy made limitless through limitations.

As a praxis of power that generates a racializing surplus of enjoyment through the perversion of knowledge, the discipline of *jouissance* thus refers to how some are limited for others' limitless *jouissance*. A false oxymoron, the discipline of *jouissance* is not a contradiction in terms since what it articulates are two different dimensions of signification—discipline produces signification through hierarchy, or disciplinary territories, while *jouissance* cannot be signified. The discipline of *jouissance* organizes in fact the academic dialectic of sameness and difference with the spatial distribution of intellectual and physical bodies. Along these contours it espouses the structure of perversion—bodies are simply the matter of the structure for which what matters is its own triumphing perpetuation at the expense if need be of ethics, laws, and rules. The discipline of *jouissance* also follows the logic of heterosexual reproduction, which bears the seeds of racialization. For its perpetuation, the noble academic family selects heirs in charge of protecting disciplinary self-sameness while they resist queer orientations—that is, any scientific and epistemological re-direction that turns knowledge production away from narcissistic celebration. As can be seen in the concomitant 2009 revolts in universities and in the Caribbean, this academic process has for larger counterpart the politics of national identity meant to restore the nation's troubled mirror-image (notably through the restoring to favor of colonization as voted by the parliament and promoted by the president).

Exhibitionistic for a didactic purpose, the discipline of *jouissance* nevertheless has to be partly dissimulated inasmuch as it must discipline without arousing political and social disorder. Philosophical universalism and scientific objectivism are thus conjured up to cover the disciplinary machinery that reproduces disciplines through disciples and according to a predefined scheme of inheritance. Meanwhile, outside the academic precinct, the masquerade of anti-racism (in the name of which positive discrimination and ethno-racial statistics are rejected) veils the collective *jouissance* that the sociopolitical domination of blacks, non-whites, and non-French individuals permits. Reclaiming the law when society nurtures itself through its transgression is a vanity. This is the reason why identifying and penetrating such mechanisms is of paramount importance. Beyond the conditions of production of knowledge, what is at stake is not the recognition of blacks—which is the colonized intellectual's own quest for the forlorn thing and the condition of its repeated failure—but the re-orientation of the republic toward a renewed self-perception and a social transformation. The narcissistic monologue of professional academics thus becomes the terrain of experimentation for determining modes of action and assessing their efficiency. In Fanon's own words in *Les Damnés de la terre*, the only way out resides in the discovery of the real and in its transformation by one's own praxis in movement.

Chapter Two

The Making of a Man

A Modernist Etiology of American Masculinities —
Trauma, Testimony, Resistance

Several aspects of James Baldwin's work have been discussed by modernist critics over the past few years. In particular, these critics focused on Henry James's influence on the way Baldwin approached identity (Johnson-Rouille; Hakutani) or, through the prism of T. S. Eliot, on the way he constructs subjectivity. Similarly, Baldwin's modernism is frequently associated with a Jamesian literary genealogy. Its African American cultural dimension, however, has been relatively understudied, and it is rarely seen as the expression of survival strategies resulting from the experience of racial domination— which is all the more devastating as it is intensified by violence between individuals and within the family. Evidence of this is found in his first novel *Go Tell It on the Mountain* (1953), his essay "Notes of a Native Son" (1955), and his short stories "The Outing" (1951), "The Rockpile" (1965), and "Going to Meet the Man" (1965), each of them revolving around the figure of a child—a child that Baldwin had never been able to be himself since, as he confessed, he was born already dead and, as such, deprived of existence (Campbell: 3). "Going to Meet the Man," translated in French as "Going to Meet the White Man" (which makes explicit the irony with which African American English indicates the racist equivalence between humanity and masculinity), is representative of the way he structures political, cultural, familial, and intra- and extra-textual spaces in a modernist formal cast, notably through the use of narrative collage and perceptual montage. Thanks to the embedding of perspectives and the play on internal focalization, the point of view progresses from that of the child *into* that of the adult—as channeled by the father. This, *in fine*, is an allegory that stands for the whole community and the whole nation. The overall sketch, resulting from the aggregation of different narrative vignettes, is only perceptible through the mediation of a (deceitfully) distant narrator. At the heart of this game of masks and of the scopic drive it determines, the way modernity perceives identity—and race in the very first place—is called into question: namely, a definition of the subject that is based on the wholeness and ownership of the self, considered as an inner space with clearly defined boundaries.

"Going to Meet the Man," which takes place during the civil rights movement, portrays Deputy Sheriff Jesse first as an adult, then as a child. This anamnestic portrait is also an anamorphic one, unveiling a description of America as an extreme and archaic country consumed by its own sexual and racial violence, and which, in addition to rationalizing its hateful rhetoric, can only be grasped through a return to childhood—a traumatic one in this case. In his recollections and through his violent conduct as a policeman (which itself becomes traumatic), Jesse is neurotically replicating the trauma he experienced as a child when he was forced to attend the lynching of a black man, who was castrated and burned alive. In Baldwin's writing and through the form he opted for, trauma becomes a modernist object in its own right, challenging the question of the point of view and blurring the boundaries between past and present, and even blurring the categories the short story should be assigned to. Indeed, it belongs to both fiction and testimonial literature, while also being a historical and cultural document. Psychoanalysis, a discipline born from the etiology of trauma, halfway between physical reality and psychological reality, has seized this mutual permeation between spaces which has divided modernity on the question of intersubjectivity.

What is at stake here is indeed the relationship from one to the other, symbolized in Baldwin's work by the motif of motion. This motif is developed through various forms: geographical, cultural, textual. It was Houston Baker Jr. who used the term "motion" (Baker, 1987: 16–17) in his study on African American modernism: both he and Baldwin agree on the deeper meaning carried by this motion—i.e., that of the subject's (re-)subjectivization, which has a highly political meaning because it relates to the conditions of existence. In the short story, at the heart of the dismembered bodies, amid the acrid smoke of burned flesh, the essential question to be heard is *Who are we in someone else's shoes?* And what—sometimes dissociative and destructive—strategies do we put in practice so as to not *actually* be there, so as not to remain within the fantasy that kills the other. "Going to Meet the Man" asks these questions about Jesse, whose Anglo-Saxon inheritance perspires through his subjectivity—that of a white and heterosexual masculinity, hermetic to any form of otherness (which is inevitably corrupting). In doing so—and through the vertiginous variations of the points of view and the montage through which the master's perspective becomes distorted—the short story makes visible the incarnate volatility of races, genders, and sexualities. As long as the reader makes the—also political—choice to look and see.

LYNCHING OR THE EROTIC FORM OF HATRED

Twenty years after his collection of stories "Going to Meet the Man," Baldwin wrote in "Here Be Dragons" (initially published in *Playboy* [1985] under the title "Freaks and the American Ideal of Manhood"):

> The American idea of sexuality appears to be rooted in the American idea of masculinity. Idea may not be the precise word, for the idea of one's sexuality can only with great violence be divorced or distanced from the idea of the self. Yet something resembling this rupture has certainly occurred (and is occurring) in American life, and violence has been the American daily bread since we have heard of America. This violence, furthermore, is not merely literal and actual but appears to be admired and lusted after, and the key to the American imagination . . . But no other country has ever made so successful and glamorous a romance out of genocide and slavery; therefore, perhaps the word I am searching for is not idea but ideal. The American ideal, then, of sexuality appears to be rooted in the American ideal of masculinity. (*The Price*: 678)

Developed in his first essay "Preservation of Innocence" (1949), this is one of the major arguments contained in Baldwin's work: under the guise of civilizational ideality, American imagination represses the fear that sex brings into racial violence (Rocchi, 2005). This unexhausted source of pleasure irrigates the whole society through the dual rational construction (in one cultural process) idealizing white masculinity and transforming the black individual into a mere abstraction, an entity devoid of humanity whose geometrical figure disappears into the landscape that absorbs, consumes it, and forgets it. At the end of the lynching scene, after the torture, the castration, and the immolation, where there once was a man is now a charred object melted to a charred ground: "Where the man had been, a great sheet of flame appeared . . . The head was caved in, one eye was torn out, one ear was hanging. But one had to look carefully to realize this, for it was, now, merely, a black charred object on the black, charred ground" (*Going to*: 251). The haunting repetition of the cardinal number *one* —which underlines the release of tension, the crowning moment in the effort to precipitate the black subject into the non-figurative and the unrepresentational that may at the same time prevent recognition, identification, and memory—is paralleled by the repeated association between the color black and the charred matter; this symbolization is all the more reductive and exclusive as the comma after the second occurrence of "black" defers any form of referentiality, as if, when all the cosmogony has been drained, the only help that earth could provide (and too late) was the modesty of its own burns. This power to annihilate, of which the story is the persistent mark and its voice the humanizing power that challenges it, continues to shape the American landscape, where very few memorial sites commemorate "terror lynchings"—a widespread practice largely tolerated by official authorities (Stevenson: 13). The reality of this situation also fosters the American national amnesia, which prevents the historic continuum from being fully acknowledged—a succession of two centuries of slavery, decades of lynchings, the racialization of life imprisonment and capital punishment decisions, and finally the contemporary resurgence of police violence toward African Americans, especially male and often young ones (Curry: 143–44; Henning; Stevenson: 17–23).

Thought over, reflected upon, applied methodically, the victimization of the African American community (i.e., resorting to barbaric treatment and physical and psychological torture) is a systemic process established in the long term. Lynchings are one emblematic example. They were at their peak during the period 1880–1945 (Stevenson: 13), which corresponds to the diegesis of "Going to Meet the Man." In the wake of African American historic and political texts such as those of Ida B. Wells ("Lynch Law," 1893), Frederick Douglass ("Why is the Negro Lynched?" 1895), and James Weldon Johnson (*Lynching: America's National Disgrace*, 1924), it may have served as a testimonial work and contributed to fill the gaps of the dominant white historiography. Other literary and artistic creations have also taken part in this process, such as the poems of Countee Cullen (*The Black Christ and Other Poems*, 1929) and Langston Hughes ("Silhouette," 1949) or, for visual arts, Charles H. Alston, who, shortly before the march on Washington, was to create the modernist group *Spiral* with Romare Bearden, Hale A. Woodruff, Norman Lewis, Emma Amos, Richard Mayhew, Alvin Hollingsworth, and Reginald A. Gammon Jr. (Soutif: 283). *Untitled* (1935), his charcoal drawing that uses chiaroscuro techniques, represents the castration of a black man, of whom only the upper part of the back and the upper part of his folded leg are visible (Apel: 249). The broken lines of the body echo the intersecting lines of a tree's trunk and branches looming over the body. In the center of the drawing, between the tree and the black man, stands the executioner, whose boney face is an ode to cubism and whose bulging eyes are the very definition of the erotic form of hatred (Stoller). Along a perfect diagonal line, the white blade of the knife is extended by the man's flexed left arm, which stretches to the sky; the contours of the sky are limited by the executioner's fist, which is raised in victory and holds his victim's semi-tumescent sex. Alston's drawing was not shown at either of two great exhibitions of 1935—namely, "An Art Commentary on Lynching," financed by the NAACP, and "Struggle for Negro Rights," organized by the American Communist Party (Apel: 239–40). But it is perhaps the softness of the charcoal technique, like a sensuous and perverse evocation of the skin's texture, that makes this representation so unbearable. This permanence of sensuality, which is lodged in horror and gives rise to a stubborn quest that is *de facto* only allowed by the experience of omnipotence, is very much present in Baldwin's short story:

> He watched the hanging, gleaming body, the most beautiful and terrible object he had ever seen till then. One of his father's friends reached up and in his hands he held a knife: and Jesse wished that he had been that man. It was a long, bright knife and the sun seemed to catch it, to play with it, to caress it—it was brighter than the fire . . . The man with the knife took the nigger's privates in his hand, one hand, still smiling, as though he were weighing them. In the cradle of the one white hand, the nigger's privates seemed as remote as meat being weighed in the scales . . . The white hand stretched them, cradled them, caressed them. Then the dying man's eyes looked straight into Jesse's eyes—it could not have been as long as a second, but it seemed longer than a year. Then Jesse screamed, and the crowd screamed as the knife flashed, first up, then down, cutting the dreadful thing away, and the blood came roaring down. (*Going to*: 250)

In this naturalist description of castration, in which the voyeur's scopic pleasure during the event is redoubled by his identification with the executioner in charge of the lynching (through the structuring perception of Jesse as a child), what characterizes Baldwin's interpretation of the lynching becomes visible. Unlike American literature from the South, which, as William Faulkner's "Dry September" (1931) and *Light in August* (1932) remind us, uses the rape of a white woman by a black man as a *topos*, Baldwin pushes into the background the frequent justification that the white woman's sacrality must be protected against the threat of black hypermasculinity, and that any (sometimes fictional) violation of it must be punished. If the motif of the lynching is only referred to once in "Going to Meet the Man" and is not further developed, it is because Baldwin is interested in a hidden reason—*the evidence of things not seen*, as one of his works is called: the racist and homophobic homo-erotic form of hatred underlying the construction of masculinity (Rocchi, 2009). Literary criticism has often focused on the edification aspect and civilizational dimension taken on by lynching in a racialized context. Apart from the teaching of terror it generates and the disciplinary aim of its sexual violence, it acts as a rite of passage and a ceremony of allegiance to the white patriarchy's law and order. Jesse goes to the lynching not knowing what he will discover there, with his family, as if he were going on a picnic for the Fourth of July (*Going to*: 244)—the only difference being that, in the words of his father, it is a picnic he will never forget (*Going to*: 245). It is actually the same secret (the naked truth of white masculinity) that Jesse summons up when, after becoming deputy sheriff of his small town and being confronted with the resistance of black civil rights activists, he hopes to contain—under his thumb and his insults (*Going to*: 234–37)—the disintegration of a changing world:

> Everyone felt this black suspicion in many ways, but no one knew how to express it. Men much older than he, who had been responsible for law and order much longer than he, were now much quieter than they had been, and the tone of their jokes, in a way that he could not quite put his fingers on, had changed. These men were his models, they had been friends to his father, and they had taught him what it meant to be a man . . . They were soldiers fighting a war, but their relationship to each other was that of accomplices in a crime. They all had to keep their mouths shut. (*Going to*: 239–41)

Policemen and military men remain silent regarding the secret of the male gender's fabrication: the proleptic announcement of a "crime committed together" (Kristeva), the lynching that establishes the community and, symbolically, the nation.

THE SHAPING OF MASCULINITY: MODERNIST WAYS OF SEEING

What being a man means, and what the figures of the sheriff, the soldier, and the father mean separately or collectively, is a matter of anxiety: the (perhaps archaic) anxiety of being part of nothing but pretense—pretense of an instituted order and control that are always threatened by the chaos of the world, to which the sacrificial rite responds by materializing on a sexual level the phenomenon of race. It is a three-term dialectical reasoning that transforms the scene displayed into a metaphor on culture and identity: the mask, thus, is the modernists' sign of signs (North: 63), which suggests the determinism of race and sex while denying its influence, so as to conceal the existential fragility of its ethos. As surely as Jesse, who is incapable of making love to Grace (simultaneously a Southern belle, his wife, and a sanctified mother-like figure [231–32]), sees his desire diminish, the structure of this motherly masculinity cracks along each breach opened on past atrocities—the blows, the mistreatment, the rapes that Jesse has perpetrated and that he tries to remember in order to maintain his desire. After each stage, in a descent punctuated with the recurring words "far away," his memory is filled with the song of resistance and the spirituals of the abhorred *niggers* who, quite literally, are spoiling his pleasure. To the lynching, the childhood, the hand-to-hand with his father, which harden his sex (*Going to*: 252).

This is the fulcrum where the narration excavates the child's eyes and voice, and when Baldwin's modernism is at its finest. In its perceptual dimension, it retains from African American literature optical aesthetics, which unlearn to look at the color of the skin to face one's fantasy. This modernism is also marked by the long teaching that Baldwin received from the painter Beauford Delaney, who taught him to see (Campbell: 21; Leeming) and to whom *Going to Meet the Man* is dedicated: to see this other reality where race stems from sexual violence, where human relationships are gripped by masochist sadism, where the adamic, unspoiled mythology of American innocence caves in on the genealogy of its masculinity. This point of view, like the childhood trauma, is all the more original and subversive, as it is white.

The lynching scene, thus, does not represent the only supremely edifying terrorism experienced by Jesse. It makes *another reality* visible, in which history and culture, their sordid horror and tenacious stench, are perverted and through which civilization and intimacy clash, the family being their meeting point. It is, within the peaceful and tidy representation of the world, the irruption of the Real, of what is impossible to symbolize (Roudinesco and Plon: 898). The text reconstructs on a visual level this psychological breaking-in through many expressions of the affect, which are symptomatic of a persistent trauma—in the burning race, the moist hand-to-hand between father and son, identified one to the other by the masochist sadism linking them and replacing the incestuous and homoerotic attachment of which the only thing left is a charred object on a land of ashes: the race. Perched on his father's shoulders, who is firmly holding his ankles, Jesse contemplates the torture scene with his entire body, which betrays his emotions: surprise and curiosity, at first ("Jesse pulled upward; his father's hands held him firmly by the ankles. He wanted to say something, he did not know what" [*Going to*: 249]); then fear ("Jesse clung to his father's neck in terror as the cry rolled over" [249]); bliss ("He began to feel a joy he had never felt before. He watched the hanging, gleaming body, the most beautiful and terrible object he had ever seen till then" [250]); sexual arousal ("but [the nigger's privates] seemed heavier, too, much heavier, and Jesse felt his scrotum tighten; and huge, huge, much bigger than his father's, flaccid, hairless, the largest thing he had ever seen till then, the blackest" [250]); and finally the oceanic ecstasy of grateful filial love ("his father's face was full of sweat, his eyes were very peaceful. At that moment Jesse loved his father more than he had ever loved him. He felt that his father had carried him through a mighty test, had revealed to him a great secret which would be the key to his life forever" [251]). The great secret of white masculinity—whose accomplished performativity stems from the repression of its incestuous homoeroticism and of which race is the exteriorized waste—will not be revealed. It is this secret that Jesse, as an adult, calls on for help during his failed intercourse with his wife. But while his reviviscence opens up on his parents' sighs of pleasure in their room the night before the lynching, it is the images of a burning man and a knife that revive his libido: "He thought of the man in the fire: he thought of the knife and grabbed himself and stroked himself and a terrible sound, something between a high laugh and a howl, came out of him and dragged his sleeping wife up on one elbow" (252). The lynching completes the (de)figuration of the American primitive scene.

This apparition—the power of the committed crime that haunts and repels the obsession of impotence—is both a veil and an unveiling, just like the secret that, for its transmission, its preservation and the value it takes from it, depends from them just as much. They are very similar to modernist techniques used by African American visual arts—namely, collage and montage. The scene within the scene, which can be distinguished without one or the other losing their fluidity, evokes, in the transformation achieved by mending the perceived object, the collages of Romare Bearden, who was Baldwin's contemporary. Upon his return from Paris in the 1940s, Bearden learned the technique of overlaying painted paper shapes (Soutif: 387). After his figurative, then cubist and abstract periods, the method of collage allowed him to provide the vision of a world "kaleidoscopically compressed in multiple spatial planes" (Greene) that connected—in a new environment that altered the reading—items that were completely heterogeneous and empirically recognizable, often cut from pictorial magazines such as *Look*, *Life*, and *Ebony* (Powell: 121–22; Cannon). The writer and gallerist Steve Cannon writes on this subject:

> Works like "Evening Meal of Prophet Peterson" and "Expulsion from Paradise" (both from 1964) are palimpsest-like collages consisting in part of cut-and-pasted images from magazines and newspapers, combined in a seemingly helter-skelter (but which is, in fact, a highly sophisticated, improvised) manner that at the same time suggests and denies narrative content. Interwoven with the photographic content are elements of painting, drawing, coloring and the entire range of modern art technique. ("The Art of Romare Bearden: A Retrospective by Geoffrey Jacques. Organized by the National Gallery of Art in Washington")

In Baldwin's work, the organization of the narration, which stems from the same aspiration for interior truth, corresponds on a textual level to the copy-paste of Bearden's images. The painter and collagist said in his manifesto "The Negro Artist and Modern Art" (1934) that beyond realism, this interior truth was typical of modern art. Indeed, each of the different micro-narratives making up this short story have their autonomy. The memory of the young black woman's rape (the first scene of the story), Jesse's brutality (as a police officer) toward the activist, and the remembrance of the lynching stand out from the flow of the diegesis through narrative, temporal, psychological, and somatic breaks such as, for example, the immersion into childhood and the fire baptism:

> He turned wordlessly toward his sleeping wife. *I stepped in the river at Jordan.* Where had he heard that song?

I stepped in the river at Jordan.
The water came to my knees.

He began to sweat. He felt an overwhelming fear, which yet contained a curious and dreadful pleasure.

I stepped in the river at Jordan.
The water came to my waist.

It had been night, as it was now, he was in the car between his mother and his father, his head in his mother's lap, sleepy, and yet full of excitement. The singing came from far away, across the dark fields. (*Going to*: 242)

In addition to their retaining their autonomy because of their specific contents, each narrated story delves deeper and sinks into an anterior temporality that reproduces the depth of Jesse's tormented psychology, into which the reader is progressively immersed. The rape reminds of other, earlier rapes, the political repression summons the white supremacism of the friends of Jesse's fathers, and the ritualized dimension of the lynching and castration brings them back to times immemorial. Incorporated in the dark mysteries of Jesse's traumatic memory after each spasm of his deficient sexuality, each episode provides its central event with a genealogy and a specific background. This background creates, on a formal level, a prominent volume that reinforces its unity, like the patches of a quilt or salt crystals. Yet these narrative vignettes are ruled by discursive chirality that, while confronting them, places their respective spheres within an asymmetrical relationship. Similar to the photograph fragments in a collage that alters their signification, the autonomy of these micro-narratives is counterbalanced by a network of internal echoes, of symmetrical effects, enabling the identification between characters. This is the case for Jesse, who, as a child, is identified with his friend Otis, an African American child who is eight years old too: it reminds the adult Jesse of the child that this civil rights activist once was. Armed with these psychological connections, Jesse's father warns his son against the potential threat that Otis represents—just before the lynching, during which the victim stands for the accomplished, castigated threat. In this exercise specific to the collage technique, which consists in veiling and unveiling and is reproduced by the short story through narrative techniques, the identifications between micro-narratives *create difference*—which is, according to Bearden, the inner truth of the modernist quest. Jesse will be neither Otis nor the man who is lynched and castrated. He will be like his father. In a staggering and totalitarian specular similarity.

Montage—the other great modernist technique—allows the reader to contemplate this similarity within the text. It is achieved by working on the point of view from which the short story's holistic cross lap unfolds. A symbol that is at once totemic and Jamesian, montage appears literally in the story's narrative entanglement through its most striking point of view, the dominant one from which the *excipit* is set ablaze: Jesse on his father's shoulders. It is the beaming chimera of a heightened masculinity connecting the bodies, where the son, heir to the sadistic pleasure, is an extension of the father. They are both indistinguishable and monstrous. This perspective that opens up on the fantasy of a hypersexualized black masculinity, whose alleged power is introjected by murder and immolation, closes the embedding of the previous points of view: successively, that of the omniscient narrator, of Jesse as an adult, of his father and of Jesse as a child.

In the same way that the micro-narratives oscillate between identity and difference, montage is blurring the structuring of the points of view. If they are distinguishable separately, they are, however, doubly amalgamated: through the narrator's point of view, the other dominant point of view in the text, which subsumes them all, but also through the ambiguous status of their perceptual modalities, which are related as much to dreaming as they are to fantasy. In the bedroom, in the *incipit*, Jesse's memories, which condense and intermingle the same motifs and the same characters—or their doubles— resemble half-awake dreams. But contrary to the first function that Freud attributed to dreaming, they do not accomplish desire (Freud, 1899). This lack is supposed to be compensated for by fantasy. But in the short story the origin of the fantasy is completely conscious. It proceeds from history and culture, and rather than the unconscious matter of dreams or fantasies, it is the matter of memory that filters representations. *Lynching and castrating have taken place*, and in their place, lurking in the darkness, remains the homoeroticism of hatred. It is between the two dominant points of view, in the space created from the narrator's point of view and that of Jesse sitting on his father's shoulders, that is produced the anamorphosis providing a way out of this point of view and delivering the truth. In the narrator's perspective, it is the sexualization of race relationships and the centrality of a masochist and sadistic psychological process; in that of Jesse, and in the theater of mascu- linity, instead of the homoerotic content of their acting, it is the racialization of actors. Thus, the scene is set in constant motion: there is a call-and- response pattern between sexualization and racialization, constructed by intertwining points of view and overlapping voices. For in the deceiving distance maintained by the narrator, the child's terror and perplexity are clearly audible: "*What did he do? Jesse wondered. What did the man do? What did he do?*—but he could not ask his father" (*Going to*: 249).

FORMED, DEFORMED, TRANSFORMED: MODERNISM'S POLITICAL PLASTICITY

Such a motion and the successive unveilings it gives rise to correspond very precisely to the essence of African American modernism. For Houston Baker Jr., it can be defined as "the mastery of form and the deformation of mastery" (Baker, 1987: 15), the form being understood by this literary critic and historian as a space with well-known dichotomies (such as those opposing the same and the other) but capable of transforming itself because it has its own power. In that respect, it is closer to "*motion seen* rather than "thing" being observed" (17).

According to Baker, who dates the birth of African American modernism from the keynote address delivered by Booker T. Washington on September 18, 1895, for the *Negro Exhibit of the Atlanta Cotton States and International Exposition* (15), what is at stake in formal mastery is the political dimension. Determined by material reality and the sociopolitical context, the dominated subject has no other option but to deform mastery. Two years later, in 1897, on the other side of the Atlantic Ocean, another important change of paradigm left its print on modernity and completely upset the vision of subject and subjectivity—namely, the inaugural stages of psychoanalysis when Freud, in his etiology of hysterical neuroses, abandoned his seduction theory, which connected his patients' trauma, such as rape, to an external event causality. He preferred the internal prevalence of psychological reality, which he began to develop from that moment on in his concept of fantasy (Korff-Sausse: 19–20; Roudinesco and Plon: 982–85). The shift from "traumatism" to "trauma" is a linguistic expression of this moment, the tipping point when the material reality and the events gave way to psychological reality and to the unconscious in determining the subject's subjectivization and, for a traumatic experience, their re-subjectivization or reconstruction. This change of perspective led to considerable debate bringing into opposition the Freudian orthodoxy and the partisans of a reinstatement of the event and material reality (Korff-Sausse: 19–22; Roudinesco and Plon: 982–85). This is also the intellectual, medical, and psychoanalytical background of the contemporary sociological phenomenon of the political recognition of trauma victims, who for a long time had been considered with suspicion (Fassin and Rechtman: 407). This is shown in the works of Freud, Abraham, and Ferenczi on soldiers injured during World War I.

Apart from being their transatlantic context, this history of ideas provides an enlightening approach to Baldwinian modernism and to the formal and political importance—to quote Baker's pattern—of the threefold relationship that the subject bears with itself, space, and the others. Such intersubjectivity blurs the boundary between material reality and psychological reality, all the while stimulating the mutual transfers and shifts between them. It also raises the question of interpretation, of how to perceive these realities, and, first of all, the possibility that both of them may coexist. Trauma, when continuous and denied, contravenes this to a great extent. Applied to the text, such a framework allows us to question the story once more, to reflect, *in fine*, no longer on what should be seen in it, but what should be heard from it. Between the two points of view that structure the lynching scene, the castrated and burned black man is the *blind spot* from which the space-changing dynamic enters in motion. The text does not provide any information on his feelings. There is only silent perplexity, suffering, and pain. This ellipsis (about which Houston Baker Jr. said that it was, along with the trope and poetic image, synonymous with the African American modernist form) is a precise reflection of catatonia and mental shock, which are the characteristic symptoms of trauma such as defined by Sandor Ferenczi: "An unexpected shock, unprepared and overwhelming, acts so to speak as an anesthetic. But how does this happen? Apparently by the interruption of all psychological activity combined by the installation of a state of passivity, lacking in any kind of resistance. The total paralysis of motility also includes the interruption of perception as well as the interruption of thought" (Korff-Sausse: 40). Ferenczi then adds,

> In the course of mental or physical torture . . . one draws strength to endure the suffering from the hope that sooner or later things will be different. One thus retains the unity of one's personality. But should the quality and quantity of suffering exceed the person's powers of comprehension, then one capitulates; ones endures no longer; it is no longer worthwhile to combine these painful things into a unit, and one is split into pieces. I do not suffer any more, indeed I cease to exist, at least as a complete ego. (Korff-Sausse: 129)

In the light of this split—a survival strategy that Ferenczi was to call "narcissistic split of the self" through which the trauma victim is split between one part that keeps on living and the other that is "encapsulated," asleep but ready to awake (Korff-Sausse: 21)—one can read the lynching scene and the whole story as an allegory of the American national trauma by comparing these two characters deeply buried in collective memory: the African American, reduced to a charred thing absorbed by the earth, and the child, whose innocence gets lost in the hateful and inculpative genealogy of masculinity. The text links them through the action of looking: "Then the dying man's eyes looked straight into Jesse's eyes—it could not have been as long as a second, but it seemed longer than a year" (*Going to*: 250–51). But this relationship in which, within a distended time, the man and the child, even momentarily, have the same identity to share, transforms the space that welcomes it and turns the lynching scene—an allegory of trauma—into a place of testimony and resistance: through its form, which speaks the two victims' silences by generating, from the extra-textual world and the political space of hermeneutics, the reader's incorporation. That by what or by whom another reality is not just perceived and discovered but created. It is a phantasmatic and literary reality bringing together the writer's and the reader's psyche through a text thanks to which the reader is the *telos* of the narration, the aim and recipient of a polyphony supported by the montage of different points of view, the repository of narrative vignettes that the centripetal force throws toward a center of gravity that provides their final meaning, the blind spot closed on a silent or forbidden voice (Depardieu): where there was a man, there is now a black object.

This ambiguous identity where subject and object are mixed up is in essence the reality of the reader who, fantasized by the text, exists without existing, remains in the objectivity when he/she is out of the text and, when inside the text, only acquires immaterial subjectivity: in a place that is not without reminding, in Freud's text "A Child Is Being Beaten" (1919), that of the son who looks at or fantasizes about his father's castigating one child and then other children—a text about which Julia Kristeva said that what was at stake there was "individuation." Halfway between subjectivization and reification, this place, in the short story, is occupied by the castrated and burned black man. It *may*, imaginarily, be occupied by the reader who, having become a full and differentiated subject, does not speak instead of the other but for him. Being the start of an exit from trauma and the action that may prevent any naturalization of the victimized position, speaking out, as well as the role of imagination, are under the reader's responsibility. Their very possibility hinges on a work on form and on the way it connects perceptual montage with narrative collage. It is also the story's ethical role, turned into a political modernist strength by Baldwin, as he brings the reader to discover humanity.

Chapter Three

Dying Metaphors and Deadly Fantasies

Freud, Baldwin, and the Meta-Psychoanalysis of Race

PSYCHOANALYSIS AND LITERATURE— READING THROUGH

Our method, which subordinates psychoanalytical theories to literature, partakes of an epistemological shift as regards identity, identity formation, the subject, and subjectivity. What is fundamentally at stake is to launch the critique of a modern Western subjectivity that conceives of the subject as being in a predetermined space that shapes its identities. To philosophical, sociohistorical, psychoanalytical, and cultural variations of this postulate, I oppose literature, where the double praxis of writing and reading not only creates the space of the text but also perpetually defers its closure. Furthermore, the common interest of Freudian psychoanalysis and literature in one figure of speech in particular—the metaphor—illustrates their strikingly obscure parenthood and the different ways space can be imagined, understood, or made intelligible. A prevalent conceptualization in both of them, for instance, consists in dividing space into interiority and exteriority, along a disjunctive tension to be theorized or transcended and reinvented. Through the act of reading, always unique and singular, literature keeps open the imaginative space it creates by substituting a bridging relation for the division between interiority and exteriority, between the text and reality, the metaphor and the object metaphorized. In this way, extra-textual reality and metaphorized objects are made utterly volatile, permanently diffracted through a kaleidoscopic perception that shifts according to time, space, and the reader's subjectivity, thus ensuring the renewal of interpretation and the possibility of a multiple relation to reality. The potentiality of literature also lies in the condition of the co-existence of subjectivities that would be equal, if not identical, starting with those introjected by the literary situation—the author, the narrator, the characters, and the reader.

Vis-à-vis metaphors, psychoanalysis has a comparable relation, but with a different objective. If psychoanalysis has recourse to the metaphorization of speech on which literature relies as well, it cannot offer itself the excessive luxury of a multiple reality that does not cohere with the ideals of science. For being accepted as a scientific theory functioning as a system, with an apparatus and a coded sociolect that articulates its own concepts and teleologies, psychoanalysis has to dry up, sip, and absorb metaphorization. Meanwhile, it is for the sake of the same coherence and scientific eligibility that metaphors cannot be cleared from the psychoanalytical text. This doubling of psychoanalysis's paradox can be explained by the condition of its own possibility—for being seen as the science that reveals the hidden truth of the unconscious, which by definition has no material reality, psychoanalysis needs to use metaphors but insofar as they are delimited, insofar as they are closed spaces bound to and determined by their location. Only in the defined space where science understands and is understood—culture—can the immateriality of the unconscious that metaphors capture be deemed scientific. Metaphors are thus necessary to psychoanalysis inasmuch as, contrary to literature, they are bereft of the limitless metaphorization power of speech, deprived of the possibility to open up the space of imagination, of (re)invented subjectivities. Inasmuch as metaphors "die" into psychoanalytical, scientific, cultural analogies. Psychoanalysis therefore strongly relies on the analogical use of cultural metaphors, such as the dark continent standing for the purposely mysterious and unknowable female psychology, the configuration of the psychic spaces represented by a landscape to be explored and colonized, or the Oedipus complex standing for family patterns and the subject's gendered and sexual formation.

In the relation between literature and psychoanalysis, and for what concerns the role of metaphors, similar conclusions can be drawn about the teleology of story-telling, which is the other great debt psychoanalysis has vis-à-vis literature. While being in literature a tension that the postulate of fiction does not allow to terminate, a circular movement that should not be interrupted, the teleology of story-telling provides for psychoanalysis the coherence and logic it seeks. Though important, rationality in literature is counterbalanced by the possibility of its failure, the uncontrolled turbulence style may provoke. In psychoanalysis, it is the theoretical ensemble that subdues such turbulence, salvaging from story-telling the pure impact of its rational unfolding. The tension has thus more to do with an arrested development, the story-telling with a vignette, a micro-story-told. When literature gives an impulse to movement, psychoanalysis controls it within the seemingly sealed off space it needs to stand for.

The story that psychoanalysis strives to tell is that of a subjectivity where psychosexual formation, gender, and sexuality obey unconscious, though rationalized, dynamics. One of the strategic means to institute this rationalization is to summon the much-spread cultural metaphor of race. This does not mean that Freudian psychosexual formation is strictly determined by race, nor that psychoanalysis does not, in turn, influence its cultural conception. Without speculating on the nature of their bond and their subsequent definition, what matters at this stage is to state that, in psychoanalysis, sex and race are irremediably related. This connection has been examined and analyzed by much of the recent critical literature that intends to explore the signification, potentialities, and limitations of psychoanalysis—as a theory of the subject based on sexual difference—when it comes to race. Nevertheless, most of the methodology therein employed rests paradoxically on a categorization that it contends to deconstruct. For instance, when Christopher Lane opens his edited collection of essays *The Psychoanalysis of Race* (1998) by remarking that psychoanalysis and race share a "conceptual interdependence" that few thinkers have theorized (7), he also posits psychoanalysis and race as categories that the collection does not apply to each other (12) but rather "implicate" "in ways which describe their joint enigmas and interpretive blind spots" (12). Exploring the "conceptual interdependence" of psychoanalysis and race while considering them *a priori* as operative concepts with differentiated terms, thereby postulated as external to each other, is problematic. One finds such a methodological shortcoming in Kalpana Seshadri-Crooks's essay "The Comedy of Domination: Psychoanalysis and the Conceit of Whiteness" (1998), where the author refers to Europe as the original space of the discourse of race (and not as the space that the discourse of race engenders), or in Daniel Boyarin's "What Does a Jew Want? Or, the Political Meaning of the Phallus" (1998), where he mentions the colony as the original space of the colonized (and not as the space, along with the metropolises, that colonization creates). A similar limitation can be identified in Sander L. Gilman's *Freud, Race, and Gender* (1993), where race, masculinity, and femininity are analyzed as social constructs whose elaboration and signification are already frozen by the cultural influence they bear. In fact, with inverted positions on the positive or negative influence that race may have had on Freud's account of sexual difference, Boyarin and Gilman follow the same logic. While Boyarin argues that "a series of potentially toxic political symptoms"—racism and an ambivalence toward homoeroticism—are generated in Freud by his self-alienation as a Jew living in an anti-Semitic cultural and historical context, Gilman explains Freud's account of sexual difference, which he criticizes, by his racial situation where Jews are feminized and homosexualized. Both these analyses speculate over race and sex by looking at each one from the perspective of the other. Meanwhile, and though their mutual implication, they refrain from examining their formation as concomitant and continuous. When race and desire can be more fruitfully regarded as spatializing each other, without interruption or limits, Boyarin and Gilman consider these spaces as already closed and, from and within them, ask the question of how Freud positioned himself racially. But, less than assessing Freud's position in the context, the point is to fathom how he created the position of psychoanalysis, and his own toward race and sexuality, *through* the psychoanalytical text. What is at stake is also how this text intends to take the "through" for an "in." This is what literature, as praxis, teaches theory—the effort to think through, a method for not considering seemingly closed spaces as hermetically sealed.

Thereby always situated in the closed spaces of geography, culture, and theorization, the relation between psychoanalytical psychosexuality and race can only be limited in scope. What these interpretations discard is the geographical, cultural, theoretical, and political reality psychoanalysis invents. This is not to claim that humanistic knowledge, and more particularly the various acceptations of race and sex, do not pre-exist psychoanalysis. But what psychoanalysis invents—or, more precisely, borrows and imports from literature—is their being encompassed within the limitless space of the psychic landscape and notably the unconscious. Meanwhile, the scientific and cultural environment of Freudian psychoanalysis requires that this limitless space should appear as being under control, with territories as delimited and differentiated as race is. Amounting to a chronologizing and interpretive misconception, these critical analyses have as a point of departure the effect sought by psychoanalysis—the idealized fantasy of itself as a science with a method (the interpretation of the subject's introspection), a field (the psychic landscape), and an object (the unconscious dynamics of sexual formation) that, though immaterial, can nonetheless be envisaged through the empirical character of race. In order not to repeat these mistakes, one needs to take psychoanalysis for what it is: a fantasy idealizing itself as scientific proof and cultural response. It concomitantly encloses and naturalizes the spaces of race, sex, and gender, but without rooting out within itself the possibility of seeing through and reopening them, provided one reads psychoanalysis through its fantasy, through literature.

While being a too neglected essence and safeguard of critical interpretation, the possibility of failing is inherent to literature. As already underlined concerning story-telling and style, leading rationality, systemic thoughts, teleological narratives, and the idealized fantasy of the Self—the Self as psychoanalysis, in Freud's case—to collapse re-establishes the free circulation of emotions, desire, and affects, while consciousness emerges as (re-invented) Self. This interweaving of emotions and reason that midwifes the open space of the text and of its multiple identities is described by James

Baldwin in "Freaks and the American Ideal of Manhood" (1985) as the overlapping of desire and imagination that fuel each other (*Baldwin, Collected Essays*: 815) to which chapter 2 has already referred. Such a statement does not only adequately encapsulate what literature and the praxis of writing stand for in Baldwin's eyes—it also refers in his text to the "possibilities of the human being." Though this can be considered as a return to the literary premises of psychoanalysis, my critical perspective is more precisely a shift. As the starting point of this analysis are Baldwin's "possibilities of the human being"—a black voice, a black subjectivity that are nowhere to be found in psychoanalysis—there is no place to return to. That place is, in fact, in black writing and literature, where being inside does not mean to be submitted to space, bound to the closed space of race and theory, as shown by Fanon, for whom the colonial experience does not limit itself to the colony, or by Du Bois, for whom being a problem within America revealed the untenable character of Tocqueville's idealized democracy. The place to shift to is where race is not a cultural metaphor, scientific proof, or the fantasy of psychoanalysis but the lived experience of being black, the open space of multiple possibilities. Black queer literature was for us such a place—but only to discover that the missing place, the lack of psychoanalysis, its absent black subjectivity, was not a circumscribed blind spot but the deadly fantasy that also engulfs identity thinking. Meanwhile, in a mesmerizing reflection, psychoanalysis invents itself through the controlled space of desire, through race as intimacy.

THE METAPHORIZATION OF THE "HALF-BREED"— FANTASY BEGINS

To understand how psychoanalysis invents itself through the closing space of race and sex, one needs, keeping Baldwin in mind, to ponder the historical moment when Freud captures the "half-breed," his sense and destiny, and gives bone and flesh to the fantasy of psychoanalysis. In his sketch of the fantasy, which will be a cornerstone in his account of gender formation and sexualities, Freud, in a complex interplay of identity and difference, draws an analogy with the so-called "half-breed" that eighteenth-century scientific racialism classified as the closest to the white race and with almost indiscernible black features. Within Freud's first topology of the psychic apparatus, which associates preconscious, conscious, and unconscious, the fantasy has the particularity of partaking at the same time of the unconscious and the preconscious. While belonging to the latter, it originates in the former. By this double nature it mirrors the supposed racial duality of mixed-race individuals. The triangulation between race, gender, and sexualities in psychoanalysis rests on this fundamental psychic location of the fantasy, whose ambivalence is compared by Freud to "individuals of mixed race who, taken all round, resemble white men, but who betray their colored descent by some striking feature or other, and on that account are excluded from society and enjoy none of the privileges of white people" ("The Unconscious," Standard Edition 14:191). Whereas Sander L. Gilman and Daniel Boyarin refer to the "half-breed" passage in their analysis of the rapport between psychoanalysis and race, they both situate their interpretation primarily in the specific frame of race *as* Jewishness, on the account of Freud's complex relation to his being a Jew. None of them relates Freud's definition of the fantasy and its near-invisible "half-breed" with his theorization of the self-blinding Oedipus whose eponymous complex terminates (through the castration complex) psychosexual formation and the fantasy of multiple gender identification.

In his attempt at demonstrating how race as Jewishness imprints its logic in Freud's construction of gender, Sander L. Gilman's exploration of their relation in *Freud, Race, and Gender* (1993) is essentially sociohistorical and cultural. Gilman argues that it was because of the strongly anti-Semitic environment of fin-de-siècle Austria that Freud elaborated an account of female gender formation that was first meant to be inclusionary and not exclusionary. Women were supposed to be a complement of men and not their opposite, a gender configuration that had, Gilman explains, an obvious racial subtext and agenda: the point for Freud was to use gender as the medium to facilitate the integration and acceptance of Jews. Since the circumcised and thus feminized Jewish male body stood as the metaphor for all Jews, the strategy followed by Freud was to project the supposedly feminine qualities of the male Jew onto the woman and use the latter as the vehicle, if not the foil, that would ease Jewish integration. While commenting upon the "half-breed" passage, Gilman also pinpoints that Freud evokes the "mixed race" when he compares the unconscious with the preconscious (21), which is, if not inaccurate, at least incomplete. Indeed, the "half-breed" does not metaphorize a comparison between the preconscious and the unconscious but a very particular state of psychic in-betweenness, that of the fantasy. The "mixed race" stands for the fantasy inasmuch as the latter is a psychic hybrid—belonging both to the preconscious and the unconscious. Gilman's analysis of Freud's inclusionary gender model parallels his reading of the psychic apparatus—masculinity, femininity, preconscious, and conscious are seen as *a priori* closed spaces to be penetrated, while Freud's textual analogy between the "half-breed" and the fantasy is more ambiguous. Gilman's implicit definition of cultural and metapsychological spaces as bounded also explains the reason why, while referring to the comparison of Jews (the so-called Negroes of Europe) and Africans, quite common at the time, he considerably downplays the anti-African and antiblack dimension present in the Freudian text. Race is the territory of Jewishness, as closed as psychic or gender spaces. But Jewishness, in turn, is more complex, divided, and divisive than it appears. As Gilman mentions, Freud acknowledged in his auto-biography that he was an "Eastern Jew" "out of his appropriate place and class and living now in the center of Austrian culture, Vienna" (14). Yet Freud was not truly an Eastern Jew: Gilman explains that Freud's family moved from Germany to the "Barbaric East" and then to Austria. This ten-sion between one place and another, between belonging or not, is quite symptomatic of the situation in late-nineteenth-century Europe of an accultu-rated Jew whom Freud liked to consider himself to be. To further Gilman's remark, one may also add that this situation of the acculturated Jew reflects, through the prism of belonging, the in-betweenness of the "half-breed" from the double vantage point of the fantasy and race. But at this point, one may ask a question discarded by Gilman: even though Jews were said to be the Negroes of Europe and Eastern Jews were associated with Africans, why did Freud illustrate the topology of the psyche and the double nature of the fantasy through an analogy with the "half-breed" and not with the acculturat-ed Western Jew since the two of them share this in-betweenness adequately fit for mirroring the ambivalent quality of the fantasy? Freud knew that any reference to Jewishness would be used against him and would harm the scientific credentials of his theory. What the "half-breed" thus metaphorizes is not only the fantasy but also what appears to be in fact Freud's fantasy of a theory of the fantasy, a rationalization in which what is at stake is the Euro-peanization of psychoanalysis thereby cleared—at least in this moment—of any obvious Jewish content that would not be Western and white. The "half-breed" comes opportunely to metaphorize the idealized erasure of this Jew-ishness that can be compared to blackness, foreshadowing the psychoanalyti-cal and phantasmatic construction of whiteness.

Gilman's restrictive reading of the racial content of the fantasy leads also to his underestimation of the role played by blackness in the psychoanalytical account of gender formation and sexualities, which also articulates phantas-matic constructions. Three years after "Unconscious" and its "half-breed" passage, Freud published <i>From the History of an Infantile Neurosis</i> (1918) dedicated to the well-known case of "the Wolf Man," where he elaborates what were to constitute the hallmark of psychoanalysis: the primal scene, the witnessing (or the phantasmatic representation) of parental sexual inter-course, and its dreamed sequel featuring the prospect of castration as a pun-ishment for such an infringement. The primal scene is a fantasy of origins where the parents are seen or imagined performing an indifferentiating anal penetration—in which both can penetrate and be penetrated. It does not cast out the possibility of a merging of desire and identification. Both parents being libidinally invested, the child can identify with his father and concomi-tantly desire him. This pleasurable drama comes to an end with another phantasmatic representation, related to the preceding one, that of the castra-tion that, in the text, takes the shape of a dream testifying in Freud's interpretation of the boy's internalization of a cultural law—a boy cannot be like his father and desire him for fear of being castrated, which is also the underlying logic of "Going to Meet the Man" as demonstrated in the previous chapter. But Lee Edelman has shown that Freud's interpretation of the child's recollected fantasy and dream is a re-construction that orientates both scenes toward the threatening castration and, thereby, represents, on the one hand, the stabilization of masculinity through the proscription of homosexual incest and, on the other hand, the establishment of sexual difference, as both a logical if not a natural outcome (Edelman: 174–83). This is also the conclusion drawn by Judith Butler's reading of the Oedipal complex in Freud's *The Ego and the Id* (1923), where she demonstrates that masculinity is already discriminated and posited before the unfolding of an Oedipus complex that precisely is supposed to lead to sexual difference (Butler, 1990: 57–78). The interest of such a construction resides in presenting the renunciation to homosexual attachments as necessary—a conclusion that Diana Fuss also reached in her interpretation of Freud's understanding of femininity, desire, and female identification in her essay "Freud's Fallen Women: Identification, Desire, and 'A Case of Homosexuality in a Woman.'"

Though most of these lesbian and queer critics' insights do not elaborate on the implications that such a reading of the fantasy, with all its destabilizing potential, may have for race—a lacuna that will be further analyzed in the last part of this chapter—a parallel examination of the two paradigms of race and gender allows us to identify both of them as phantasmatic and closed spaces. In fact, if we were to unfold the different layers of the initial "half-breed" metaphor within the narrative where it is embedded, we could eventually envisage the metaphor for what it stands—the psychoanalytical fantasy as both whiteness and heterosexual masculinity. Besides scientific objectivism, Freud's lack of sympathy or compassion for the "half-breed's" misfortune can logically be explained by the fact that the latter is an embodied absence of subjectivity without history, consciousness, or feelings. He is reduced to a phallic presence that penetrates without consent the white world to "enjoy [its] privileges" and that should consequently be punished, a catastrophic *mise en abyme* of what could be Freud's destiny in the anti-Semitic universe of science. By being thus unmasked as black, he is skinned, literally cut into two halves ("half-breed"), and the phallus he was is textually and metaphorically circumcised. He becomes a Jew by no longer being white.

Is this a contradiction of the earlier conclusion drawn? Or, conversely, does this (re)doubling of the Self represent, in the midst of his own fantasy as scientist, Freud's most dreaded scenario that, while foreshadowing the "Wolf Man's" primal scene and dream of castration, would confirm that Jewishness not only is to be seen as white but also *has* to be seen as white? If the "half-breed" is a metaphor of the fantasy that engenders the psychoanalyst's fantasy of himself as white, once inserted in a narrative that also functions as a metaphor standing for circumcision, the whole passage has then to be read as an allegory of psychoanalysis—visibly renouncing Jewishness, visibly indulging in racism but invisibly re-inscribing a Jewish identity, which is *potentially* black. A coded reflective mirror, the text delineates the space for an identification between Freud and the "half-breed." But, as Butler points out after Jacqueline Rose, identification being not identity is bound to fail. To determine the extent to which psychoanalysis invents a modern, white, straight subjectivity, one needs to explore the reason why this identification should fail in the first place, and this implies looking at the relation between Freud and the "half-breed," within the unconscious of psychoanalysis— where there is more to see than what meets the eye. As Slavoj Žižek argues in the essay "Love Thy Neighbor? No, Thanks!" any power relation is sexualized as soon as "an intrinsic ambiguity creeps in, so that it is no longer clear who is effectively the master and who is the servant" (170). What kind of sexual content is there to understand in the bond that the textual circumcision—the coming to the fore of the black skin—seals between Freud and the "half-breed" and how the black Jew of the text loses his Jewishness?

THE FANTASY OF RACE AND THE FATHERING OF PSYCHOANALYSIS

In the literary and cultural heritage of the father of psychoanalysis, who dreamed of a Judaism without God while identifying with Moses, there is a passage from the Old Testament of particular interest to us. Ham's curse can well stand as the hypo-textual primal scene of psychoanalysis that the "half-breed" text re-constructs. In this perspective, Ham's punishment would be internalized, translated into a textual circumcision, a literal and crippling blackness that foreshadows the ominous threat of castration that, incidentally, Freud identified as "the deepest unconscious root of anti-Semitism" in *Analysis of a Phobia in a Five-Year-Old Boy* (*SE*, 10:198–99; quoted by Daniel Boyarin in Lane [214]), where the term "castration complex" appears for the first time. The "reading through" of the biblical passage reveals that the deepest unconscious root of psychoanalysis—as a response to anti-Semitism—is the excision, the rooting out of homoeroticism cryptically metaphorized in the Freudian text by blackness. In a fantasy of origins of sort, the book of Genesis situates the genealogy of Ham's descent—which apologues of slavery would conveniently see as black—in a well-known family drama featuring a troubled father, Noah, and a troubling son, Ham. Catching sight of his father's nakedness as Noah is lying drunk in the vines, Ham is punished for his transgression of the divine rules through his descendants. His son, Canaan, will be the slave of his uncles Sem and Japhet, and Canaan's sons will be the slaves of their descendants. Not only does Ham's transgenerational curse enclose his descent in the differentiated sphere of a specific lineage singularized by its social status—a race that is different and inferior—it leaves Noah's patriarchal power unharmed. Indeed, the castration of Ham's homoerotic gaze onto his father has no consequence for his position.[1] The son being punished through his sons, the son's father escapes punishment and therefore guilt. While Ham's descent is trapped in the closed space of a different race, Noah safely remains the father of all his sons, including Ham, as long as homoeroticism is punished and cast out. The condition for a tenable identification between father and son is the banishment of the possibility of homosexual desire between them. The renunciation of the homosexual possibility founds the father-and-son relationship. The bond prevails over the bonding. Of course, the return of the cursed within the primary circle entails that homosexuality is again visibly present, justifying retroactively that the renunciation of homosexuality as well should be transgenerational. It has thus to run through sons and fathers until God, substituting the rainbow that symbolized his bond with Noah, seals with Abraham, son of the sons of Sem, the new bond of circumcision—the naked truth of Jewishness as homosexual bonding castrated.

In the psychoanalytical text, where nakedness is metaphorical, homoeroticism is present inasmuch as it is textually castrated through blackness. The father-and-son relation has to be searched in discernible traces that Freud may have disseminated within and without the "half-breed" passage while he fathered psychoanalysis. As previously pointed out, the "half-breed" echoes intra-textually other instances of the fantasy, particularly fantasies of origins, such as castration in the "Wolf Man" case or as it completes the Oedipal complex. In both cases, the repudiation of male homosexuality in a family context is at stake. But more importantly, in Freud's text, the "half-breed" himself is defined as belonging to a "specie" engendered by drives of which he is the "Abkömmlinge," the German term for "descent" or "offspring." As fantasy, the "half-breed" is the son but only as what can be called "the son of a drive," a biological impulse with no other history than the narrative psychoanalysis that unfolds and encloses upon him with no father. It is the absent father that ensures the failed identification between Freud and the "half-breed" and the subsequent impossibility of homosexual bonding between father and son. There cannot be any homoeroticism since there is neither father nor son. Or, more precisely, like Noah and Ham, they do not belong to the same sphere, the "half-breed" being sent back to drives, biology, and race. Meanwhile, if the "half-breed" is a black Jew, the text encrypts his Jewishness and no father acknowledges him. It is precisely from this emptied space of asserted fatherness that metapsychology supersedes biology, history, and religion, engendering a fantasy of race where whiteness is the color metaphor of a successful repudiation of homosexuality. It is kept in the shadowy depths of the unconscious, surfacing only as text and skin.

BALDWIN'S SHIFTING PERSPECTIVE—BACK TO BLACK

For James Baldwin, whose whole life and works revolved around the exploration of white consciousness, the text and skin are not the porous surface
where the unconscious (homo)sexual roots of race emerge but the acknowledged synecdoche of the black lived experience in America. From a vantage
point that Freud's text does not frame—that of Ham, whom Baldwin identifies with the African American, notably in *Go Tell It on the Mountain*
(1953) and *The Fire Next Time* (1963)—Baldwin elaborates an etiology of
the white man's fantasy *as* reality. In this reality, not only are blacks and
homosexuals differentiated between and confined to specific spaces, but they
are also raped, castrated, and burned alive, as "Going to Meet the Man"
testifies. Freud's theorized construction of whiteness, with its intermingled
conscious and unconscious algebra, is here physically inscribed on landscapes and faces. In what could be a vibrant response to Freud's silenced
voice of the "half-breed," this is how Baldwin reads the text, mind, and lips
of white America, captured in their absence on the African face:

> They face each other, the Negro and the African, over a gulf of three hundred
> years—an alienation too vast to be conquered in an evening's good-will, too
> heavy and too double edged ever to be trapped in speech. This alienation
> causes the Negro to recognize that he is a hybrid. Not a physical hybrid
> merely: in every aspect of his living he betrays the memory of the auction
> block and the impact of the happy ending. In white Americans he finds re-
> flected—repeated, as it were, in a higher key—his tensions, his terrors, his
> tenderness. Dimly and for the first time, there begins to fall into perspective
> the nature of the roles they have played in the lives and history of each other.
> Now he is bone of their bone, flesh of their flesh; they have loved and hated
> and obsessed and feared each other and his blood is in their soil. Therefore he
> cannot deny them, nor can they ever be divorced. (Baldwin, 1998: 89)

A moment of *anagnorisis* that the "half-breed" passage failed to be, Baldwin's text is striking in the resemblance it bears to Freud's. Nonetheless, if
one can contend that, like the "half-breed" vis-à-vis the Jewishness-white-
ness rapport, the African enables us to question the relation of black and
white Americans, the latter triangulation is not a subtext or a context but the
kernel of the passage. Furthermore, the African represents the point of departure of the emerging consciousness at the backdrop of which "alienation" has
to be understood. Indeed, the Negro is estranged not from the African but
from what he embodies in his eyes—the immensity of a boundless time and
space, fathomable only through the traumatic stigmas ("conquered," "too
heavy and too double edged," "trapped") the situation of the encounter encapsulates. A Freudian "hybrid" in reverse that, through the history and
geography that were missing in Freud, has become another self. In this un-

canny moment of dis-alienation, the two selves are in fact reunited. In a logic exactly opposite to Freud's, where subjects are determined by discriminated spaces, the encounter on the Seine puts in perspective two *re*-locations. The first one is the Negro's in his face-to-face with the African whom he *recognizes* as an other self. This recognition dries up the source of estrangement. The second interlocks the three spaces of Africa, Europe, and America. The blurring of their frontiers is achieved through the encounter itself, a *mise en abyme* that doubles the dis-location in Paris and in Africa of an American scene thereby manifestly bound to the triangle of the slave trade. This is what white Americans do not recognize, their "alienation," that maintains them out of consciousness and within fantasy. To the "half-breed" fantasy in Freud, Baldwin responds with whites' lack of consciousness. The "alienation" at stake is thus not the Negro's, who is no longer estranged from Africa and the African, but the white American's, for whom the closed spaces of racial and national identity rationalize the split between a phantasmatic self-idealization and the unbearable horror of reality. Besides, the African is not cast out for the purpose of a scientific demonstration but is included in a narrativization that aims at showing the opposite.

Much more in accord with the tenets of psychoanalysis than the Freudian text itself, Baldwin's "encounter" puts to the fore the failure of speech ("an alienation too vast . . . to be trapped in speech")—beyond rationality what the text addresses is the desire and imagination the Freudian fantasy has cut itself from. In this perspective as well, the intertextual identification of the two "hybrids" breaks against another major difference: the use in Baldwin of a highly emotional style that unveils the sophisticated grammar of self-consciousness. It is through its literary quality that Baldwin's text comes to "signify" on Freud's subterranean teleology of fantasy and identity. While Freud's "half-breed" betrayed by "some striking feature or other" (191) the truth of biology and his black ancestry, the Negro's living in Baldwin betrays, first and foremost, memory and history, which are obviously absent from the psychoanalytical "hybrid" portrait. Moreover, whereas betraying equaled betrayal and entailed exclusion in Freud's narrative, it expresses revelation and announces communion in Baldwin. As a subjective experience further enhanced by the "tensions," "terrors," and "tenderness," the Negro's memory unfurls along this ternary rhythm into a bridging history between white Americans and black Americans, already associated with Africans. This unacknowledged communion would remain a sheer drama, unreal and artificial, if, as it falls into the "perspective" the text creates, "the nature of their roles" were not revealed by the empirical fact of miscegenation. Its truth imposes itself naturally, as it were, and all the more so that it is thrust forward with the authoritative force of biblical scansion and metaphors: "Now he is bone of their bone, flesh of their flesh." Whereas the Freudian text relied on implacable logic, freezing cultural metaphors and story-telling, Baldwin's narrative strategy founds itself on an emotional intensity meant to strengthen and quicken the process of signification. The first part of the last-but-one sentence of the passage—"they have loved and hated and obsessed and feared each other"—is exemplary of this technique. It is a syntactical unit whose continuity rests on the haunting repetition of "and"—the lexicalized obsessive bond, the nature of which is the key to "alienation"—that the phrase translates into affects, the historical communion between blacks and whites, past and present, to which the use of the present perfect testifies as well. But the awakening that emotions mediate would not be complete if history and emotions, as communal as they might be, were not being returned to the "hybrid" for an empowerment of which the "half-breed," castrated by the text, was deprived. The power of the Negro is the text, which unveils truth and within this truth gives him the features of resistance, face to face with the fantasy. The Negro's empowerment, through consciousness and desire, history, and emotions, is discernible in the key metaphor of the "happy ending," coordinated to the "auction block." Behind the scathing irony that, in the fashion of the pastoral-like narratives of antebellum plantation life, re-casts the purchase of the slave into the "happy ending" of an American wedding, creeps the ugliness of reality—the incomprehensible bond of economic exploitation and sadistic violence through collective rape and mass murder. This is the *raison d'être* of white Americans' continued denial of the Negro, despite the fact that they cannot "be divorced." While necessary to the system and indelible in memories, if not in history, the white fantasy as idealization continues to keep horror at bay and produce another reality based on falsehood and bad faith. The text and the "hybrid" make this reality of the fantasy inescapable. Reflecting the "encounter" on the Seine, while giving it its hidden sense, the "auction block" is the theater of another scene, the "hybrid" and the white American's own primal scene, which is here the object of an ellipsis. Like the bond between the "hybrid" and the white American, recalling Freud and the "half-breed's," the scene is visible only through the trace it left, the "impact of the happy ending" between the master and the female slave. The "impact," the offspring of this probable rape, is the "hybrid" himself. As "his blood is in his soil," his self is reflected in the white man who is thus unmasked as father while the text draws the Negro's face as America.

Decontextualized in Freud's "half-breed," the repudiation of homoeroticism in the construction of whiteness is central in Baldwin's works. Alluded to in "Encounter on the Seine" through the use of vocables such as "tenderness" or "loved," the homoeroticism of male bonding is often re-coded elsewhere in contexts of explicit sexualized violence. A passage from Baldwin's "Nobody Knows My Name" (1959) stands for the American version of Freud's "Wolf-Man" and of his primal scene. It re-casts castration not as the universal fantasy that stabilizes masculinity through the rejection of femininity but as the cultural law of white America, and particularly the law of the South, which forbids manifest homoerotic bonding and, first and foremost, that between father and son, through a racialized and sadistic violence. In "Nobody Knows My Name," Baldwin develops the "very bitter interracial history" (*Baldwin, Collected Essays*: 203) he had sketched in "Encounter on the Seine," re-uniting this time the artificially opposed spaces of Southern and Northern America, which form the same nightmarish reality. As in "Encounter," the "bitter interracial history" is "written in the faces of the people" and on the "Southern landscape—the trees, the silence, the liquid heat . . . [which] seems designed for violence, seems, almost, to demand it" (203). Desire is everywhere to be seen, while invisible, inconceivable in its horror, only conceivable as a fantasy of origins requiring historical revision. While on the outskirts of Atlanta, the writer's mind's eye visualizes it as a hallucinated scene, discovered "out here; over this fence, behind that tree, in the darkness, there" (203). As striking as Noah's nakedness, this scene of desire betrays more than the memory of the auction block, more than the awareness of being the offspring of a rape, it opens wide the incommensurable gulf of nothingness onto the self. In the Southern primal scene where black and white fathers merge in hatred, where desire originates in crime, the writer contemplates his conception as non-being. For him, in order to be and keep open the possibilities of his being black, re-invent himself and survive, the recourse to imagination is the only way out from the maddening trap of history, the deadly abyss of consciousness. The essay therefore rewrites the historical reality of black women's rape by white masters into an improbable romance between the white man and "his concubine, the sensual-looking black girl" (204). But the ugliness of reality is not evaded by the writer's fantasy that includes the possibility of its unveiling as imaginary and false. Contrary to Freud's double sequence of the "Wolf-Man's" hallucination of his parents' intercourse, the primal scene, and the subsequent dream of castration, Baldwin's narrative joins both the fantasy and castration within the same unit. In this indifferentiating textual space, the ambivalence of the rape/romance micro-narrative is thus dislocated—dissolved as it is being shifted—into the ambiguity of the black man's castration that closes the passage and gives back to the rape/romance its reality as sexualized violence. Meanwhile, it also reveals the significance of homoeroticism in the family/national drama, both phantasmatic and historical:

> And the white man must have seen his guilt written somewhere else, seen it all the time, even if his sin was merely lust, even if his sin lay in nothing but his power: in the eyes of the black man. He may not have stolen his woman, but he had certainly stolen his freedom—this black man, who had a body like his, and passions like his, and a ruder, more erotic beauty. How many times has the Southern day come up to find that black man, sexless, hanging from a tree! (204)

The white man's guilt is eventually determined by the homoerotic attraction of the black male body, whose castration identifies him as the transgressor. While giving centrality to homoerotic desire, Baldwin's fantasy of origins makes manifest the latent logic of Freud's insights in the "Wolf-Man" case and in the "half-breed" passage. What castration aims at is the punishment of a homosexuality that blackness metaphorizes and that is a threat for the white father. One can incidentally recognize him through the homoeroticized identification between the white man and the black man that echoes, in "Encounter on the Seine," the "tensions," "terrors," and "tenderness" the "hybrid" saw reflected in white Americans. Patriarchy and power, as white and heterosexual, thus consolidate themselves through the same rejection of homosexuality, the same psychological matrix, in fin-de-siècle Vienna, in Paris-on-the-Seine, or in the Southern cultural context where strange metaphors, "sexless, hanging from a tree" (204), recall that the violence of fantasy is a reality.

RACE RELATIONS AS SADOMASOCHISTIC POWER STRUCTURE

Indeed, only through violence—onto the Other and/or self-inflicted—can the closing spaces of race and sex, and of the father's position within them, lead to the idealization the fantasy produces. The violence of the "half-breed's" castration and his exclusion from the white world enhance the mastery of the psychoanalytical discourse, while masking any too obvious Jewish content. The violence of white Americans' denial and alienation in "Encounter on the Seine" is the condition to keep afloat the mythology of a benevolent white paternalism, a history of lies and crimes in which the writer of "Nobody Knows My Name" blinds himself before acknowledging its full signification. This is also Baldwin's own phantasmatic idealization of himself as father of the text, as a writer in an ontogenesis that, after transcending the biographical family in "Notes of a Native Son" (1955), transcends now the historical one, securing for himself the possibility of self-transformation. The violence transpiring through the maddening text being the price of his and the reader's ticket, provided the idealization of literature is safe.

Baldwin was well aware of the role played by violence in the phantasmatic construction of identities, and more particularly in the idealization of white American masculinity, as already argued in chapter 2 through the reading of "Freaks and the American Ideal of Manhood" (1985). Baldwin explains in this essay that the reality produced by the fantasy—the idealization—can be obtained only at the cost of a divorce between "the idea of one's sexuality" and "the idea of the self" (815). In this respect, he is close to Jacques Lacan, whose "fundamental thesis is that a minimum of 'idealization'—of the interposition of phantasmatic frame by means of which the subject assumes a distance from the real—constitutes our 'sense of reality': 'Reality' occurs insofar as the real is not (and does not come) 'too close,'" as Žižek argues (166). But in the American context, the distance from the "real" (the ugliness of reality), from, in Baldwin's terms, "the idea of one's sexuality," is covered by a "violence [that] is not merely literal and actual but appears to be admired and lusted after, and the key to the American imagination," adds Baldwin (815). This also means that the violent distancing from sex relocates the sex it meant to repudiate in the very midst of the idealized self. It is within that perspective that Baldwin frames his understanding of American interraciality, where discourses on race, pregnant with idealization, supply through violence the resolution to a sexuality that cannot be controlled or mastered, which is inherently in excess. Violence per se is sexual. Race provides the good reason to unleash it in the blackness of pain and pleasure, onto the Other and in oneself—a reading frame that a critical return to Baldwin's "Going to Meet the Man" (1965) sustains.

As the Freudian "half-breed's" textual circumcision/castration tentatively bore the possibility of an identification between the Jewish psychoanalyst and the "hybrid," the castrated black man of Baldwin's short story supports an identification with Jesse, the discontinuously impotent white sheriff, until the racist, masculinist, and heterosexist American ideology puts an end to it. Two elements identify them with each other in the story: Otis, Jesse's childhood best friend, whom the unnamed castrated black man reminds him of, and the physical castration whose scene, witnessed when he was a child, Jesse needs obsessively to recollect to overcome his impotence during sexual intercourse with Grace, his wife. This interracial identification and its homoerotic component shifts at the end of the narrative into a father and son one when Jesse, still a child, seated on his father's shoulders, watches, in the middle of the roaring crowd, a black man being castrated and burned. The lynching scene ends on the paroxystic form of love that Jesse then felt for his father. It also signals his entry into the community of white men that the South and the American nation extend. Seen through the synthetic prism of psychology, ethics, and politics, the spectacle of torture that the story stages and that narrativizes what Baldwin would call in "Freaks and the American Ideal of Manhood" "the key to the American imagination" can only stand as a cultural aberration allowed by ideological and political wrongs. It is reason gone astray. Indeed, when not considered in a utilitarian or didactic perspective, lynching, public humiliations, and other forms of spectacles of pain—minutely analyzed by Saidiya V. Hartman in *Scenes of Subjection, Terror, Slavery, and Self-Making in 19th Century America* (1997)—can only be seen as a psychological deviance of a sadistic kind, easily dismissed for being pathological. But as Baldwin's accounts recall, the frontier between strict utilitarianism and pathology is tenuous. There would have been, for instance, no slave system—culturally accepted while legally endorsed and protected—without slave breeding or rape, and therefore without a primary sexual arousal that, in this context, cannot be deemed abnormal. When it comes to the notion of spectacle, one may follow Hartman's Butlerian analysis and claim that it is through its display that torture performatively justifies itself beyond ethical or cultural contradictions. This is what Baldwin's texts make manifest in Freud: the racializing psychosexual dynamics that fulfill their role in the elaboration of white identity through the violence of their textual display. In relation to identity formation, the question is therefore not "how can violence and torture be ethically and culturally accepted?" but rather "how can they be sustained within an idealization of the self?" In "Going to Meet the Man," the scene of torture is saturated with similes comparing the black man's bodily parts to the white father's and son's, as in "Nobody Knows My Name." These comparisons underline in the child's vision the shared humanity without which there cannot be any identification, be it compassionate or sadistic. Seeing himself and his father in the man in flames, the child recognizes his humanity. Meanwhile, it is the scene of torture that unfolds in its conclusion the rational explanation to the excess of emotions, fear, anxiety, fascination, and intense pleasure it has aroused in the child, his father and mother, and their friends: from a human body the black man has been turned into "a black charred object on the black, charred ground" (950). The rational explanation the torture scene provides, while securing the minimum of identification for the circulation of emotions, is This is not a man like us. But for this rationalization to take place, identification has to fail and, as Judith Butler suggests in *Bodies That Matter: On the Discursive Limits of Sex* (1993a), identifications are bound to do so:

> Identification is constantly figured as a desired event or accomplishment, but one which finally is never achieved; identification is the phantasmatic staging of the event. In this sense, identifications belong to the imaginary; they are phantasmatic efforts of alignment, loyalty, ambiguous and cross-corporeal cohabitation; they unsettle the "I"; they are the sedimentation of the "we" in the constitution of any "I," the structuring presence of alterity in the very formulation of the "I." (105)

From the Other in a failed identification the black man becomes subhuman, animal, object. It is also the logic of racism, as Lewis R. Gordon explains in "African-American Philosophy, Race, and the Geography of Reason."

> Since the Self-Other dialectic constitutes ethical relationships premised upon a hidden equality (each self is another's other and vice versa), and since antiblack racism depends on a fundamental inequality (a human-below-human relation from the standpoint of the white, a human-other-human relation from

> the standpoint of the black), a system of unilateral ethical relations results,
> wherein blacks experience ethical responsibility in relation to whites but
> whites do not exemplify such reciprocity. The consequence is that racism
> destroys the Self-Other dialectic and collapses into the double world identified
> by double consciousness: a Self-Other *and* Nonself-Nonother structure. It is, in
> other words, the denial of the humanity of the black as *another human being*
> before the white. (L. R. Gordon and J. A. Gordon: 12)

What violence thus displays and enables the implementation of is a rationalized and racialized hierarchization between a Self and an Other that *a
priori* were related as equals and could thus be identified with each other.
Running counter to Elaine Scarry's argument in *The Body in Pain: The
Making and Unmaking of the World* (1985), according to which the suffering
body and the agent of the suffering are absolute opposites, or to Hannah
Arendt's when she suggests that Nazi camps were beyond logic and rationality in *Auschwitz & Jerusalem*, the present analysis also implies that there is a
disjunction, a rupture in the humanizing emotional identification that will
allow the corollary dehumanizing rationalization to occur. This disjunctive
moment is central in the unleashing of violence and in the torture scene. It is
the moment when rationality and affects collapse into each other, when consciousness is suspended, when the Self is being shattered by the spectacle of
death whose image of ultimate failure reflects its own. It is this anguish of
being shattered and the murderous aggressiveness toward others that brother-
ly love, as sublimation of sexuality, is supposed to assuage, as Freud argues
in *Civilization and Its Discontents* (1930). But according to Leo Bersani in
The Freudian Body, Psychoanalysis and Art (1986), Freud had understood at
an earlier stage that sexuality was necessarily about failure, that one could
not in sex relate to others or assuage the anxiety stemming from the anguish
of being shattered. From this realization he felt the need to rewrite sexuality
within a historical and teleological perspective—salvaging pleasure, sexualization, and procreation—so that it would not be meaningless. Though he had
already sketched in *Three Essays on the Theory of Sexuality* (1905) an analysis of sadism as a masochistic identification with the suffering object—which
he would develop ten years later in "Instincts and their Vicissitudes"—Freud,
Bersani adds, could not come to terms with this unsettling truth about sexuality: bound to fail, sexuality in itself would be a form of sadism, a masochistic
identification with the suffering object.

While proffering an idealization of itself and borrowing coherence, logic,
and power of conviction from science and literary narratives, psychoanalysis
would therefore stem from the catastrophic fantasy that the intrinsic failure of
its object study—sexuality—could be (like) its own. In this perspective, the
"half-breed's" textual castration can be re-interpreted as Freud's sadism or
masochistic identification, reflecting in fact his own suffering as a Jew in an
anti-Semitic world. In Freud's cultural environment, where anti-Semitism is

expressed through utterly sexual forms, particularly misogynous and homophobic, the circumcised Jew also mirrors the failure of sex, and the subsequent illusion of gender and race, all unbearable to his persecutors. Freud's idealized self as scientist and his positioning as white would thus be the mask concealing his masochistic identification with the "half-breed." In a hide-and-seek dialectic, this would be the meaning of the violence of Freud's "half-breed" and Baldwin's torture scene: the outcome of a structure of failure where necessarily unachieved identifications—like the homoerotic one between father and son—find their resolution into pain, onto others, and self-inflicted. But the difference between Freud and Baldwin is that the latter shows what the former hides, and, in this display, it is the violence of white consciousness as heterosexuality that is disclosed. The sadism with which Baldwin's "hybrid," "Negro," and "black man" are treated in his essays, short stories, and novels encodes a form of masochistic identification typical of white American Puritanism whose homophobic undercurrent also founds masculinity, as Baldwin explains in "Freaks and the American Ideal of Manhood." It is in such a paradigm that he locates most of his white male characters. Besides Jesse in "Going to Meet the Man," there is also, for instance, David, the first-person narrator of *Giovanni's Room* (1955) whose long, self-flagellating confession as a guilty, closeted gay man parallels the semiotic castration of a black presence invading the text, but always in the guise of signs, and never as fully embodied subjects.

In these narratives, homoerotic desire is the agent of punishment whose pleasurable pain is already within the law. As such, race relations incarnate a (sado)masochistic power structure where, bound to fail in violence, inter-subjectivity is maddening or murderous. Incidentally, madness, in its para-noiac, psychotic, or neurotic forms, translates the emotional upsurge of the shattered Self that, in a racist context, does not equate the failure of reason. Baldwin's white male characters are not mad. They live in a madness of race and sex masquerading as normality. Contrary to what Henry Louis Gates Jr. argues in "Talking That Talk" (1986: 205), the racist's error, and theirs, is not one of thought, simply because it is not an error in the first place—reason has not gone astray. Rather, the cultural injunctions to master one's pain and pleasure with one's emotions are no longer complied with, either because the social conditions of the racist environment no longer provide the means for channeling emotions, through, for instance, idealization, or because these conditions are in conflict with other powerful sources of emotional arousal, since to dehumanize and torture requires great strength and mastery. It is thus a conflict between what is and what should be, or what society asks for, that Baldwin depicts in his anatomy of American racism. In "Going to Meet the Man," Jesse's paranoiac and neurotic symptoms do not betray his guilt at being a racist but his guilt at not being a good enough one: a good enough white man whose racism proves the castigation of his homoerotic desire.

Therefore, it is not reason that fails; it is the call of racism for not failing in the repudiation of homosexuality.

The safety net or, according to the point of view, the deadly fantasy, is provided by race and the ideologies of hierachized differences. They maintain the illusion that pleasure is not in the pain that cultural, religious, or psychoanalytical laws inflict. A phantasmatic idealization that contains the return of a shattering and threatening ugly reality. Meanwhile, within the structure of failure that masochistic identification unfolds, these systems preserve their *jouissance*, an unacknowledged "surplus-enjoyment" that finishes reifying the other—as alluded to in chapter 1 when applied to academia. While desire is defined by the "gap between a positive object of desire and desire itself," "jouissance emerges when the very reality that is the source of unpleasure, of pain, is experienced as a source of traumatic excessive pleasure . . . In clear contrast to desire, jouissance (or libido, or drive) is by definition 'dirty' and/or ugly; it is always 'too close,'" as Žižek demonstrates in Lacanian terms (158–67). One easily recognizes here the features of the castrated black man, Jesse and his father's *jouissance*, or those of the "half-breed," which is Freud's. The "half-breed" is the offspring of drives, possibly ugly and dirty, at least with striking features, and too close since already within the white world. As such, he is Freud's source of unpleasure and the embodied reminder of his Jewish condition and of homophobic anti-Semitism. But this displeasure soon gives way to the irrepressible vertigo to be in, to be part of, to belong to the world of science, white and gentile, and straight. Though excessive, this pleasure is also contained within the psychoanalytical fantasy the "half-breed" has become: a conceptual tool, working as the lever of Freud's self-idealization as scientist—his own "black charred object on the black, charred ground."

To quell the prospect of its own destruction, the Self therefore needs to be idealized through the creation of an Other. An Other like it, for the idealization to be possible, while unlike it for it to be continued. This combination of identification and differentiation is the metapsychological matrix of race where, while opposing identity and difference, ideologies endow them with values. The same relation binding identification and differentiation underlies the elaboration of metaphors for which speech is the initial matrix, the space where signifieds and signifiers take on their respective value in function of an all-mighty referentiality. Most erring readings of race and desire, taken separately or considered together, originate from this underestimation: race and desire, alike, are a movement until they are arrested. To make the terms of this simile metaphorize each other is already to be ideological and to fall into the ready-made trap of chronologizing sex over race and vice versa, or hierarchizing them, since while being isomorphic, race and desire are not parallel but perpendicular. They are not their mutual and respective Self and Other. Each contains the possibility of the other's Self-and-Other binary. As an ideological construct, what race represents is the lever that dissociates hetero- and homoerotic desire, masculinity, and femininity, while allowing their hierarchization. Similarly, ideological constructs of gender and sexual difference provide the categories for thinking of races as separate and unequal, or mixed and degenerated. The cross-like framework the two perpendicular structures form together delineates the closed space of the family or the nation where white fathers rule, oppose, castrate, punish for fear of being unmasked in the frailty of their power, pleasurable and self-destructive. Freud, Noah, and Jesse's father are in this respect emblematic figures, immersed in pain and pleasure and whiteness that the literary text exposes in the nakedness of their fantasy.

OF THE FAILURE IN THE METHOD: TOWARD A META-PSYCHOANALYSIS OF RACE

In order to pursue this exposition and the exploration of the "metapsychological matrix of race," it is necessary to return to the lacuna earlier on identified in contemporary lesbian, gay, and queer psychoanalytical critique and that prolongs Freud's subordination—if not complete absence—of race in the conceptualization of both gender and sexuality.

Indeed, from Freud to subsequent critiques of him by lesbian, gay, and queer studies, race has been manifested primarily through its absence or its effacement. This racial void is freighted with consequences: it in part invalidates the recourse to the method of applied psychoanalysis, which would produce a psychoanalytical reading of black literature, whether in its African American, diaspora, or postcolonial forms. Consequently, it requires the use of an inverse method, which Pierre Bayard calls "applied literature" (43) in *Peut-on appliquer la littérature à la psychanalyse?* [Can Literature Be Applied to Literature?], and which consists of inventing new conceptual and methodological psychoanalytical tools from literary texts that make manifest how much race has been absorbed in the discourses and the systems addressing sexuality—which has so far been the point of the reading of Freud through Baldwin.

Because of the organic link between psychoanalysis and literature, Bayard establishes his method on the latter. Constructed on such a loose foundation, the edification of the method ends up collapsing. In effect, an analytical method based on literature is in itself a paradox; as it can only exist through a singular reading, it eludes the very idea of transmission. Bayard's impossible method thus reveals what psychoanalysis refuses to admit about its own method: it is impossible to theorize successfully an object that resists constituting itself as such. For Bayard the object is literature; for Freud it is sex. The theory and the method that fail are, for the former, literature applied to psychoanalysis, and, for the latter, a psychoanalysis that works. I will retain Bayard's method of "applied literature" complete with its failures since, as Lewis R. Gordon (in keeping with Frantz Fanon) reminds us, failure is productive when correctly interpreted.[2] The point is to show that it is precisely through failure that applied black literature can succeed, though this may not be the successful idealization that psychoanalysis proposes.

The queer criticism of the past few years attributed success in psychoanalysis to Freud's sheer strength of will exhibited in the face of evidence relative to the failure of sex. Beyond this and because such failure, as has been argued so far, is consubstantial with psychoanalysis, literature, and identity, it must be integrated into the method itself, as must the relationship of the failure to the method to be considered. According to this perspective, race is to be considered as an identification destined by its very nature to fail, but one that has been forced to prevail as a form of identity. The successful circumvention of this failure has its roots and its expression in sexuality. It remains, however, perceptible in Freudian texts, and in the queer texts that criticize them, through the disappearance of race as a fully constituted object and therefore "theorizable" on the same level as sex.

No matter how productive they are methodologically, the theories of sexuality, whether they are superseded, as in psychoanalysis, or reintegrated, as in queer criticism, fail to deliver their anticipated returns. Within the very method itself, what these failings reproduce time and again is race—not as an object, but as a primary condition so that sexuality has an object—that Freud circumscribes by the use of psychoanalysis. The very grounds upon which the Freudian argument posits the results of its analyses are called into question by queer readings. Because it is not considered as an object, race becomes the condition for the existence of sexuality in so much as the latter is a failure that one dissimulates. Thus race, as either an object or a condition, is not doomed to this failure, which promises to save the method from the black hole of its object. As a result, conditions are created that allow both psychoanalysis and queer criticism to lapse into racism by default. The examination of the conditions and their effects, on the one hand, and the attempt to begin to elaborate another method, on the other hand, are what I call the "metapsychoanalysis of race." It has its origins in the results of the method of applied literature—that is, its failure. Its objective is not to circumvent the implicit foundation of psychoanalysis—that is, its failure. It follows the same critical pathways as the queer Freudian method, but backward, with a point of departure that queer Freudian method does not envision: race. In fact, it does not attempt to destroy it, as Frantz Fanon started to do. The failure is tamed by literature, through successive readings of James Baldwin, Melvin Dixon, or Rozena Maart, as the content of this book aims to show.

To understand why lesbian, gay, and queer theory in the Freudian tradition fails to think about race, one must retrace its intellectual heritage. Influenced respectively by feminism, on the one hand, and post-structuralism and post-modernism, on the other hand, the lesbian and gay theory of the 1980s and its queer variant of the 1990s are Euro-American hybrids. The history of ideas and the American cultural context are important for several reasons in understanding the limits of Freudian homosexual criticism. They contradict the idea that the influence of psychoanalysis in the United States would be limited to the evolution of "Ego Psychology," a therapy that aims at an ideal of adaptation, so dear to American pragmatism, and, additionally, toward the evolution of a sort of psychiatric medicalization. In fact, it produced a variety of currents, some of which contributed to culturalism and differentialism.

From the anthropological conceit established by the former that each culture is irrevocably particular, the latter takes the idea of a generalized difference applicable to groups and to individuals. Both break, then, with the universalism of psychoanalysis without totally rejecting it. Testifying to this is one of the most important vectors of psychoanalysis in the United States, the works of the cultural anthropologist Margaret Mead. The second reason why the history of ideas and the cultural context are heavy with significance is that in Europe, as in the United States, the transatlantic framework finds itself cracked down the middle by the racial demarcation at its very heart. It is in this American cultural perspective, where the theory of difference advocates the rapprochement of races through the acceptance of their specificities and from which feminism also emerged, that it is necessary to consider the particular underestimation of race, which lesbian, gay, and queer criticism brings to Freudian psychoanalysis.

If, through its study of infantile sexuality, psychoanalysis universalized and removed the guilt from sexuality—or, indeed, took it away from the psychiatric nosology of the end of the nineteenth century—its progressivism, with the unconsciousness causing an epistemological revolution, stopped however at homosexuality. Homosexuality was no longer conceived of as a pathological abnormality but understood from the equally simplistic, though less stigmatizing, perspective of immaturity (Rocchi, 2003). In their Foucauldian or Derridian commentaries on Freud's texts, American lesbian, gay, and queer theorists—among whom the influence of Diana Fuss, Judith Butler, and Leo Bersani should be cited—criticize this stigmatization and this reductionism. By attempting to dismantle the difference between the sexes, they show that the opposition between masculinity and femininity is a construction (Butler, 1990: 35–78). The stability of this construction depends on a primordial division between homosexuality and heterosexuality that psychoanalysis uses according to the principle that desire and identification are mutually exclusive (Fuss; Freud, 1920). In other words, a child can only identify with the parent of the same sex if he/she does not desire him/her.

The reading of Freud through homosexual criticism participates, in fact, in the change of intellectual viewpoint on sexuality, which translates, at the university level, into the emergence of queer theory. This theory is anchored in lesbian feminism, but, in this case, its break with social movements was cleaner and more rapid. Certainly, it conceptualizes sexuality in a more labile, plural, and fragmentary form, thereby renouncing the gender categories to which gay studies and lesbian feminism are historically more attached. But, as the last stage in homosexual criticism in its organic evolution, it does not integrate the notion of race into its approach anymore than its predecessors did. In the 1970s and 1980s, American lesbian feminism had already seen its logic of class and race questioned. Since then, even as lesbian and black workers took on the term "queer" to underscore the fact that they detached themselves from this monolithic lesbian feminism, the racial question still remains peripheral to queer theory (Garber).

Thus, over the course of her work on the Freudian concept of identification, and notably in her works *Gender Trouble: Feminism and the Subversion of Identity* and *Bodies That Matter: On the Discursive Limits of Sex*, Judith Butler explains that the identification with heterosexuality is produced by the identification with homosexuality as an abjection (1993a: 112). This cultural construction encourages the renouncement of homosexuality, which recalls the melancholy and homoerotic childhood attachment to the parent of the same sex (Butler, 1990: 57–65). In *Bodies that Matter*, Butler maintains that one can find this same logic of repudiation in a racial context (Seshadi-Crooks: 370); however, the analysis does not go beyond this observation. It is essentially from a pre-established theoretical body of work that Butler confronts herself with the question of the racialized subject, as some of her essays on Frantz Fanon prove.[3]

Another example, the queer reading of James Baldwin, Frantz Fanon, and W. E. B. Du Bois in *Homographesis: Essays in Gay Literary and Cultural Theory* (1994),[4] relies on Freudianism and Lacanianism, corrected from a homosexual viewpoint, though still not conceptualized on the basis of race. Finally, the same remark can be made in regard to *Homos, repenser l'identité* (1998), in which Leo Bersani references race in an analogous fashion (47, 59, 82–83, 87–88, 109). In its psychoanalytical approach, queer theory thus makes race a "non-thought," confined to the terrain of experience or reduced by analogy to its own consolidation.

For European Freudianism as for American queer criticism, the "non-thought" of race is the remnant of an essentialist tradition of difference that has been rationalized in France from the end of the seventeenth century in the form of a racial hierarchy. It is transmitted to psychoanalysis through biology and to queer criticism through the cultural anthropology underlying feminism. Constructed on the refusal of a scientific heritage that asserts the primacy of essence, psychoanalysis and Freudian queer criticism, nevertheless, inherit from race a balance that they equally owe to such an epistemological rupture. In terms of biology and of the organization and functioning of human societies, in Europe as in the United States, the most probing proof that race, sexuality, and gender draw from the same source as essentialism is provided in the nineteenth century by the virulent menace posed by degeneration. Just as miscegenation is linked to infertility, homosexuality is a social scourge; and both are held to contribute to the decline of civilization. And yet theories of sexuality continued to develop separately. So much so that race appears not just as a "non-thought" but also as politically inconceivable (in the strategic sense of the term). Queer criticism takes root in the possibility of existing within differentialism such that the American university is its privileged fortification. As for Freudian psychoanalysis, it tries to distinguish itself from biology of which it is partly a result. When considered as much a cultural manifestation as a theory, the relationship to race of both queer criticism and Freudian psychoanalysis is analogous and not genetic, which prevents them from viewing themselves from a subjective distance and moving beyond their flaws.

THE POLITICALLY "INCONCEIVABLE" OF RACE: FROM EFFECT OF SEXUALITY TO IMAGINED DESIRE

Such an analogy is primordial. Because it brings psychoanalysis' new outlook on sexuality, the unconscious, and the subjectivity of the subject back to race (Rocchi, 2004c) while continuing to make sexuality an effect of race without envisioning the complementary perspective by which race is an effect of sexuality. This is the hypothesis I have sketched in the first part of this chapter in the Baldwinian reading-through of Freud's text, starting with the Freudian fantasy and the observation of its *métis* in its psychic and spatial duality.

The result of this reading-through is that contrary to the approaches of lesbian, gay, and queer theory and to the racial criticism of Gilman and Boyarin, the subject should not be considered within a predetermined space but rather for his/her possibilities in creating it. In Freud's case, he invents the space of psychoanalysis. Enclosed upon itself, this space also becomes that of a white consciousness conceived as a renouncement of homosexuality. Revisiting the psychoanalytical space renders visible the racial effect of a renouncement that, according to queer theory, also establishes the foundation for gender. It also reveals from the text that it is a subjective and political space that can be universalized, in so much as it remains particular, and open to identity, in so much as it stays imagined—a possibility best proffered by art and literature.

It is art and literature, in effect, that best compensate Freudian psychoanalysis and queer theory in their "non-thought" of race. Thinkers of black consciousness, W. E. B. Du Bois, Frantz Fanon, James Baldwin, and Steve

Biko, for example, are also writers who, expressing themselves through a permanent hybridization, combine intellectualization and feeling, rationality and affectivity, abstraction and emotion, consciousness and desire—cleavages that Robert Misrahi reminds us are present throughout Western philosophy (1991: 204, 212), as pointed out earlier in the introduction. The texts *The Souls of Black Folk* (1903), *Peau noire, masques blancs* (1952), and also *Notes of A Native Son* (1955) or *I Write What I Like* (1978) use the reconciliation between consciousness and desire to abolish the border between the interiority of the subject and its exterior, to dismantle categories and to escape from the closed spaces of literary genres, of the taxonomy of the human sciences and of the racial divide, which Freudian psychoanalysis and queer theory fail to do, or rather, in their effort to circumscribe their own space, succeed in maintaining.

Inversely, Fanon refuses to make the subject into a closed space, "a substantialized tower"[5] as he says of the past. The most beautiful illustration of this abolished frontier between interiority and exteriority appears on the last page of *Peau noire, masques blancs.* The key phrase is "O my body, make of me a man who always questions!" where missing knowledge is a source of introspection that remains open to the exterior, without this same exterior being the limitation or manifestation of lack, which is already posited. In this way, the black consciousness of Fanon breaks away from the Hegelian desire in which the Other is the basis for self-consciousness and rather conceives of desire as the space of possibilities embraced by the subject to transform himself—a lack therefore that is not a call for recognition. It is, through the body, the consciousness of a man-in-the-making, a vision that recalls the Baldwinian concept of race as an imagined desire. In effect, the comparison of the African American author to the Martiniquan-Algerian author is justified beyond the fact that they were contemporaries. Like Fanon, for whom the "Negro consciousness" is "self-adherent,"[6] for Baldwin black consciousness is not determined by its relationship to white consciousness but by the relationship to desire that subsumes them both. Then, in the etiology proposed by Baldwin, the sexual dimension, by dint of its fantasying character, shifts race into the psychic space of the subjectivity of the modern subject. This psychic space, to which Freudian psychoanalysis attributes a white and heterosexual syntax, surpasses its American geographic and cultural framework and thus recovers that of the colonial situation. If Fanon's treatment of sexuality is often understood as the masculinist or heterosexist reflection of racism, it also corresponds to a social psychopathology in which all forms of sexuality are a metaphor for an alienating colonial position (as much for the black as for the white, the colonized and the colonizer, the colony and the metropolis), making race and sexuality indissociable factors of the same psychic space that, while white consciousness defines itself, are also hierarchized and rendered discreet.

This can be black consciousness's contribution to the meta-psychoanalysis of race, a psychoanalytical anti-theory issuing from applied literature, a method that Pierre Bayard reminds us "would not attempt to project an exterior theory onto literary texts, but, on the contrary, would produce theory from these texts."[7] The matrix texts would be black, in the Fanonian sense of the term. That is to say that they would not be black by the skin color or culture of their authors but by the consciousness of what the black condition signifies: to be reduced to an identity by the essentialist substrate of race. And of what it *could* signify: the incarnation of the open field with multiple identifications. Because they are literary and they allow for an evasion of meaning that, moreover, is integral to them, these texts give way to an anti-theory that would resist systemic authority. As the inverse reflection of psychoanalysis, the anti-theory leads to the failure of hierarchized identities through a continuous and successful multiple identification.

In addition to concepts, black literary texts and the anti-theory would produce their own tools, thereby revealing what doesn't work in psychoanalysis: a dysfunction of which race and the renouncement of homosexuality are the symptom and the cleavage between consciousness and desire, the profound cause. The creation of these tools would also enable us to return to the origins of psychoanalysis, which borrows so much from literature to forge its Oedipus and Electra, or notions such as narcissism, sadism, and masochism. It is the consciousness of this return that would prevent the tool from enclosing itself in the concept, and the practice from exhausting itself in the verification of the theory. The origin would no longer be the point of departure from whence it is necessary to distance itself, but a marker to which to return to re-imagine it. Henceforth, it would be vain to construct the anti-theory on the repudiation of psychoanalysis. This is comparable to sapping the source from which its theory and its practice ceaselessly reinvent themselves. The meta-psychoanalytic tool of race would, however, permit the correction from the black and homosexual point of view of its perspective and its effects, from the black and homosexual point of view so that it would no longer need to be one. Literature through its own strengths provides glimpses of this.

The desiring black consciousness of Baldwin, or that of Fanon, is one of these tools. Others would be added to them. They would propose a different reading, one pregnant with connections between fantasy and reality, sadism and masochism, desire and identification. The Freudian categories would no longer be limited psychic spaces for the creation of differences in order to inoculate sex, but the literary tools destined to inflict political effects.

An emotional method of consciousness, black literary texts and the conceptualization stemming from them would thus aim to render the reader singular, above and beyond the identities that were transmitted to him/her, including those of which he/she is unconscious, while eventually questioning what our experience of the text—with the identifications it creates—says about our identities.

Chapter Four

Desire as "E mag e nation"

*South African Black Consciousness and Post-Identity in
Rozena Marrt's "No Rosa, No District Six"*

POSTCOLONIALITY AND POST-IDENTITY

Up until the 1960s and 1970s, self-image in the black literature of post-slavery and postcolonial societies was used more as a pretext to underscore the caesura between the Self and the Other than as an occasion to examine more closely the re-creation of separateness and its underlying psychosocial and historical motivations. For the new generation of black writers of the 1990s, the literary aim is not to represent a self-image that, like the negative of a photograph, inversely reflects the image of the postulated Other it was before the political changes of African American desegregation, the decolonization of Africa, the advent of *négritude* and *créolité* or, even more recently, South African liberation. For these writers, this consists of making the text and its signification into the mirror of a Self rendered continually fissionable by the energy of sexual desire. Not that the fission of a black Self is absent from the works of Baldwin, Lorde, Morrison, and Walker, to only cite African American authors, but the desire at work in their texts—though central to their project of the diffraction and complexifying of self-image, most notably through female and homosexual prisms—are contained within the framework of identity in its familial, communal, and national declensions, which form a system of reference through which desire signifies.

Emerging from the dying ideologies, paradigms, and certainties of the twentieth century, this new generation of black writers has a marked defiance toward any predetermined identity—including those fixed by the theoretical-cultural literature of psychoanalytical, sociological, and historical inspiration that represents all or a part of their intellectual training. They make sexual desire and its literary metaphorization into the active principle of excess: rather than having desire included in identity, the point is now to overflow its boundaries. The Self thus erupts from the image and, by the fission dynamizing it, regenerates, transforms, and expands over multiplied spaces like so many contiguous territories adding on to themselves.

Whether specializing in gender, sexualities, or geographical-cultural spheres, these novelists, short story writers, poets, and artists—such as, among others, Sapphire, Essex Hemphill, Joseph Beam, Randall Kenan, Melvin Dixon, Adrian Stanford, Assotto Saint, Norman G. Kester, and Rozena Maart, to whom this chapter is specifically dedicated—are the writers of the regeneration of the "after" through desire.

Conceived as both an act of the imagination and a carnal encounter between the reader and the text, their writing, which one could qualify as of "post-identity," follows the deterritorializations, the circumvolutions, and the transformations of consciousness tied to desire, freed from historical determinism, territorial confines, and societal injunctions. The weight of the *post* in the post-slavery or postcolonial heritage is thus lightened, and the very idea of chronological rupture, of spatial disjunction or of the schize of the subject thus becomes obsolete. Intended as a new self-image, post-identity does not so much signify a desertion of political territory as its reconfiguration around the subject, singled out by his/her lifestyle choices, singular in his/her aesthetic options.

At the heart of this reconfiguration of the subject, whose identity crisis reflects those of the social and political bodies, exists a free and multiple identification in opposition to those that would continue to prescribe or proscribe allegiances to race, nation, gender, and sexuality. These allegiances are indeed problematic inasmuch as they absorb both the subject and his/her subjectivity to the detriment of other options of identity. The subject is entirely engulfed in an impulse toward a singular idea of him-/herself—an impulse that is all the more powerful as it stems from the trauma of a rupture. This rupture is catastrophic for Paul Gilroy when he defines the unitary space of the black diasporic diversity through the common experience of slavery (Gilroy: 187–97). It is phantasmatic, and no less traumatizing, for Freud when he makes heterosexuality out to be the univocal and culturally logical expression of masculinity under the constant menace of castration as the two previous chapters have illustrated. From the viewpoint of postcolonial studies or traditional psychoanalytical discourse on the subject, and beyond their scientific and/or disciplinary expectations, the rupture works paradoxically in the same way for the continuity of values that it induces: there is *in fine* only a rupture in the changing of paradigms and not in the justification of their axiology. The *post* here is pretext: it circumscribes nothing more than what was already postulated about the becoming of the subject. No matter what prevails from an epistemological rupture—which is, in fact, illusory—these discourses consequently come back to an unmistakably essentialist conception, marginalizing the multiple identifications through which the subject identifies him-/herself, for example, as both male and homosexual, black and queer, South African and lesbian. Very much in accordance with the desiring black subject as a reading method and the meta-psychoanalysis of race, studying black and queer literature thus offers possibilities for theoretical and political deconstruction, not only because the authors' complex subjectivities reveal the blind spots of the doxas about the subject but also because the literary position, the bringing into play—the play of desire—of plural, dissimilar, contradictory identifications, accepted or rejected in the course of reading, create a *mise en abyme* on the identifications underlying the construction of individual and collective identities that the theories of the subject strive to synthesize and simplify to rein in and put in place. Here the *post* is political. By the term "writers of post-identity," one therefore does not so much designate those who come after the generation of affirmed identity—as implied in "postcolonial"—but, in a primordial manner, the authors and intellectuals who strongly deny the nature of the political role given to *post* and to the mirage of the monolithic definition of the subject, his/her identifications and his/her identities, and where writing about desire is just as political.

Influenced by queer culture, Deleuze's identity theory, feminine and feminist writing, Baldwin's anatomy of the subject's multi-positionality, Glissant's rhizomes, and Derridian deconstruction, post-identity is a practice that explores in-betweenness, indetermination, and intersectionality while challenging the subject's enclosure in historicity and in teleological designs. It also calls into question the imposed and refuted cultural identifications that make identity into an invariable state and the subject into the subject of an "after," of the melancholy-of-the-too-late—his/her gaze fixed on the individual and collective past by whose yardstick he/she never ceases to measure him-/herself and die. As the driving force of this challenge, sexual desire also takes on the color of black consciousness. This places these writers at the exact confluence of, on the one hand, black texts remaining under the dictates of identity—and even those preoccupied by the representation of sex—and, on the other hand, contemporary Western literature in tune with the lesbian, gay, transgender, bi, and queer social movements but ignorant and/or unconscious of the existential and transnational dimension of the present-day black being.

Making their lives and their works the place for connection in which there is neither a before nor an after, neither a rupture between the political and the aesthetic nor a hiatus between the becoming of the subject and the future of the community, between the black being and sexual desire, post-identity writers question the construction of identity and the excessive role that "the after" plays in it. Forming a wall upon which the free and multiple identification of the subject hits a stumbling block, "the after" and the caesura that open the field of identities become, through the text, the opening for the rebirth of the Self. A desiring Self, the same as everyone else, like the text in which desire signifies the possibility of many concomitant and complementary identifications, where one's self-image is always displaced and indeterminate, an identity freed from predetermination, liberated from the genitive tyranny of the "of" that cuts, links, and binds the Self to the image and its social introjections. The text of desire as the location of a metaphorical Self. South African writer Rozena Maart is an example of this ethic and this aesthetic: black, sexual, political, and continually plural.

"NO ROSA, NO DISTRICT SIX" — POST-IDENTITY AS WRITING PROJECT

In the short story "No Rosa, No District Six," for which she won the Canadian *Journey Prize* in 1991, South African writer Rozena Maart describes the awakening of a black female consciousness through the witnessing of a lesbian primal scene. Through the coalescence of the discovery of desire and the rediscovery of the South African nation, the "e mag e nation" of the child Maart was under the apartheid regime in the Cape Town neighborhood of District Six is channeled through the writing of the adult she has become. Through old stigmas of memory, now transformed into textual interstices, the child's imagination and the adult's writing project a new image; from the white traces of dislocation, the *nation* of apartheid is recomposed by the *imagination*/"e mag e nation" of the writer and the child, reunited.

A fictional self-portrait, the story opens with an uninterrupted flow of words from "the female-child" (122) whose fertile and dissident imagination cannot be contained by familial and institutional authorities. Rosa's imagination resembles her speech. A phonetic mix of English, Afrikaans, and a "patois" whose unique rhythmic accentual chain imposes its surging parataxis on the text, unpunctuated until the final period that closes the long first sentence in which the little girl's entire discourse is contained:

> Mummy and mamma always say dat I make tings up and dat I have a lively e mag e nation and dat I'm like der people in der olden days dat jus used to tell stories about udder people before dem and dats why mummy and mamma orways tear my papers up and trow it away but tis not true I never make tings up I orways tell mamma what happened and mamma doan believe me and I tell mummy and mummy doan believe me too and den I write it on a paper or on der wall or behind Ospavat building or in der sand at der park and Mr Franks at school he don't believe me too cos he says dat I orways cause trouble wi der teachers and I talk too much and I jump too much and I doan sit still too much. (118)[1]

Prescriptive vectors of censure and, at the same time, passers of memory, the ambivalent figures of the mother and the grandmother place Rosa in a matrilineal relationship and the fruits of her "e mag e nation" in the myriad popular stories that compose the collective South African history of District Six. This setting is reflected moreover in the structure of the collection *Rosa's District 6*, in which each story develops a particular narrative depicting different inhabitants whose stories and destinies are nevertheless unified by Rosa's viewpoint and words, which first introduced them in "No Rosa, No District Six," the opening text in the collection. In their ambivalence, the mother and grandmother are trigger elements and a point of departure toward which the childish logorrhea returns.

This circularity combines two heretofore distinct temporal spheres: first, the present of the little girl's narration that anchors her story and creative imagination and, second, the sphere of her story-told, including the vexing reprimands of the George Golding Primary School teacher, Mr. Henson, who teaches the official history of European colonization in a white, male perspective soon subverted by the little girl's off-centered re-reading:

> And today Mr Henson ga me four cuts cos he says dat I was dis o be dient and dat I cause trouble in der class but tis not true cos you see last week we celebrated Van Riebeeck's day on der sixt of April wit der flag . . . and four weeks ago Mr Henson toal us dat Van Riebeeck made Cape Town built a fort and erecticated a half way station for food and supplies for der Dutch people and der European people . . . and den Mr Henson also toal us dat Van Riebeeck's wife was Maria de la Quelerie . . . and den Mari der big girl in my class, she has her periods oready she toal us she wondered where Maria de la Quelerie put her cotton clot wi blood on it in der ship from Holland cos Mari's mummy toal her not to tell her daddy her broder or her uncles about her periods cos men mus never see or know dees tings . . . and Mr Henson ga me four cuts on my hand cos I drew a picture of Maria and not Jan and Mr Henson say der assignment was about Van Riebeeck and not Maria and I say is der same ting cos it was all part of der same history lesson and Mr Henson screamed at me to shut up. (119)

Represented by the drawing of "Maria and not Jan," Rosa's rewriting of history associates European colonization with male power. Marked into the South African landscape by the transformation of the fortified city of Cape Town and in Rosa's flesh, bruised by her beating at the hands of her history teacher, the double violence of colonization and male dominance becomes the source of a female and feminist reappropriation through the motif of menstrual blood.

Menstruation is such an object of fascination for Rosa and her friends that her classmate Mari, who has already had her period, wonders if Maria de la Quelerie could have hidden hers from the curious males who had embarked with her on her transcontinental voyage. An intergenerational and transracial secret shared by Rosa, her classmates, and Maria de la Quelerie, brought back from the past by the historical-comical fabulation of children, menses are the point of the overlapping of individual and collective history, spheres of the past and present, the creative imagination and historiographical determinism. It is from this red blood, symbol of violence suffered and the indelible trace of femininity, that Maart defines a series of displacements, which are themselves subsumed by the merging of the double autobiographical "I," the surpassing of an identity fixed by the "after," the birth of a self-consciousness in the process of becoming: *the child as female, the female as child, the child and the female as female-child.* The inner workings of the *mise en scène* of consciousness, these displacements are deployed on spatial-temporal, historiographical, and feminine textual terrains.

DISTRICT SIX—THE LOCATION OF "E MAG E NATION"

The first displacement is geographical and historical. It concerns the passage of colonists from European ports to South African shores and is mirrored locally by the deportation of sixty thousand essentially black and mixed-race persons, forced to leave District Six between 1966 and the early 1980s. An inner neighborhood of Cape Town where harmonious cosmopolitanism, a spirit of brotherhood, and opposition to the apartheid regime defied the fascism and ideological racism of the Nationalist Party, District Six was declared a white zone by the promulgation of the Group Areas Act in 1966.[2]

This is the context in which the story is placed, as indicated by the date that closes Rosa's first-person narrative ("*r. 29 April, 1970*": 120) as well as by the other stories in the collection, all taking place in 1970. Reviving the trauma of colonization, the deportation of the inhabitants of District Six nevertheless opens up a space for transcendence; from the location of her new life in Canada, a chosen displacement, the writer re-establishes the memory of her childhood in District Six, *topos* of the "e mag e nation," a fictional nation unfettered by boundaries and rules.

In the writer's memory and in Rosa's vision, the child, after skipping school, immerges into the heart Cape Town. The city is vibrant, full of noise, sounds, and rhythms that Maart attaches to women, children, and men in their daily lives and most mundane moments. Cape Town is re-created by the imagination, brought back from the writer's past and offered to the eyes of the little girl, making a memory into an active and subjective place of historical significance, frontally opposed to the alienating commemoration of colonization. The city suspends time outside itself in a memory that is not stalled in the past but is oriented toward transformation, a memory nourished by the past but freed from its laws and its univocal sense. Confined to the space-time of colonization, Cape Town enters, liberated, into the consciousness.

From the first description of the city, a living body, it is this dimension that jumps out at us and unfolds once again in a very long sentence:

> The shuffling of feet, the racing of pulses, the screams of little children being bathed by older sisters and brothers in the backyard, the green hose pipe curling itself up among the plants, the sound of several liters of urine being flushed down the toilet in the backyard, where its circular swashing motion competed with bundles of early morning hair awaiting its disposal, the sound of creaking floors as boys and men raised themselves from their place of sleep, the smell of fire as the stove brewed its first round of morning tea, the ravenous chirps of gulls circling the street for morning bread crumbs, the sound of peanut butter jars being emptied by eager hands clenching sharp knives . . . the disgruntled noises of dockyard men walking the charcoaled streets, their feet removing chips of wood and cigarette butts from the previous nights fire, their eyes looking ahead matching their place of work—the sea, with the sky above the heads—and spotless Table Mountain—grey with not a speckle of white on its top—these formed the backdrop of this early morning Black experience. (122)

Reinforced by the anaphoric value of the final demonstration that also constitutes the intention of the sentence, the use of topicalization here pulls the text toward the past but is in conflict with its object: the long enumeration of nominal phrases and gerunds that render the past present. The syntax plays with temporal categories and with the semantics that they generate, the images of the past give way to vision of the consciousness, where the reminiscence is a means of taking up the past in order to change it, to give it another meaning. It is not the memory of colonization that runs through the alleys and streets of Cape Town but the intemporal meaning that Rosa/Rozena's consciousness gives to it.

WALLS AS WORDS AS WEAPONS AS WOMB— DISPLACEMENT AND TRANSFORMATION

Transgressive, the second displacement is historiographical in nature. By refocusing the point of view on Maria de la Quelerie, women rejoin the national history from which they are held apart ("it was all part of der same history lesson": 119); this marks a gendered separation of the history-making that also refuses to consider the fight against apartheid as exclusively masculine.[3] Thus, with the pretext that she writes on the walls of the house, Rosa's mother, fighting against injustice, succeeds in having her daughter reintegrate the school after her expulsion (120). From this return back to the place of imposed knowledge, the desire is awakened in the little girl to render to women what they had given her: a black and feminine consciousness that reinvents the Self just as the words written on the walls of would-be fortresses can rattle their very foundations. Personal and collective, black female consciousness is passed through education and a matrilineal transmission of knowledge that come, nevertheless, essentially from the familial sphere and not from the institutional space of the school, as Mamma Zila, Rosa's grandmother, recalls in "The Bracelet" (183).

A surface for dissident writings, the walls in "No Rosa, No District Six" are Rosa's friends, as the third-person narrator immediately explains when taking over the second part of the story: "Her sticky fingers cupped the flesh around her cheeks as she eagerly observed the friendly wall upon which her writing spoke her truths" (120).

Before Rosa stands the wall overlooking the George Golding Primary School, the surrounding wall where one commemorates the humiliation of colonization ("last week we celebrated Van Riebeeck's day": 119) and where one teaches alienation by recalling the so-called benefits of colonization for the local population. On the wall, a dominant erection of colonial power, the symbol of a national story whose stones and cement are white, Rosa, through her writing, speaks *her truths*. This polymorphic rewriting of history makes women into its principal object, prefers graffiti on a wall to institutional formatting and makes the studied object into the subject living her own knowledge: an ensemble of truths made fluid by speech and implicitly opposed to scientific truth—whether historiographical or anthropological—that by its racial taxonomy fixes, typifies, and underlies the apartheid regime. Compared by her mother and her grandmother to the elder members of the community who never stop gossiping about their neighbors, Rosa's written truths retain the power of speech: the creation of a network of signification as an experience of plurality. Because the ambivalence of the wall and its historiographical symbolism do not only allow the dominated subject to reappropriate her history, by passing through the place of the alienated Other to that of the liberated Other, transcendent and ready to make the Same eat dust: however European she may be, Maria de la Quelerie is an integral part of the little girl's rewritten history.[4] The wall represents rather a changing of worth, a displacement in the operation of meaning: the Same is no longer opposed to the Other; *it is identified to the Other as the possibility of multiple identities*. The Same is no longer the truth; it is the Other's truths. The gap between the official truth of colonial history and Rosa's experience becomes the space for a polyphonic rewriting of history where Rosa, her friends, Maria de la Quelerie, Mummy and Mamma Zila, and all of Cape Town have their place.

Moreover, the historiographical rewriting gives another meaning to history. The break represented by postcoloniality and its shadowy promise of an after-colonization identity, triumphant but confined to itself, are in fact now the slit through which meaning is regenerated, the possibility of a plural-signification transcending the arbitrariness of the sign. It is also, by anticipation, the birth of a South African nation liberated from apartheid that makes the diversity of its communities its credo. Reaching farther than the walls of the George Golding Primary School, a symbol of state oppression, the dream of individual and national liberation is not realized through destruction but through transformation: that of a postcoloniality open to the cosmopolitanism and diversity incarnated by District Six before its destruction, and which Rosa, at least in the diegetic reality, is on the point of discovering and *recognizing*. The space of the "after-wall" represents then the resistance to both the apartheid and the black South African nationalism in whose waters the New South Africa risks foundering.

A metaphor for the black South Africans left in the shadows of the national narrative, the crevices between the stones allow little Rosa to climb and pass over the wall with the agility of a grasshopper, to rejoin the lively and multicolored world of Cape Town where her adventures continue.

As in its geographic-historical dimension, the historiography and the synecdoche of the wall have consciential implications. The re-subjectivization of the dominated subject, the reappropriation of a unique identity, is not then a freeze frame of an image, the image of the liberation from the tyranny of the Other, or from a self-sufficient and insular after, but rather an opening of the singular onto multiple possibilities. A program of political philosophy that blends into the very aesthetic of the texts that incarnate it. On the linguistic front, Rosa's manner of expressing herself is a form of multilingualism that gives the little girl's testimony a plural singularity by embedding within it both the national South African narrative and the female consciousness developed in the second part of the story via the motif of sexual awakening. The white/space that underscores Rosa's first-person testimony and separates it from the third-person narrative of the rebellious little girl's adventures is not the wall of the textual "after" that imprisons her in a new identity— "Rosa," "she," or "the female-child"—whose force would be so alienating that she would be unable to verbalize it. On the contrary, the "after-text" is not only dedicated to plural identities; it also keeps the memory of its before and the singular signification that Rosa gives to it. Here the "after-text" becomes the pretext for exposing the chimera of the before and for denouncing the rupture and discontinuity in the text that become the base for the reconstruction of identity. Thus when the narrator confides that the conflict opposing Rosa and Mr. Henson is only one episode in a long history of such confrontations—including a clash between the professor and Mamma Zila, who was ready to come to fisticuffs to reintegrate her grand-daughter into the school—it links the third-person narrative to Rosa's previous account of the threat of expulsion weighing on her. The first and second part of the story are not a "before" and an "after" that the "I" and "she" signify on a horizontal and chronological axe in a textual order, itself a carbon copy of the colonial political order and its official historiography, but rather two sides of the same coin: the consciousness of Self and the conscientization, active principle, and process by which consciousness comes to the Self.

In this order, superior to time and space, as just seen with the representation of Cape Town, the Self happens *by and as* becoming: the before and after are meaningless. All that matters is the interaction and the concomitance between the consciousness of Self and the process that brings it into being. As the active principle of the text, the third-person narrative actualizes the "I" of the first part of the story, renders it reflexive by echoing the "I" in its own narrative, whose words, moreover, would not resonate if they had not already been said. The third-person narrative is then the gap, the textual slit in the text, the narrative passage that makes Rosa's testimony into the performance of a polymorphic narrative in which she is the actress and, in an ultimate example of reflexivity by which the action becomes testimony and creates the story, she plays the role of witness.

Through the gap in the wall, through the slit in the text, flows an "I"—black and female—that reassembles the multiplicity of identities and narratives through the motif of blood, and more particularly, menstrual blood. The blood is, by the "e mag e nation," the object of a third displacement. After having been spatial-temporal, historiographical, and feminine, this third displacement is sexual, lesbian, and feminist. If, after mentioning her friend Mari's historical speculations about Maria's period, Rosa wonders about the possible filiations between Van Riebeeck and Maria, the little girl then quickly discovers that menses announce not only the capacity to engender but also the advent of adult femininity and with it the promise of sexual fulfillment whose spectacle is worth the displacement. Put into images through the medium of a Sapphic love scene, the intrinsic *irregularity* of sex curbed by the normative discourses of which it is the object, like the relationship between history and historiography of colonization, is not in itself exceptional. Homosexuality is neither over invested with nor emptied of meaning here; it simply is. It is an epiphany in Rosa's eyes, the consciousness of entering into the community of women that seals, by the pleasure that it conceals and the love of *a Self that is the same as all others* that it represents, the female South African body. Feminine and feminist, homosexual and black, it is *simply* a South African experience that "No Rosa, No District Six" describes, in the same way that, in "The Bracelet," male homosexuality crosses all social categories to the point of losing all its intrinsic particularities in them, with the exception of the desire to signify South Africa through the culture of District Six.

WRITING AND CLIMAXING—THE IMAGINED NATION
OF SOUTH AFRICAN FEMININITY

It is at this point of cultural, consciential, and political entanglement that the third displacement of the story overlaps the two precedent displacements in order to denounce the dismemberment, and the partition of the national consciousnesses along ethno-racial, sexual, and gender lines. The first sign of this denunciation—and more precisely the denunciation of a certain European and American LGBTQ academic intellectual colonialism—is the absence of the distinctive qualifier "lesbian," which is never used in reference to Auntie Flowers or Mrs. Hood, the female couple caught in the act of lovemaking by Rosa and who, moreover, all District Sixers identify as cousins. However, this absence of communal nomination does not mean that their homosexual acts exclude them from the patriarchal and heteronormative criticism of South African society, as demonstrated in the second part of the short story, which mentions the constraints and frustrations imposed by marriage. By leaving the act and its identification unnamed, the field of identities remains open: the place reserved for South African cultural specificities of lesbian desire is thus preserved. In "No Rosa, No District Six," one may cite among these cultural specificities the relationship "mummy-baby," metaphorized by the sexualization of nutrition, particularly breast-feeding.[5] Male homosexuality also has a dimension particular to South Africa. In the story "The Bracelet," neither Nathaniel Chambers nor his brother-in-law Neville Collingwood nor Matthew Michaels identify themselves as gay or queer. To designate the social identity that their homosexual practices confer upon them, the men use the term "Moffie," etymologically linked in the final glossary to "hermaphrodite": "*Moffie:* From 'Hermaphrodite,' thus 'Hermaffie,' which then became 'Maffie,' and later 'Moffie'" (231). Although stigmatized during and after apartheid, notably by the Black Nationalist discourse making the African identity of the renaissance into an essence incompatible with homosexuality—which was seen as a Western importation—the Moffies are an integral part of South African social life (Gevisser and Cameron; Krouse). This is particularly true in Cape Town, where their feminization of the male gender is rejected less than it is in Europe or North America. In South Africa, the masculine-feminine division in effect leaves a larger intermediate space for gender negotiation than in the West, where, since World War II, heteronormativity assigns people to one gender identity rather than to another and does this much more than during the first half of the century when sexual practices and gender identities had a less coercive, mutually defining relationship. In fact, the specificity of male South African homosexuality depends on the combination of racial and social hierarchies. The racist ideology of the apartheid, its social expression that links social ascension to the privileged classes to clarity of skin color, and the bourgeois morality that condemns any corruption of these rules, come up against the reality of Cape Town and above all of District Six: a racial and social mixity, a space of intersection and exchange that favors a form of sexual liberty. This relative fluidity of the sexual expression[6]—which does not equate at all an absence of homophobia—does not mean, however, that Mrs. Hood and Auntie Flower's sexual play in the bathtub in "No Rosa, No District Six" can be practiced outside the private and protected space of the domestic sphere. But there is no doubt that, in regard to the colonial and postcolonial situation, in the racial and racialist setting of the division of social classes and the interaction of the ensemble of these parameters, the signification of homosexuality requires a specifically South African interpretive framework, capable of de-centering the Euro-American perspective of LGBTQ studies by revealing the sexual and gendered blind spots of postcolonial approaches (Spurlin: 199–200). It is also this avant-garde[7] displacement that Maart makes Rosa first accomplish empirically, through experience and sensation.

Finding herself in the already agitated early morning of Cape Town, Rosa searches for a place to hide from Mamma Zila's certain punishment and chooses the home of Mrs. Hood and Auntie Flowers, who were supposed to have gone shopping. When the two women return home earlier than expected, Rosa is forced to slide under Mrs. Hood's bed, a space all the more confining as it reeks with the pestilential odor of Mrs. Hood's urine emanating from a chamber pot. The smell of the urine is so acrid that Rosa can only breathe through her open mouth, thus giving vision primacy over speech; however, the urine later proves useful in drowning a little spider who threatens to reveal her hiding place. From her place under the bed, Rosa observes a fascinating spectacle that begins with Auntie Flowers removing the bobby pins one-by-one from her hair, followed by the caresses and kisses exchanged by the two women as they fill the metal bathtub with hot water and flower petals and slowly immerge themselves, singular and together in their nudity:

> Auntie Flowers unbuttoned her dress and there, nakedly, the two women faced one another, each with her own shape. Each put her left foot into the bath at the far side of it, allowing for some space for the right foot. Auntie Flowers was standing at the back of Mrs Hood, who had her arms round both of them so as to embrace Mrs Hood. As both women placed themselves in the bath, splashes of water fell to the floor and small lavender petals stuck to the outside of the bath. The two women remained locked together for quite a while, their silence perturbing Rosa greatly. Mrs Hood lifted her head backwards and placed it gently on Auntie Flowers shoulders. Her clavicles made their appearance and her long grey hair made big circles on the nape of her neck, sculpturing her clavicles in a somewhat vivacious manner. The room was silent. Both women were breathing deeply. The release of their breaths shook the room. "Woooooow," they both breathed out repeatedly. (129–30)

The dance of the bodies entangling to the rhythm of the lovers' breath leads to another silent exchange, this time of fluids. First, saliva:

> Auntie Flowers stroked Mrs Hood's hair and made rings with it, placing water on the already curly bits. Some of the droplets nestled themselves onto Mrs Hood's lips. The two women put each's finger in the other's mouth. Rosa thought it was exciting to see grown women exchange spit. (130)

Then blood:

> The rays of sunlight shone brightly on Auntie Flowers's face and enhanced the sharpness of her clavicles, its wetness bronzed like a medal, waiting patiently to be touched and admired. Mrs Hood's teeth met the temptation, sucking dearly at its warmth until blood filled the gaps between her teeth. (131–32)

Just as the slit in the wall and in the text transform the writing of the story and the story of the writing, the opening of Mrs. Hood's mouth, reduced to the space between the teeth filled by Auntie Flower's blood, transforms the cultural myths of vampirization and transubstantiation that give the body the signification of repressed desire and disembodied spirituality:

> [Mrs Hood's] kiss planted a red glowing print on Auntie Flower's face and the woman's sparkling eyes made Dracula seem like a hopeless case for seduction against the wishes of frightened, chaste women. Both women ate graciously from the blood, their tongues curling with lust and their palates seeping with its nutritious contents. There was passion, love, admiration, an exchange of caring moments, stolen from the heavy load which the constraints of marriage bore. No body of blood of Jesus Christ could fulfill the spirituality of body, of being, that these women felt and allowed themselves to indulge in. (132)

Wet and glistening, the scarlet letter of Mrs. Hood's kiss on Auntie Flowers' face is not the signifier of male law, Mr. Henson's corporal education, Dracula's blood-stained and gloryless seduction, or the transubstantiation of Christ that only transforms himself as suggested by the chain of genitives that concludes with the name of the Son, and reduced to nothingness by the "no [/] body" that generates it. Silent, the mark of the red lips is a barrier to the rule of men and the rule of their words. It is the mark of the body that opens itself to female consciousness and that, in doing so, incorporates it: "the spirituality of body, of being, that these two women felt and allowed themselves to indulge in" (132). The spirit is in the body, the body is in the spirit and the lips do not breathe out the Word, but kisses of saliva and lovers' blood, exchanged together and at the same time, literally incarnated.

A form of sexual initiation, where the combination of cannibalism and sensual pleasure fill the bodies, the spectacle of Auntie Flower's mouth on Mrs. Hood's breasts, of her legs twined around her lover, of her fingers clenched on the edge of the bathtub, is for Rosa a very different lesson than those taught by Mr. Henson. While his lessons commanded silence, this lesson, like Rosa's truths written on the walls, tells the secret of sex ("It's a secret and noborry knows anyting, [Rosa] uttered," 135). The separation between those who know and those who remain ignorant of this secret is filled by the profound breath of sexual pleasure, which comes from the stomach, inflated with pleasure or inflated by the air that gives voice, that holds a note or makes an unpunctuated logorrhea speech, as Rosa does at the beginning of the story. The women's grunting retrospectively gives breath to Rosa's speech; they animate it and make the little girl's voice part of the concert of the community of black South African women. In this same way, the breath of sexual pleasure becomes retrospectively, and between the two parts of the story, the third-person narrative authority of Rosa's "I" and is now the active principle of her conscientization. It allows the voice of the conscience to enter on the path of the consciousness of Self, a Self conceived—reborn rather than engendered because it had been created—from the image of other black women:

> Heavy breathing like a voice lesson, Rosa thought again, was the medium through which these two women communicated their desire . . . Auntie Flowers's feet, crossed one over the other, made the shape of a bow. Is this what Auntie Spider spoke about when she referred to white women being scared of Black women's powers and how our women can wrap men up like Christmas presents? . . . [Rosa] recognized the visual image implanted in her mind, one created by the words of Auntie Spider, also known as Auntie Legs, who regularly told stories about Black women's sexuality to girls in the neighbourhood, preparing them for their approaching womanhood. Is this like sex? the female child asked herself, having been told that it being when a woman allows a man into her vagina. (132–33)

Embracing the religion of black femininity and of a multiform sexuality, Rosa baptizes herself with the same water used by her elders. In the water reddened by the blood of their pleasure, poured into the courtyard by Mrs. Hood and Auntie Flowers as they are about to leave for Hanover Street, Rosa, like the two lovers before her, wets her foot and becomes conscious of her inclusion in a community. The blood that the little girl makes flow from her finger after having stuck it with a splinter seals this entrance into the black female and feminist South African community. This childish form of sealing a secret also returns her consciousness of Self on her like the retrospective and interiorized gaze whose circularity enchains the child, the adult, and the writer. This journey transformed colonization, historiography, male and heterosexual power into the writing of a black climax, the imagined nation of South African femininity on which the walls of District Six open, and upon which Rosa, this time, will not write her new secret, will not affix her bloody signature:

> It had dawned upon her to speak to one of her many walls—her companions—and this event needed to be recorded . . . Having pricked her finger, as she usually did when writing on walls and implanting her print, she swore to secrecy and vowed never to talk about the events she had witnessed . . . Touching her nipples and remembering the fullness of Mrs Hood's breasts, she climbed over the wall and rested herself among the wooden logs in Mrs Benjamin's backyard. There was nobody home and she could climb all the walls to the end of the street. (136)

In a successive order, the walls that little Rosa gets ready to scale to return home are the images of her identities, captured in the cinematic cross-fade of her consciousness. They split the horizon of the text on the historical reality of the text's present: 1989, the year in which the story was written, one year before the wall of apartheid begins to crumble. The moment and the momentum that rendered all the returns to District Six—proscribed by the double negation of the title, dreamed up by the very "e mag e nation," only possible in "writing" and "climaxing"—can now be realized.

Chapter Five

"The Substance of Things Hoped For"

Melvin Dixon's Vanishing Rooms;
or Racism Intimately

Ecrire dans le noir?
Ecrire jusqu'au bout?
En finir pour ne pas arriver à la peur de la mort?
— Hervé Guibert, *Cytomégalovirus*, 1992

INTERRACIALITY AND SADOMASOCHISM —
DIXON'S TEXT IN CONTEXT

In the United States, the political and aesthetic project of queer black male writers and poets, such as Essex Hemphill, Melvin Dixon, and Assotto Saint, is framed by the historical and cultural context where the influential literary representation of desire among the previous generations *in fine* partly failed to thoroughly challenge the social disconnection of racial, sexual, gender, and class-related identities. Testifying to this is the black nationalistic and conservative backlash of the Reagan years, along with the political apathy in the AIDS crisis that severely struck the African American community, as Cathy J. Cohen explains in *The Boundaries of Blackness: AIDS and the Breakdown of Black Politics* (1999). Besides, racism among white gay men and lesbians remains an issue reflected by the conspicuously deficient representation of the lived reality of blacks in both mainstream (white) LGBT and queer literature and criticism. It is thus between black homophobia and white gay racism, both reinforced by the AIDS crisis, that 1990s authors face their literary and political agenda, where self-transformation should not alienate

the subject from the continuity of the community, and the existential significance of one's being black not be divorced from sexual desire.

The 1990s represent a turning point in black contemporary literary history
because sexual desire is not only the motif articulating personal fulfillment
and collective emancipation but, first and foremost, the vehicle of excess in
the writing itself, a literary practice that illustrates black queer authors' defiance toward predetermined identities, sharing in this respect the same positioning as their South African counterparts as argued in the previous chapter.
Essex Hemphill is for instance quite emblematic of this writing of excess.
Besides African American bigotry and bourgeois nationalism, he adamantly
denounces public and normative discourses on identity as inherited from
W. E. B. Du Bois's moralistic elitism. For him, poetry is provocative in
essence. Like the anus, the form of the poem is holy, and it is through this
glory that the poet is "looking for signs of God / as [he] sodomizes [his]
prayers" ("Heavy Breathing," in *Ceremonies, Prose and Poetry*, 1992). To
such a rejection of the norm, which confines one's being black to the public
sphere and one's being gay to the private one, queer black male authors add
other political and philosophical standpoints that they translate into aesthetics. They refuse, for instance, to occlude the subject in historical determinism, frontiers and territorialization, teleological discourses, or compulsory
identifications through which identity is traditionally elevated to a transcending and immutable state—another characteristic of contemporary black literature also testified to by Rozena Maart's writing. In doing so, they also
reduce the black subject's so-called split identity—the rupture of slavery or
colonialism still defining the former generation—to an inaccurate, ready-
made label. They subordinate allegiances to race, nation, gender, and normative sexuality to the subject's life choices and aesthetical motivations. While
atomizing the black Self through multiple identifications and the writing of
desire, they also question the meaning of blackness, sex, gender, and identity
formation as a whole.

It is in this perspective that their exploration of the American scene of
desire *par excellence*—interracial sex—should be considered. The epitome
of American intimacy, interracial sex stands for the relation between Self and
Other where both history and mental sanity are engulfed. It conjures up the
conflict between individual desire and a narrative of American race relations
that carries, deeply ingrained in the collective unconscious, its cluster of
maddening metaphors of subjugation that pervade both social and psychic
lives.

Unsurprisingly in this context, sadomasochism is in recent black queer
poetry and narratives a much favored trope of intimacy, and violence and
madness are both recurring themes and narrative strategies. Defying sheer
mimesis, such a representation of extremes always verges on textual catastrophe. It resists visualization, impedes the generation of signification, and,

by confronting aesthetic pleasure to identifications with the abject, challenges the reader's comfort zone where his/her ethical and political responsibility is left unharmed. A good case in point is the poem "Heaven in Hell" (*Spells of a Voodoo Doll*, 1996) by Assotto Saint, the Haitian-American poet, writer, playwright, performer, and activist who died in 1994 from AIDS complications. A parody of William Blake's marriage of contraries, the poem intends to reconcile historical determinism and free choice, pain and pleasure, one's being black and one's homosexuality, the melancholy of belatedness and the satisfaction of being still here, breathing, and declaiming poetry. While being an elegy for the loved one, a white man slain on the battlefield of the AIDS pandemic, the poem overlaps a sex scene in an SM club and the cross-racial pantomime of a familiar sexual subjection, cornerstone in the regime of terror on slave plantations. As in African American visual artist Kara Walker's shadow shows, this adumbrated historical background is the source of the poem's consciousness-raising power. History here is unfolded through one single verb: the infinitive "to slave." But the referentiality of "to slave" is twofold; while pointing at the historical and collective trauma, it also maintains history in the background, a "behind-the-scene" that does not invalidate the intensity of the playful, theatrical, and pleasurable SM scene, where slaving bears another signification. In this way the persona's memory of pleasure and its subjectivity are not absorbed into the lethally moralistic definition of race inherited from the past.

Another, more traumatic, instance is provided by Melvin Dixon's *Vanishing Rooms* (1991), which is the main object-study of this chapter. The multiple viewpoints and polyphonic narrative of the novel mirror in themselves the maddening conundrum of American intimacy that Jesse and Metro's interracial love still (or up to a point) embodies, though it is stifled by the tight embrace of homophobia and gay racism. Dixon's novel encapsulates one of the most eloquent contemporary images of the madness of intimacy, echoing in many ways Baldwin's "Going to Meet the Man" (1965) and Tennessee Williams's "Desire and the Black Masseur" (1948). American interraciality is here seen as a cultural and political configuration unveiling pleasure as the logical end and means of domination—a point made in chapters 2 and 3—shifting sadism and the enjoyable subjugation of others from the acceptable status of a contingent aberration to that of the *raison d'être* of white Americanness.

IN THE BOWELS OF DESIRE — RACISM AND INTIMACY

Written ten years before *Vanishing Rooms*, Melvin Dixon's poem "Tour Guide: *La Maison des Esclaves*" finishes with these words: "We leave quietly, each alone, / knowing that they who come after us / and breaking / in these tides will find / red empty rooms / to measure long journeys" (1983: 33). In 1991, a few months before his death from AIDS, Dixon published *Vanishing Rooms*, a literary choreography in which his writing dances around and in these same red and empty spaces, disappearing. In the space of time separating the poem and the "choreo-novel," these long voyages— gages of memory and vessels of identity—became one-way and terminal. There is no "us," much less an "after us," and "knowledge" is useless. In the meantime, between the writing of the texts, as reflected in another of Dixon's poems, "Angels of Ascent, " the angels who haunt the unnamed spaces of the dark valleys of Heaven in search of absolute gravity, stopped their ascent. Stopped suddenly where those of Essex Hemphill—the self-proclaimed angel fucker and desperate revolutionary—cease to fall ("The Edge," Hemphill, 1992: 162–63). There is neither ascension nor descent in the novel, neither horizon to erase nor other God except the one who sodomizes the world, fills it up, pulls out, and abandons behind him a red and empty space; "Oh my fucking God," as one of Metro's rapists exclaims (Dixon, 1991: 66). There is something in the disappearing spaces of *Vanishing Rooms* that is more than the African American nihilism that Cornel West describes and denounces (1993b: 17–31). That is more than the poisoned presence of history in intima- cy like Baldwin's sadomasochistic trope of interracial relations, or Wright's materialist determinism. And neither is it the uncertainty of a vacillating, post-modern subject glimpsed in the *pliés*, *pas de deux*, and *jetés* of one of the African American voices of the novel, the dancer Jesse Durand. Between Jesse and Ruella, his friend and temporary refuge, his lover Metro, a member of the Louisiana white middle class, and Lonny, "regular white trash" (Dix- on, 1991: 30), who participates in a gang rape of the latter, is the atrophying space of the inter-human relationship—that is, the risk we run in establishing it, the failure we meet in trying and the futility of the attempt when faced with the consciousness of death. The vanity of being, the progressive vacuity of space, redoubled by the writing itself that is limited by lack of sufficient pages to sketching an incomplete picture of all this, and yet, tries anyway, resolved to fail. In dance also, there is no space but that created by the body. Tired, some bodies keep dancing anyway. *Vanishing Rooms* is the story of this "dancing anyway," the surreptitious return, in the contemporary African American geographies of identity, and, in the era of AIDS, of the hostility of the world; less a resistance than an expectation, a letting-go in the form of writing and dance that fills the empty space of impending death.

On the buttocks of Jon-Michael Barthé, renamed "Metro" by his lover Jesse Durand because he knew how to adventure underground, Cuddles, Maxie, Lou, and Lonny, his rapists, leave traces of their passage: like a cartographic outline, the lacerations of reclaimed territory, the place taken back from the lost essence of their masculinity. In "Tour Guide: *La Maison des Esclaves*," the central poem of the collection titled *Change of Territory*, the words of the house tour guide on the Senegalese island of Gorée fill the red and empty rooms that house the history and the memory of the out-bound bodies: the kneeling forms of young, uncertain virgins resurging, and in the third room near the ocean, the sick and dying who will not make the journey (Dixon, 1983: 32). The empty space of the poem and the scarlet laceration of *Vanishing Rooms*, its transatlantic prolongation, belong to the same structural model in Dixon's writing that articulates race and sex to revisit the relationship between geography and identity—in a sort of guided tour of the American house. In the novel, each of the stories incited by Metro's murder and recounted in turn by Jesse, Ruella, and Lonny are peopled by metaphorical variations of the laceration. This is true for the urban landscapes of New York in the fall of 1975, pierced by flashes of the subway, while above, the night breaks on the towers of slivered bones of metal and light (Dixon, 1991: 14). In these dark corners, the city's skin is also lacerated: on the asphalt, delimited by police chalk, is the void recalling the fatal rape and torture endured by Metro and where Lonny, in the middle of the dead leaves, lies down his murderer's body and his guilty logorrhea. A verbal laceration of reality, his phobic delirium pollutes these same dead leaves, which are to him like so many little mouths opening on the escaping truths (Dixon, 1991: 118). The confessions that hold the intimate secrets that the prison doctor hopes to collect from Lonny's mouth-down-below, as he examines the adolescent, raped in his turn by other inmates (180–81). Whether geographic or historical, material or corporal, psychic or linguistic, the spaces deployed in *Vanishing Rooms* come into being from a void, a cavity, a breach, a gap—often violently forced open. Then they disappear into themselves and, transfigured by fiction, come to signify the central space around which they are organized, that of intimacy opening in the folds of desire and history, where the "you-and-me" is the laceration.

Early in the novel, Jesse recalls certain episodes of his relationship with Metro for Ruella, who temporarily gives him the much-needed vital space that had disappeared with Metro's death:

> Eyes like reaching hands. When he looked straight at me, I felt pulled into his whole face. His stare made me feel weightless, light, angled toward him on wings suddenly fluttering from inside me and begging for air. I wanted then to get under his skin, travel at breakneck speed through his veins and right to his heart. (Dixon, 1991: 38)

The flight of the angel, the emancipation from gravity, the power of attraction molting into yearning, the geometry of the bodies are emblematic of Dixon's poetic prose. But this description of the meeting between the black dancer and the white journalist, at the time both are students at Wesman University, is important also for what it lets us glimpse of Jesse's odyssey to come, between his almost complacent passivity and willing desire. It is one of the formal characteristics of the novel that plays on contrary sentiments or antonyms to blur the differentiated representation of spaces. It is also the heart of what is at stake when the sphere of the interracial couple's intimacy implodes. Jesse does not recount this passage to Ruella, whom he has renamed Rooms (Dixon, 1991: 13). He barely admits it to himself, unconsciously and in his sleep, so strong is the shame and detestation of the feelings evoked by the truth of his relationship to Metro—because it his truth as well:

> I held him tight in my arms that night. He was pale, thin, and more nervous than I remembered him being before. He seemed to change there in my arms into someone more fragile, more vulnerable, as if the night was wearing him down and the gray, thick asphalt was draining him daily. I kissed him everywhere: forehead, eyes, nose, lips, neck, nipples, navel, and there. I held him tight. His penis responded to my wet caresses, and I kissed it again and again. Metro held me, his thighs tight, and his fingers knotting my hair. His moan, my moan, some kind of song from his deep chest and mine. But it wasn't a song and his chest wasn't filling with desire or love that could hold safety and assurance for us. It wasn't that, but his teeth edging like a razor on one word: "Nigger." (Dixon, 1991: 113)

Underscored by the pendular movement of the author's style, the physical call-and-response encloses the two lovers in the singular and double spaces of intimacy: at first identified by the same actions, the repetitions, the moaning in unison, they are then recalled to their essential difference by the final laceration of the insult, "Nigger." The effect of this verbal switch is multiple as it touches on the signification and the distribution of the spaces, as well as personal identity. At the very heart of the refuge of their intimacy, the debasement, the reification, and, finally, the psychic murder represented by the insult is brutally repatriated by Jesse in the here-and-now. The protective interiority of intimacy hits up against, penetrates, and dissolves into the racism of the exterior world just as Metro's teeth do on the word itself, "Nigger," placed at the border between the two spaces, ready to fall into one or the other, without knowing for certain to which of the two it belongs in the first place. The question is important because if "Nigger" has its origin in the space exterior to Jesse, then Metro's racism reflects what Jesse carries within himself, which Metro latches on to and consumes at the same time that he devours his lover's body. The ambivalence of the enunciation's origin is moreover reinforced in both the interior and exterior of the passage. In echo to the protean character of the insult, at first a moan and then monotonous chant, the source of the term is indifferentiated: it emerges from the depths and lungs of both characters. The scene is followed by Clementine's clarifying commentary. Formerly Clement (like Albertine was previously Albert), she represents the monstrous stereotype of the crazy flamboyant black queen, fat and greasy with the same exorbitant eyes as those one finds in Baldwin's works. A sort of avatar for the Greek chorus, he/she embodies the conscience and memory's all-seeing eye, and very much like the old guide in the House of Slaves, he/she haunts the corners of Paradise Baths, the sauna where, after having left Ruella's apartment, Jesse comes to try to sleep and to recall the paradise of his lost lover by retracing his footsteps between the empty stalls of the sauna, between the thighs and the parted lips of potential lovers, with the cheap and stereotypical decorum of second-class gay pornography. In a scene that recalls the gay militant discourse of the 1990s constructed around the axiom "Black men loving other black men. Loving being black and men together" (Dixon, 1991: 115), and notably popularized by Marlon T. Riggs's 1989 film *Tongues Untied* and Joseph Beam's anthologies, as well as Essex Hemphill's poetry, Clementine lifts the veil on the ambiguity of "Nigger," the imagined word:

> That's what you get being a snow queen . . . I was watching you. You must have been asleep. You were yelling "nigger, nigger," in some high girlish voice so I knew it really wasn't you saying that. You wouldn't call yourself a nigger, would you? . . . You was his nigger. Face it. Your college degree wasn't shit. All he wanted was your cock or your ass, but he was afraid to get it off the real streets he walked on. (Dixon, 1991: 114–15)

Jesse does not awaken in the intimate refuge that was lacerated by the word "Nigger" but rather in the illusion of the non-adherence of the Self to hatred, as if by the annihilation made metaphor by the word "Nigger," what mattered were not so much the language that ripped him from the real but his shattering fall that engulfed him in the vast and impalpable space of a real other, the psychic world where the subject is lost from view and disappears.

GEOGRAPHY OF THE INTIMATE AND LACK OF DIFFERENTIATION

Through this psychic configuration of intimacy and desire, Dixon organizes the spaces of the Self and the Other. The geography of the intimate that he traces also allows him to join history via the African American literary canon that he himself had studied through the perspective of space and the reinvention of the Self. In *Ride Out the Wilderness: Geography and Identity in Afro-American Literature* (1987), Dixon proposes in effect a hermeneutic of modern African American literature founded on space and its various structures of signification, arguing that black American writers' reaction to alienation and segregation had consisted of making language an alternative space, propitious to the health of black culture and identity, as well as to self-transfor-

mation. In putting down roots through language, the imagination and literature are used as a means to erase or transcend the stigmatizations of being
rootless. Among these places of refuge and regeneration, Dixon notes three
recurrent spaces in African American literary history: the vast and desolate
space of "the wilderness" that one finds in slave songs; "the underground"
that Dixon explores using Richard Wright's short story "The Man Who
Lived Underground" (1944); and "the mountaintop" that unites, among others, Martin Luther King Jr. and John Grimes of *Go Tell It on the Mountain*
(1953; James Baldwin's first novel), as well as Pilate Dead and Milkman, the
main protagonists of Toni Morrison's *Song of Solomon* (1977). A psychic
landscape articulating the reinvention of the Self and the relationship to the
Other through the experience of desire and fantasy, intimacy is the fourth
place in Dixon's geography of identity in African American literature. Adding up the spaces that Dixon identifies—that is, the space in front of, underneath, and above the Self—intimacy in contemporary black literature can
then be said to be the place of permanent transformation through desire that
plays on, moreover, the spatiotemporal categorization of structures of signification, epistemological frameworks, and community allegiances. In the era
of uncertainty and diversity, intimacy represents the entry of black writing in
post-identity, the open-ended "after" where identity remains a question—
a thematic and formal feature analyzed in chapter 4.

The space in which Jesse finds himself, the intimate lacerated by insults,
has yet to become the place of self-transformation just described. It is in fact
a perversion of it, a nightmare revealed to be reality, or what one would call
the "extra-real." The extra-real designates this exhaustion of the Self in
which psychic space and real space are entirely subsumed in the fantasy of
the Other. In all places exterior to the Self, and just as "Nigger" appears in
multiple spaces—in Metro's mocking mouth, in Jesse's dream, at the Paradise Baths sauna, and finally on the very streets of New York—the fantasy of
the Other's perception of the Self takes shape and expands to the point that,
more terrifying than being the plaything of another, one realizes that he/she
is playing the same game as everyone else and is more and more indifferentiated from them. One becomes the fantasy of the Other, a fantasy that is not
oneself and yet is corroborated by reality and sustained by desire. "You was
his nigger," as Clementine puts it more simply (Dixon, 1991: 115).

In this American variation of Maupassant's "Horla," there is no refuge
from racist and homophobic hatred: the spaces in front of, underneath, and
above the Self are similarly saturated.

Dixon thus completes the spatial and psychic genealogy of African
American identities. Here the alienation of the subject from the world is not
vectorized by the veil as it is for Du Bois, or by violence as it is for Wright,
or desire as it is for Baldwin. The extra-real leads to the annihilation of the
subject because there is no Other, no elsewhere, no refuge, no possibility of

regeneration. Between the You and Me, space shrinks away and closes itself in the chaos of orgasm and violence combined:

> I hit him once, and I hit him again. He didn't hit me back. I hit him again, harder, so he'd hit me back, but he just lay there moaning and fighting the air. He wasn't fighting me. He wasn't even seeing me. He was pulling at himself. I stopped and watched him pulling and punching at himself and pulling and punching again until he moaned again and stopped as abruptly as he had begun. The bed was wet, his groin was wet. His hands slippery with his own semen. (Dixon, 1991: 114)

Jesse's violent physical response to Metro's insults and to the justification that he gives to them ("You want it low. You want me to take you there. Down under. Well, down under you ain't nothing but a nigger. A coal black nigger" [114]) recalls the force with which, in LeRoi Jones's play *Dutchman* (1964), another mixed-race couple embarks in the underworld, also represented by the subway. Clay teaches his mistress, Lula, about the relationship between words and reality in African American culture: "Just let me bleed you, you loud whore, and one poem vanished" (cited by Dixon, 1987: 79). Writing to sublimate violence is essential to the African American experience. And if its literature abounds with metaphors of race and racism—as varied as color, the veil, the tree, the bastard, or invisibility—it is not to substitute an image for reality but to try to redefine it using emptiness as a starting point, the intangible object, this hatred that drives Du Bois to the edge of insanity, pushes Rufus to jump from Washington Bridge and Sethe to kill her daughter, and explains how Horace, the protagonist of Randall Kenan's *A Visitation of Spirits* (1989), decides to blow his brains out. The black American metaphor does not replace a truncated reality, the intangible object that is hatred; it transfers it to another structure of meaning, African American culture that, like Dixon, one can observe through the prism of space, which makes sense for the largest possible number of individuals sharing that experience. But what sense should be made of it when racial violence is not sublimated but acted upon and realized through the search for sexual pleasure, all the more troubling because this racial violence is shared? Because, faced with Metro's sadomasochistic racism, Jesse's attitude remains as ambiguous as the enunciation of the insult. He becomes not only the one who hits but also the one who watches and, many times in the novel, gives consciously or unconsciously different and incomplete variations of the scene (Dixon, 1991: 3, 42–44, 114–17, 209–11). The repetition of the scene betrays the protagonist's obsession with this humiliation, or is it rather that his controlled representation of the repeated humiliation procures him pleasure? It is in fact through intertextuality that Jesse's adherence to Metro's racist fantasy becomes clear. If in *Ride Out the Wilderness* Dixon is interested above all in *Go Tell It on the Mountain*, the study of which leads him to

isolate in Baldwin's works the paradox of feeding his liberating writing with
the very religious faith that condemns him for his homosexuality, it is the
short story "Going to Meet the Man" that crisscrosses *Vanishing Rooms*.
Besides sharing the name of the main protagonist and the suffocating representation of racialized sadomasochism that unites intimate history with
American history, the two texts are also linked by the themes of childhood
and territory. The short story to which chapter 2 is entirely dedicated takes
place in the South, the very soul of America, to quote Baldwin, and little
Jesse, as it is to be remembered, has a black playmate named Otis. In *Vanishing Rooms*, Metro also has a childhood friend with that name and who smells
of burning wood and tobacco, which Metro associates with Louisiana and
which leads to his first stirrings of desire (41). An olfactory memory charged
with horror through intertextual dialogue. When Metro detects this same
smell on Jesse Durand during their lovemaking, it foretells the worst of the
revelations made at Paradise Baths (42). As the site of this intertextual revelation of an American apocalypse, Paradise Baths also recalls the pyre in
"Going to Meet the Man." In *Vanishing Rooms*, the site represents the baptis-
mal fountain celebrating the beginning of the transformation of Self, while
the pyre makes the burning of a black man into a ceremony that seals the
allegiances of the members of a Southern white male community. Through
intertextuality, history's underground that houses its testimony and transmission and assures the survival of a black American culture, the Jesse of *Vanishing Rooms* prolongs the American destiny of the Jesse of "Going to Meet
the Man," accomplishing, at the end of the novel, the liberating metamorphosis of which his fictional homonym is deprived. By bringing together the two
textual spaces, Dixon effects several significant displacements. His parody of
Baldwin's text makes interracial desire and sadomasochism the novel's point
of departure, the terrible truth about intimacy that Jesse Durand learns to
confront and to transform. In the short story, interracial desire and sadomasochism are the result of the story's finalism in which they are the hidden
meaning, metaphorized by the lynching.

   This change of focus goes along with the lesser importance given to the
religious dimension in *Vanishing Rooms*, where transcendence is impossible
because verticality, the rules of geography, and the differentiated spaces are
only illusion. Jesse Durand does conserve a few stigmata of the black Christ,
a recurrent figure in African American literature: the splinters that lacerate
his feet and legs (128) as he dances on the wood floor of the empty warehouse where Metro comes to look for him, where, against the wooden pillars
and in the odor of tobacco, he finds the pleasures of humiliation once again.
And yet, in spite of this, Jesse is not the redeemer, or the sacrificial victim, or
scapegoat—or at least not only that. His responsibility and moral quandary
haven't disappeared; he just lacks the space to evaluate them while the
sphere of intimacy is cracking. Before admitting to the racial dimension of

sex with Metro, Jesse thus recognizes, in the midst of the naked men of Paradise Baths ready to take their pleasure or revenge on the insolent well-being of youth (103), his attraction to pain: "'But you want pain,' a voice inside me said. 'Don't you? Why then did you come here? It's not because of Metro anymore. He's dead'" (103). At the end of the novel, Ruella even accuses him of having pushed Metro to hate him. Jesse is therefore not the victim of puritan American masochism that, in a racial projection of bodily taint, makes the black person into an instrument of punishment and a vector for the expiation of sin. This representation is as central in Faulkner's *Light in August* (1932) as it is in "Desire and the Black Masseur," the short story by Tennessee Williams where, in the steam of a sauna and the wet heat of the South, an office worker goes to a big black masseur, day after day, and asks him to crush his bones. In these hypotexts, the Protestant ethos reintroduces, through the racial stakes of submission and domination, the pleasure in the law that condemns it. In *Vanishing Rooms*, it is not just a religious crisis but an ontological one that engulfs the characters. Their similarities to their intertextual elders are such that they struggle to exist by and for themselves. Their universe is a lack of differentiation—of spaces, of beings, of sexual pleasure; without any relationship to law or transgression, their world is more in resonance with the chaos anterior to civilization, as Freud described in *Civilization and Its Discontents* (1930). And Dixon does not preach for the primacy of law and the revitalization of social differentiation that establishes categories of identity—to which Freudian psychoanalysis is no stranger. He wants to recover the spaces necessary for human fulfillment, the intimacy that disappears as a result of being so saturated with violent and hateful expressions of identity, like those employed by Lonny, of which he is also the victim (153). The white double of Bigger Thomas, just as Jesse Durand is the black double of Baldwin's Jesse, Lonny is characterized by, in addition to Richard Wright's materialist realism, an existential anguish: "The bodies and the voices attacked me this time, and I had no room to hide in or get away to. No fucking where to go" (119). His white identity and heterosexuality, which he emphasizes to Jesse and Metro many times, are significant, like black identity and homosexuality, inasmuch as they carve out a necessary space of being.

PAS DE DEUX: A KISS DANCED WITH DEATH OR THE DISAPPEARING SPACE

While anchoring *Vanishing Rooms* in the literary and cultural heritage of black America, intertextuality, as a space of multiple identifications, does not entirely define the novel's objective: to open the field of identities to a more personal and intimate quest, freed from the traditional frameworks of geography, religion, materialism, or psychoanalysis that are at best ineffective, and at worst generators of violence. After having realized that his relationship with Metro does not provide the intimate space necessary for self-transformation, Jesse finds this space in dance and choreographic creation, which draws a human geography of the liberated body inventing its own space and its own identity:

> I had a chance to choreograph something. And to dance. I decided upon a simple dance for two men. A *pas de deux* to Ellington's music. I watched black men everywhere for movement: in barbershops, on street corners, some reading the *New York Times*, some going in and out of expensive hotels by the front door and some by the service entrance. And I watched myself: my bend of waist while making the bed, washing dishes, stretching on the parquet floor . . . I watched white men and black men and short men and fat men and men who were interested in my watching them and others who were not. (Dixon, 1991: 197–98)

In the same way that the reader experiences the influences of jazz in Baldwin and Wright's works, Dixon's *pas de deux* carries the reader in a written dance where, to a binary rhythm, the duality of white and black, of the Other and the Self, meld together, opening on to the non-predetermined space of a desire. The fusion of dance and language is for Dixon and Jesse, who becomes a choreographer through his narration of the story, the regeneration of the intimate, the disappearing space reinvented by the writing of the body in motion. And when Jesse executes his *pas de deux* with Rodney, his new lover, "black and lovely" (208), the fourth wall of the theater crumbles as the audience breaks into applause, making a wave of light appear before the space that held the dancers disappears (211).

This ending is like the novel itself—ambiguous. How to define this last disappearing space re-created by the dance? Is it an apotheosis or an apocalypse? This uncertainty, this resistance to interpenetration from pre-established frameworks is perhaps the *raison d'être* of the novel, the space by which it survives and that requires creativity—if not literary, at least interpretive. The hermeneutic of uncertainty also reflects the structure of the novel: balletic bodies replacing words and that disappear as they rediscover the interior force to be in movement once again. What, then, should be made of the impalpable promise of nothing, which words—useless, ineffective, empty—cannot grasp? It is perhaps this speechlessness that is represented by the luminous disappearance at the end of the novel.

All that remains is the other space—the memory of the text, intimately embodied.

Chapter Six

Writing as I Lay Dying

AIDS Literature and the H(a)unting of Blackness

AIDS WRITING — A POLITICAL AND CULTURAL OVERVIEW

Confronted with the AIDS pandemic that struck the last two decades of the twentieth century, contemporary African American and black literature, and particularly queer texts, have shed a significant light on the uncertainties of identity formation. In *Invented Moralities: Sexual Values in an Age of Uncertainty* (1995), Jeffrey Weeks has charted such an analysis about contemporary sexual ethics but without specific reference to race. In fact, praxes of sexual identity, notably in the context of AIDS, seem at first sight to go beyond the color line. Though with striking differences in use and signification, the key metaphors of collapse, failure, and nothingness haunt black and white writings of the AIDS era alike. For example, black and white American authors obsessively scrutinize the human body that collapses in a disintegrating world. Collapse and disintegration are indeed classical *topoi* of AIDS writing. Among them is also the imminent death that Ross Chambers, in *Untimely Interventions: AIDS Writing, Testimonial, and the Rhetoric of Haunting* (2004), eloquently metaphorizes as "death-at-the-door," or the paradoxical nature of the body in pain, which, according to Elaine Scarry in *The Body in Pain: The Making and Unmaking of the World* (1985), is a certainty for the sentient and suffering body, while always remaining a site of doubt for witnesses around, be they characters, narrators, or readers. In extra-textual reality, as in the testimonial literature about AIDS, to watch the body in pain summons the suspension of disbelief. This is what is aimed at by the salvaging of language and a restored rhetoric that pain precisely applies itself to destroy—an allegory of the blurred frontier between fiction and truth that

119

literature reflects and questions. This preoccupation is also equally shared by black and white authors.

"What does AIDS writing say about the nature of literature?"—the force of such a meta-literary question lies in the fact that it is all but an abstraction. It is the human subject that returns here, less as an occasion to pursue post-modernist speculations about the end of the sovereign and unified Self than to face the bewildering catastrophe announced by the body that materially dwindles and disappears. Craig G. Harris describes this apocalypse in his text "I'm Going Out Like a Fucking Meteor" (1991), where the narrator ponders his shrinking flesh, his vanishing body, his bowels flushed out in the toilet as the text darkly shimmers with the unanswered question "What does it mean to write as one is dying?" (Harris, 2005: 137–50). Beyond the text, and throughout AIDS literature in black and white, the question reverberates an address to the reader, a hailing about his/her commitment and collusion with the world. It also renews the labyrinthine meaning of intimacy and the nature of the bond with the Other. Writing out the dying from the world into the text—be it a brother, as in Jamaica Kincaid's *My Brother* (1997); a companion, as in Paul Monette's *Borrowed Time: An AIDS Memoir* (1988a); or oneself, as in Melvin Dixon's *Love's Instruments* (1995) and David Wojna-rowicz's diaries—frames the relation between literature and the human subject with ethical, political, and aesthetic concerns: "Is it right?" "What is it for?" "How to?" All these questions expand from the realization that in such an extreme experience of intimacy, the sense of identity becomes transient, as selfhood and otherness are more than ever ethereal. No other's touch can connect the dying Self with its vanishing physicality. The witness is more-over left alone with his/her growing alienation, which also becomes the very condition of survival, his/her only resistance while facing the other's death. What writing encapsulates and problematizes in a conundrum as unsolvable as that of desire is the estrangement from oneself, the other, and the world. An existentialism without choice, a desire without lack—since all has vanished.

Yet in this panorama that the literary experience of/in/as death tentatively universalizes, identity and consciousness, both racial and national, quickly reappear as primary and inescapable characteristics of the American experience. It therefore comes as no surprise that the AIDS crisis should also have been of paramount importance in the shaping of a contemporary black queer literature. The transience of the life it carries casts a tragically ironic light on black queer writers' existential stances of depicting their "lived reality," as Joseph Beam and Essex Hemphill aimed to show in their respective anthologies *In the Life* (1986) and *Brother to Brother* (1991). Like them, many writers, artists, and activists of this aborted generation were lost to AIDS that, besides the human tragedy, also had political and aesthetic repercussions in the defining paradigms of black queer literature.

Both the individual's relational complexities with the community and the indeterminacy of identity took on new meanings in what revealed itself to be the black queer paradox. On the one hand, with the palpable return of death into life, identity matters reached a transcending dimension that outgrew mere attempts at redefining blackness. The urge to translate racial and sexual categorization into a matter of life and death—as James Baldwin called for at the end of "Notes of a Native Son" (1955) and which was now prompted by the imminence of death—added to the dissenting positions that, with their proclaimed non-heteronormative sexualities, black queer writers occupied within their communities. Such a combination also laid the foundation for a revolutionary understanding of black identity that would connect black consciousness to desire in the open array of self-transformations that the finiteness of life restores to favor. Melvin Dixon's *Vanishing Rooms* is certainly exemplary of this endeavor shared, across the color line, by David Wojnarowicz's *In the Shadow of the American Dream* (1998a), another literary *tour de force*. On the other hand, and as the condition for such a new black identity was also its terminating limitation, it is a strong communal sentiment that responded to the "fierce urgency of now" with a nationalistic rhetoric sometimes akin to that of the black arts movement. The sociopolitical awareness that AIDS decimated African Americans, and among them gay men in particular, reinforced in black queer writers the impulse to belong to the community, a phenomenon that also altered the terms of their conflicted allegiance to the group. The counterpart of this withdrawal into nationalistic expression is, in white American authors, the persistent racialization of sex, now combined with a black metaphorization of contamination, infection, alienation, physical decay, and death, as in Paul Monette's *Borrowed Time* (1988a). As the disease of the Other, AIDS is the contemporary metaphor of an American intimacy eaten up by murderous race relations. Textually, it also regenerates a deep-seated American fantasy: constructing an Other to be destroyed, and preserving an idealized whiteness from madness.

VANISHING—BEING DEAD AND NOT REMEMBERED

With its cohort of deaths and vanishing bodies, AIDS in the 1980s and the 1990s inaugurated an irresolute conundrum in American homotextualities, both black and white: How to represent a reality that disappears or, in photographer David Wojnarowicz's words in *In the Shadow of the American Dream* (1998a), "How do you describe emptiness without using words?" (242). The complex relation to metaphors in AIDS writing, concomitantly rejected and regenerated, is exemplary of this tension between refusing the fact that language masks the horror of reality, thus evaded in bad faith, and the acute awareness that only a new *poesis* can spur the return to a reality that is all the more elusive in that it is disintegrating. The human disaster, verging on the unspeakable, resists a metaphorization that also appears as sheer indecency. Several pieces in Assotto Saint's *Spells of a Voodoo Doll* (1996), for instance, bear the title "No More Metaphors." Another is titled "No Symbols." They bear witness to the life and death of AIDS victims in a very material and direct way, reproducing obituaries, court statements, notes written for the AIDS Memorial Quilt project—a tribute to AIDS victims—and intimate recollections of the deceased.

Many texts testify to this concreteness in their recourse to a war-like rhetoric, as in Essex Hemphill's poems "The Occupied Territories," "The Edge," and "When My Brother Fell," all published in *Ceremonies, Prose and Poetry* (1992). The warfare against AIDS also casts an ironic light on Assotto Saint's pseudonym, an apocopate of Toussaint Louverture, the Haitian revolutionary hero who inspired Saint as poet, playwright, and AIDS activist. War is total, either massive and launched on a large scale, as in David Wojnarowicz's photographs in *Sex Series* (1988–1989), or in the intimacy of daily life, as in Melvin Dixon's poem "Turning Forty in the '90s," which describes how "vials of Septra and AZT line the bedroom dresser / like a boy's toy army poised for attack" (*Love's Instruments*, 1995: 69). These texts denounce apathy and indifference and call for action. Hemphill's "When My Brother Fell" is, for instance, dedicated to Joseph Beam, both a writer and an activist who died in complete isolation. In this poem as well, Hemphill strongly rejects the recourse to metaphors and allegories, including the quilt.

Nevertheless, in this danse macabre where the dying and the slain are no abstractions, the more metaphors are claimed to be rejected, the more they are regenerated, binding AIDS writing in its various forms. The angel metaphor haunts both Hemphill's and Dixon's poetry, while in Tony Kushner's theater it becomes the allegory of America's rebirth through AIDS. A similar ambivalence toward metaphors can be found in George Whitmore's *Someone Was Here: Profiles in the AIDS Epidemic* (1989). Whitmore's documentary-like narrative echoes Judith Butler's concern in *Precarious Life: The Power of Mourning and Violence* (2004), where she argues that the lack of national mourning for AIDS victims in particular reflects the deep-seated American belief that some lives, because deemed worthless, can be forgotten. Close to Hervé Guibert's *Cytomegalovirus* (1992), in its factual tone of voice and abundance of minute medical detail, Whitmore describes several individuals' struggle for survival, using a journalistic prose that, though distanced and paralleled by very informational footnotes, is never bereft of emotion. Powerful metaphors, scattered throughout the text, carry the pathos of these destinies while urging readers to wake up to reality. The most striking is at the outset of the text. It represents, set among many others, a human skull, whose empty eye socket encapsulates in its "black hollow" the nothingness left by the epidemic. But the *vanitas* is not vain, and as the metaphor is being regenerated, it is the text itself that springs from the eye socket. The indifferentiation of the title dissolves in the "here," in these textual catacombs. In his introduction, Whitmore's writing foregrounds the skulls to be arranged, the lives of the dead to be remembered.

With the regeneration of metaphors, one can identify many other formal characteristics recurring throughout these texts: the power of language to derealize through style; the deconstructive representation of reality through narrative strategies; the extended lexical field of vision and perception; an intertextuality that celebrates gay literary forefathers or the systemic call-and-response between authors. But the politics of forms, the pertinence of a figurative language, differ from all other American literary and poetic movements or traditions, such as those of the 1930s "Objectivists" and of the 1970s–1980s "Language-Poets"—for whom the form aimed at social transformation—and from African American literature in general that, as an aesthetics of optics, endeavors to reveal whites' fantasies and re-establish the reality of a racist America. In the 1990s, the world to be transformed, the reality to return to, or to re-establish, is vanishing, and to bear witness to this contemporary tragedy and be acknowledged for this dedication is what is at stake for many authors. Though it duplicates the paradox of any so-called minority writing whose aesthetic specificity is to become a defining feature, an identity, once it has been acknowledged by mainstream literature and criticism, AIDS writing goes beyond the false opposition between aesthetics and politics to take on, across the color-line, an ethical and existential dimension that is perfectly rendered by the following statement by David Wojnarowicz in *In the Shadow of the American Dream*:

> I'm not so much interested in creating literature as I am in trying to convey the pressure of what I've witnessed or experienced. Writing and rewriting until one achieves a literary form, a strict form, just bleeds the life from an experience—no blood left if it isn't raw. How do we talk, how do we think, not in novellas or paragraphs but in associations, in sometimes disjointed currents. (235)

To witness and be witnessed in return exceeds the form but does not suppress it. It is possibly the only thing that remains beyond the vanishing of authors and artists—their dying without being remembered as if they had simply not existed. For want of being meaningful in the world's indifference, most of the works in the AIDS era express this obsession with vanishing through both the object and the medium of their representation. David Wojnarowicz, who signed an essay for the catalog of "Witnesses: Against Our Vanishing," a controversial November 1989 Manhattan AIDS show, composed a self-portrait in which his face disappears while being covered with earth ("Untitled," 1993, in Meyer, 2002: 273). The image echoes the work of another photographer, "Untitled" (1991) by Felix Gonzalez-Torres, which shows an empty bed with crumpled white sheets and pillows, shaping the hollow of the already absent lover and the memory of Eros (Meyer, 2002: 269). The photograph is in dialogue with Wojnarowicz's still present lover and its anticipation of Thanatos. The same metaphor of vanishing can also be found in Paul Monette's *Borrowed Time* where Paul, the narrator, back home from the hospital where Rog, his lover, has been taken to die, stares down at his empty bed "where the sheets still swirled with the shape of his sleep" (1988a: 334). Time, and means for achieving the impossible representation, are also dwindling to nothingness, as thousands succumb quickly to AIDS, a human and artistic helplessness that Melvin Dixon voices in his poem "One by One": "Another telephone call. Another man gone. / How many pages are left in my diary? / Do I have enough pencils? Enough ink? / I count on my fingers and toes the past kisses, / the incubating years, the month ahead" (*Love's Instruments*: 59).

Vanishing contaminates everyone and everything: people, art, the possibility and the reason to create. Even literary and artistic works, once they are finished, offer no guarantee that they will last, be preserved, and fulfill their mission to bear witness. Vanishing also comes in the form of censorship as Wojnarowicz warns before "The Suicide of a Guy Who Once Built an Elaborate Shrine over a Mouse Hole." In a note addressed to readers, he explains that the following pages disclose a set of Dakota's recollections, salvaged by his friends, since everything that Dakota wrote, played, shot, and painted had been burned by his parents when he died from AIDS (*Close to the Knives: A Memoir of Disintegration*, 1991: 164). Assotto Saint feared the same fate for his works. Of course, censorship, especially when it comes from close relations, gives to vanishing—being dead and not remembered— another, even more destructive meaning. What it inscribes in life and others is erasure as memory: being dead and being remembered as a non-entity, a non-existence. Linking AIDS and the gay experience, beyond epidemiology and the sociology of sex, this awareness consolidates a crucial dimension of gay consciousness: being dead among the living, being a specter in one's own family and entourage, transparent and seen through AIDS as the vanishing of the vanished. The struggle not to vanish, in the context of AIDS, has therefore to be put in perspective with the life-long fight for existing as gay. Within gay writing and art in general, works about AIDS reproduce the same irrepressible attempt to connect.

LACK-WITH-AN-OBJECT—LOVE: THE URGE TO CONNECT

For African American novelists and poets such as Dixon or Hemphill, the primary connection is between black and gay experiences. As a member of the black gay writer collective Other Countries, Assotto Saint took part in this aborted revolution, which, as Patrick Moore claims in *Beyond Shame* (2004), "seemed on the verge of bridging the gap between black and gay identities until nearly all of [these writers] were lost to AIDS" (160). Being black and gay, synonyms of social opprobrium, taken separately, may be deeply alienating when cobbled together since heteronormativity and homophobia in the African American community is often the reflection of internalized racism while antiblack racism from whites is in part sexual, in both motive and expression, as the previous chapters have illustrated. Poems such as Dixon's "Etymology: A Father's Gift" (Beam, 1986) or Hemphill's "Family Jewels" and "The Photographs" (1992), poignant calls for escaping erasure from the collective picture of the black experience, testify to the urge to be acknowledged, celebrated, and remembered by the black community. It is the same connection with the group sought in Dixon's short piece "Aunt Ida Pieces a Quilt" (Hemphill, 1991), where he links the deceased, the loving African American grandmother, and the fabric that is meant to be integrated in the AIDS Memorial Quilt metaphorizing a national community of which to be part as well.

While radically alienated from the Puritanism and materialism of American society, Wojnarowicz's attempt to connect is paradoxically pursued through warfare and violence, which also figure among his preferred literary techniques to convey his atrocious isolation as he dies from AIDS. In a fragment of his diaries, partly collected in *In the Shadow of the American Dream*, Wojnarowicz wages a war against "the rich," "their armies halfway around the world," and "their useless bank accounts." They hide behind the "shades on their three windows, long black slats of designer materials" under which "they hear very little of our lives, they hear little of our hollers our screams our hunger our choking." But Wojnarowicz has his weapons: "small explosives and crude brand-name missiles temporarily made from stove matches tinfoil and now small steel cups" (241–42). His most powerful one, however, is his nakedness, which "shows his hunger," "a difficult thing for anyone to ignore," and which he flaunts through the window of his cheap hotel room. The warfare is one of violent witnessing and forced acknowledgment, but the intrusion of the gaze of the rich into his room is never actualized. The only intruding viewers are the readers who concentrate on Wojnarowicz's mind's eye—the scene of his destructive nakedness and sexuality witnessed by fleeting peeping Toms. Meanwhile, the textual voice hammers the estrangement of the rich and insists, through the anaphoric "they," on their aloofness. "My image can go where my voice would falter and dissipate" (241–42), claims Wojnarowicz, but it is the textual voice, with the stylistic markers (the repetitions and coordinations, the opposition between "us" and "them"), that gives the image of nakedness its profound meaning: an ultimate striving, despite, beyond, or along with the desire to murder, to connect, a despair betrayed by the concluding anticlimax "I wave periodical-ly" (242).

Subsuming the gay literary and artistic landscape of the 1980s and 1990s, connection at all cost is pursued to the extreme, including life-threatening and anonymous hard sex in meat-packing warehouses or derelict buildings. They are a recurring setting in Wojnarowicz's diaries, his memoirs, and his photographs (the *Arthur Rimbaud in New York* series). They also appear, more precisely located by the Hudson River, in Dixon's *Vanishing Rooms*, which we analyzed in the previous chapter, and whose title also refers to the rooms where Metro enjoys being beaten up. The texts and artistic works of these decades reflect each other through the New York gay underworld of the 1980s. Men's loneliness and tragic attempts to connect in porn movie thea-ters, described by Wojnarowicz, are also painted by Patrick Angus in *Hanky Panky* (1990), and in this landscape, shame and self-disgust are never far away, as Assotto Saint's poem "Black Fag" shows. The scene is set in the Mineshaft, a sex-club as popular as The Saint, whose devil-may-care atmos-phere has been captured by Marc Lida's watercolor *The Saint* (1982). In "Black Fag" the persona ponders his participation in white gay men's fanta-sies and their instrumentalization of his blackness: "Beyond the dreams of bathing in a thousand white dudes' cum / to wash a dark shade off my skin / beyond the dreams of their fingers grasping my head still / to wave the wooliness out of my hair / beyond the dreams of their golden showers" (*Spells of a Voodoo Doll*: 393–94). What is to be reached on the other side of the cumulative and anaphoric "beyond," on the other side of the warehouse wall, the screen of porn theaters, is this lack-with-an-object—love, the urge to connect that AIDS, and the prospect of a precipitate termination fuels and magnifies.

Against the countdown of the vanishing process, the attempt at connect-ing often takes the form of a suspension—of time, or of consciousness. As-sotto Saint's "In the Fast Lane" represents both as they are transcended by the poetic form. "Riding / . . . / on Los Angeles's freeways" a rented red Honda, the persona and his lover, free and carefree, renew in a gay version the cliched image of a blissful and prelapsarian America. But the wheels of the motorcycle stop turning as the poem jolts mid-way on the line "I looked at you look at me." In this *anagnorisis*, the two lovers understand the lethal meaning of the "strange gay plague" the radio bulletin blares about (*Spells of a Voodoo Doll*: 45). From now on, the wheel of fortune takes over the red Honda's wheels of desire. But the poem supersedes this substitution with a transubstantiation of its own. If life, bliss, and time are suspended, the poem nonetheless continues its due course for them, unfolding itself permanently, spinning a regenerated text from the pivotal line "I looked at you look at me." The poem is repeated from the start but with its lines now inverting the order of italics and block characters, as though reflected in a mirror—the mirror of AIDS that the two lovers face in a transience that will not befall the poetry.

When time cannot be suspended, it is already too late, and, continuously and compulsively, death calls at the door as if it were not the one not to be remembered. The watch alarm that goes off to remind people that they should take their AZT sounds in both Sarah Schulman's novel *People in Trouble* (1990) and Paul Monette's *Borrowed Time*, where, moreover, the narrator avows that "the whole idea of calendars [is] a horrible mockery" (1988a: 192). Writing AIDS is a Janus with two faces—deferring the fatal outcome but also propelling it, making denial sound like another mockery. Before featuring denial as a topic, AIDS writing itself was the subject of denial. In *Confronting AIDS Through Literature: The Responsibilities of Representation*, Paul Reed, the author of *Facing It* (1984) recalls that "as early as 1983 the mysterious plague was a burning theme in Dorothy Bryant's *Day in San Francisco* and Armistead Maupin's *Baby Cakes*" (Pastore: 91). But the writing of AIDS was a personal matter to writers who had to face their friends' death and their own, both of which require time and acceptance. In the same respect, Melvin Dixon remembers George Whitmore as the writer who "struck a Faustian bargain with AIDS: If he wrote about it, perhaps he wouldn't get it" (*Love's Instruments*: 75). Nevertheless, as Dixon confesses in his text "I'll Be Somewhere Listening For My Name" (*Love's Instruments*: 76), if "one becomes afraid to write because one's wildest speculations may in fact come true," writing, beyond the procrastination of time and consciousness, imposes itself as a tentative reminder of the self, others, and the world, as the only connection left—with one's own vanishing. In a dystopian version of Whitman's multiple self, encompassing all "gropings, impulses and desires," Wojnarowicz sets out what is essentially at stake:

> I'm afraid I'm losing touch with the faces of those I love. I'm losing touch with the current of timelessness . . . Maybe nothing can save me. Maybe all my dreams as a kid and as a young guy have fallen down to their knees. Inside my head I wished for years that I could separate into ten different people to give each person I loved a part of myself forever and also have some left over to drift across landscapes and maybe even to go into death or areas that were deadly and have enough of me to survive the death of one or two of me—this was what I thought appropriate for all my desires and I never figured out how to arrange it all and now I'm in danger of losing the only one of me that is around. I'm in danger of losing my life and what gesture can convey or stop this possibility? What gesture of hands or mind can stop my death? Nothing, and that saddens me. (1998a: 229)

Vanishing and the corollary estrangements from the Self and from others are the basis of Wojnarowicz's artistic experimentations. In *In the Shadow of the American Dream*, which borrows its strong visual quality from Wojnarowicz's photographic art, itself obviously influenced by the narrative dimension of his diaries, one of the final passages gives a minute and vertiginous account of what being aware of the imminence of death entails for the Self and for one's sense of identity. Duplicating the loose structure of AIDS as a virus, vanishing is here represented as a network of metaphors—the author's "invisible words," "invisible arms and hands," "the glass human disappearing in rain," the vanishing of physical sensations. Progressively the metaphors gnaw at the fabric of the text and isolate the opening proclamation of existence and its vain litany of "I am," repeated seven times in four lines. "I am" disappears and dissolves into its "new persona as a stranger," itself metamorphosed into objects, more and more ethereal, or sheer abstractions—volume, "blank spot," "a smudge in the air." Transubstantiation from materiality to abstraction, this growing invisibility separates the Self from others and from oneself: "I am a stranger to others and to myself." The symptom of this (self) estrangement is the failure of connection and communication: "[I] can no longer speak the right language . . . What I make has meaning that circulates inside rather than outside, which defeats communication other than with myself." With an internal circulation of signification, the text also is bound to disappear as it cancels its own *raison d'être*—being read and connected to the world out there, its context. Unsurprisingly, the author does make thus clear that there is no such thing as a context in death: "I'm not ready. What does that mean; there is no context for that statement." Between the self-assertive first lines, which rapped out their "I am," and the concluding "I'm not," which conveys almost timidly one's rejection of death, the text has already swallowed itself. Without context to provide either otherness or difference, the "I" has first become a stranger to the Self and to others and then a non-entity in a literal and written emptiness. Vanishing within a context that has vanished, the author's interior space "is [his] location at this time like an invisible map, invisible even to [him] but [he] embod[ies] or carr[ies] it and it is now [his] identity, it is [his] emptiness, it is [his] loss of reflection in the mirror" (*In the Shadow*: 262–63) This is what facing it—death or the mirror reflecting the loss to come—implies: what is perceived in a glimpse by the dying subject, and translated into text, is the death of the Self and, in the adherence to one's own vanishing, the vanishing of mundane identities.

Against its propensity to submerge the voice, the vanishing "I," and social identities in nothingness, the text also proffers the possibility of a resistance that articulates identification and identity. In a radical alienation, the Self is metaphorized into an Other, becomes that Other, retrieves itself from it and lets the Other die. From the "Self-as-Other" to the "Self-is-Other," the transformation exactly follows the development of the progression of AIDS at a cellular level. In other words, the text becomes the virus that destroys it to save its voice. Materializing Arthur Rimbaud's statement of uncanny revelation "*Je est un autre*," Wojnarowicz had already pictured the first stage of this transformation—the "Self-as-Other"—in his collection of photographs the *Arthur Rimbaud in New York* series where a man, a mask of the French poet on his face, wanders around New York, the gloomy and artificial setting of his loneliness, while he exposes himself, masturbates, or uses drugs. A process that irremediably underlies writing, especially in the autobiographical mode of diaries and memoirs, the "Self-as-Other" transformation in *In the Shadow of the American Dream* still achieves a complete identification and reaches identity. The Self is the Other before being split again into two entities, equal but different, as one dies and the other survives. Or so it seems:

> I feel like it's happening to this person called David, but not to me. It's happening to this person who looks exactly like me, is as tall as me and I can see through his eyes as I am in his body, but it's still not me. So I go on and occasionally this person called David cries or makes plans for the possibility of death or departure or going to a doctor for checkups or dabbles in underground drugs in hopes for more time, and then eventually I get the body back and that David disappears for a while and I go about my daily business doing what I do, what I need or care to do. I sometimes feel bad for that David and can't believe he is dying. (212)

In another fragment, "David, but not me" wears the mask of the child the two Davids were once. In a nightmarish dream the author wanders on the sidewalk of Broadway, suspended in time and space while the neighborhood of his "childhood hustling days" rustles with "movements of bodies, legs, pedestrians from the chest down." As he crawls in the luminous wonders of his dystopian Broadway dream, he finally finds himself at the intersection of Eighth Avenue and Seventh Avenue. He is now in a "ten-year-old's body and that body is full of life, full of flesh and muscle and veins and blood and energy and it all produces and propels this scream, this scream that comes from twenty to thirty years of silence . . . And it is here in the midst of that scream in the midst of this sensation of life in an uninfected body in all this blurry swirl of dusky street light that [he] wake[s] up" (224). The Munch-like scream is ambivalent. It voices the triumph of life over the virus but reproduces the conversion of cells and the progressively blurred lines between them. Expanding and saturating the text through widening circles, the scream equalizes all and everything: the scream and the author, David as an adult and David as a child, the thirty years of silence and the dusky street light. In the struggle between the screaming textual voice and the text, between life and death, the voice seems to have the upper hand and to save the Self in an Other who supposedly is not going to die but actually founders on reality and its powerlessness—"I wake up." The child was a dream, and both are already dead.

RESISTING INDIFFERENTIATION,
TRANSCENDING IDENTITY (?)

In its resistance to a growing indifferentiation, Wojnarowicz's text bears a striking resemblance to a passage from Melvin Dixon's *Vanishing Rooms*. The movement from "Self-as-Other" to "Self-is-Other" is more explicitly conceived in the perspective of insanity. Guilty of Metro's rape and barbarous murder, Lonny is one of those lost kids in America who "never had a chance," as his mother kept telling him. In an earlier variation of the passage quoted in chapter 5, he comes back to the crime scene to lie down on the asphalt, in the space left by Metro's body, now vanished. The contrast between the stark reality referred to by Lonny's confession and the matter-of-fact style, with its verbless short sentences and its repetitions, gives Lonny's hallucinatory narrative a harrowing dimension. Madness creeps in under the form of talking autumnal red leaves that give voice to Lonny's troubled conscience. To escape from the leaves and allay his conscience, Lonny thinks of inhabiting another body, the empty space of Metro's corpse: "So I walked around the outline, seeing it from different angles. How funny to see something that fixed, protected from people or from falling leaves or from the slimy drippings from sides of beef. The outline wasn't Metro. It was somebody like me" (68). Soon the metamorphosis is finalized: "The chalk shape was glowing like crushed jewels under the streetlights . . . I crossed the barricade and sat inside the chalk. The glow was on me now. It was me. I lay down in the shape of the dead man, fitting my head, arms, and legs in place. I was warm all over" (68). But, as in Wojnarowicz, the change does no good. The old self continues to fall into October red leaves and madness while, for the new Lonny, regenerated from a dead body, only rape and prostitution loom on the horizon.

In their common attempt at transcending identity in the face of imminent death, Wojnarowicz's *In the Shadow of the American Dream* and Dixon's *Vanishing Rooms* both stand out as remarkable literary pieces of the 1990s. The connection between them is all the more powerful in that they are bound together by an invisible tie that, in *Vanishing Rooms*, has vanished. To my knowledge, AIDS has never been a prism through which the novel has been be read. The main reason of this lack is that, although published in 1991, the novel is set in 1975, a cultural and political context when the intricacies of racial and sexual identities fueled a heated debate. In their introduction to *A Melvin Dixon Critical Reader* (2006), Joyce and McBride therefore conclude that

> this latter period was further complicated by the height of the Aids epidemic, a topic Dixon may have wished to avoid by choosing to set *Vanishing Rooms* in 1975 so that the AIDs epidemic would not overshadow the other very impor-

tant problems central to this novel: the nature of interracial intimacy, relationships between gay men and heterosexual women, the violent manifestations of
homophobia, and the relationship between love and desire to name but a few.
(xxi)

But one may contend that it is precisely in the shadow of the AIDS
epidemic that *Vanishing Rooms* shines the most and proves Paul Reed wrong
when he argued that "no single, major masterpiece of fiction has yet emerged
from the AIDS epidemic to take its place alongside the great novels of
illness—Camus' *Plague*, Mann's *Magic Mountain*, Defoe's *Journal of the
Plague Year*" (Pastore: 93). In its very form and structure the novel conveys
the invisibility of the virus and its undercurrent process of general vanishing,
achieving the *tour de force* of representing not only what cannot be—the
vanishing of space and bodies—but also what cannot be represented since it
exists only negatively—a virus that is identified by the destruction it pro-
vokes. The entire novel *Vanishing Rooms* can thus be seen as a metaphor of
AIDS bestowing textual space on the temporal quicksand the disease sym-
bolizes. Though the diegesis is set in 1975, time has no meaning in the grip
of AIDS where the future is already enclosed in the space of the past. In this
indifferentiation, room for certainty, for racial and sexual identities, and for
sanity vanishes. This is reflected in the novel's polyphonic structure that
collapses. First, the different characters' narratives are juxtaposed and narrate
the central event of Metro's rape and murder and the consequences. Progressively, the narratives sound alike and, as they contaminate each other, one
voice merges with another, erasing from the quilt-like fabric of the text the
seams and stitches separating self and other. Indifferentiation stemming from
AIDS thus appears as both structural and thematic.

As paradoxical as indifferentiation in AIDS writing might be—it signals
the subject's death and, as a result, the possibility to transcend identity—
American literature of the 1990s nonetheless retains race as the irreducible
point of difference. In the contemporary writing of death, race remains the
reductive metaphor of the black lived experience and the condition of a
phantasmatic white survival. While in both Wojnarowicz and Dixon the Self
failed to engender an Other to be sacrificed in its place, thus paving the way
for the death of identity and its literary transcendence, most AIDS texts are
enmeshed in American racial antagonism, betraying a return to the unavoid-
able reality but also, for AIDS literature and its aesthetic and political pretensions, an insuperable limitation.

The social context of black gays and lesbians in the 1980s and 1990s is
one of double exclusion. Writers, poets, and artists of this period are part of a
stigmatized group that, in "I'll Be Somewhere Listening for My Name,"
Melvin Dixon calls "the sexual niggers of our society" (*Love's Instruments*:
73). In the same text, which is an adaptation of the keynote address he

delivered at OutWrite in 1992, just before his death, Dixon describes the "double cremation" that black gays and lesbians have to face:

> We must, however, guard against the erasure of our experience and our lives. As white gays become more and more prominent—and acceptable to mainstream society—they project a racially exclusive image of gay reality . . . As white gays deny multiculturalism among gays, so too do black communities deny multisexualism among its members. Against this double cremation, we must leave the legacy of our writing and our perspectives on gay and straight experiences. (77–78)

In this context, Essex Hemphill's poem "Object Lessons" can be read as targeting both black conservatives' hypocrisy and whites' sexualized fantasies of blacks. Representing itself as a sexual object, oiled and passive, the persona seems to consent to the penetration of the reader's/viewer's gaze but holds for itself the signification of this visual possession. It is deferred by a series of anaphoric "if," which ends on the reappropriation of both image and meaning by the textual voice: "The pedestal was here / So I climbed up. / I located myself. / I appropriated this context. / It was my fantasy, / To do so / And lie here on my stomach. / Why are you looking? / What do you wanna / Do about it?" (*Ceremonies*: 69–70).

In this perspective, transcending identity and returning to reality cannot be but a double-bind in AIDS writing since the reality to return to is over-racialized while death is not the great equalizer expected. Though writers try to dismantle racial categorization, their attempt at connecting breaks on a sociohistorical and cultural determinism to which their texts also testify. Very significantly, if most writers and artists working in and about the AIDS epidemic want to be remembered and acknowledged, self-identified white ones address themselves to the national community. While being a dissenter castigating the indifference of the American public opinion, the injustice of health services, and the negligence of the administration, George Whitmore nonetheless re-creates in *Someone Was Here: Profiles in the AIDS Epidemic* the allegorical and mythical national narrative where, from the trauma of AIDS, is to emerge a regenerated American consciousness. On the other hand, when African American and black artists express their fear and rage at being excluded or their commitment to a collective experience and memory, it is, first and foremost, for and within the black community. Besides the divide between black consciousness and American-consciousness-as-white, another significant feature of the permanence is the haunting presence of blackness. Returning from a cultural and literary heritage where what is foreign exerts an uncanny fascination mingled with repulsion, the specter of blackness, and its ideological content, is to be found in analogies, metaphors, allegories, and similes throughout most of AIDS writing by white authors. The prevalence of blackness is such that it becomes in itself a set of figures of speech, both syncretic and rhizomatic. The literary phenomenon Toni Morrison analyzed in *Playing in the Dark: Whiteness and the Literary Imagination* (1992) is thus continued in the contemporary era where the transgressive attraction of sex makes room for the fatal rejection from AIDS but always with black ghosts haunting whites' words and imagination.

In the same way as connecting in AIDS writing needed to be contextualized in gay literature and art at large, images of blackness in 1990s AIDS narratives and poetry prolong a tradition where homoerotic desire is associated with otherness, be it national, racial, or ethnic. For David Wojnarowicz, who defines America as the kingdom of sameness, being gay is already a state of "foreignness" within the federal state. Besides, there is no distinction to be made between the 1970s sexual revolution and the AIDS era of the 1990s since America was and remains a "one-tribe-nation" struck by the "fear of diversity." In *In the Shadow of the American Dream*, he recollects his teenage travels across the United States, symbolically seated at the back of the bus, his eyes riveted on "the large rearview mirror" where he watches the driver who inspires in him his 300-mile-long "hard-on." Meanwhile, the other passengers are "clustered like flies." They embody, in a reminiscence of Ginsberg's Moloch, this "self-destructive or suicidal amoeba" that America was at the time "when everything was reformed and rebuilt to look the same in order to ease people's fears of foreignness and to induce them to travel without having to risk making new choices" (244). In *Close to the Knives*, Wojnarowicz continues to put American conservatism and conformism on trial. Twenty years later the same reductionism devastates Americans but now the metaphor, though still organic, is that of "an extreme disease," "just like a pimple on the face of a society." Both the metaphor and the simile recall the skin lesions related to AIDS whose social stigmatization is thus returned to the face of the nation:

> A disease that shows itself in the prevalence of FEAR OF DIVERSITY and is characterized by various symptoms. Among them are sweating palms, angry outbursts, hysteria, the discharging of handguns, the passing of certain legislation, the invasion of foreign countries, the burning down of homes, the running out of town, and ultimately the legalized murder of those who are diverse in their natures. (154)

America is no place for desire and has never been. Joining Rimbaud, Gide, Genet, Burroughs, and Baldwin before him, Wojnarowicz mainly conceives of desire as deterritorialized. In this respect he perpetuates the mystique of sailors whose quest for freedom and self-reliance encrypts a homoerotic desire that cannot be fulfilled on land. Established by Melville's *Typee*, *Moby-Dick*, and *Billy Budd*, this paradigm also crosses American painting and visual arts, from Charles Demuth's *Two Sailors Urinating* (1930) and Paul Cadmus's censored *The Fleet's In!* (1934) to Tom of Finland's *Untitled (Sailor's Orgy)* (1959) and the more recent *Read My Lips (Boys)* (1988) by Gran Fury that, before being an ACT UP poster, was a more daring 1940s photograph showing two sailors crossing their erect penises. It is in this heritage and context that should be read Wojnarowicz's "*invitation-au-voyage*-addressed-to-oneself" within *In the Shadow of the American Dream*.

September 19, 1977
SEEING MYSELF SEEING MYSELF SITTING BY AN OPEN WINDOW

> When dawn comes on after a night that has spent itself by the window, dark ships ease into the frame of sky taking the place of clouds. Upside down they are sailing on and on toward an imagined horizon where the seekers of love stand to the side of the curtains peering out. There is great mystery, one of foreign soils and oceanic breath disappearing beyond the fine line of water and sky. We are growing steadfastly, fingernails and hair and subtle gray curves in the head. Lessons come in all forms from every direction, out on the bench by the river an old man sits swayed by neither water nor air, yet from this porthole several stories up I am seized by a continent of my own making. (35)

As often the case, sailing away and the emancipation it foreshadows are explicitly associated with foreign lands while the expected self-transformation is metaphorized by blackness, here encoded as night. "Spend[ing] itself by the window," the night thus personified also reflects the author. The passage is a striking reminder of the incipit of Baldwin's *Giovanni's Room*. A young white American and closeted gay man in the South of France, David in the novel cannot see himself literally becoming black as the night falls through his reflection in the window-pane behind which African shores remain invisible.

Within the prison of America or deterritorialized, literary white homoerotic or homosexual desire seems consubstantial with a sense of otherness. Particularly so when this desire can be encompassed by a black shape that can explicitly refer to an African American presence, as in Jack Kerouac's and Norman Mailer's use of "the black cool cat" stereotype or the latter's problematic self-identification as a "white Negro" in *Advertisements for Myself*. In the context of the "extreme disease" of AIDS in America, the metaphorization of blackness reaches a terminal stage where, contrary to Wojnarowicz's and Dixon's attempts to resist vanishing, the splitting of the "Self-(a/i)s-Other" results in the preservation of whiteness and the sacrifice of blackness.

THE H(A)UNTING OF BLACKNESS

In the same fashion as Freud's etiology of the fantasy retained the "half-breed" metaphor for the cultural conjuring-up of racial difference at the expense of the black lived experience and subjectivity, as previously contended in chapter 3, most of white AIDS narratives, poetry, and literary criticism consider African American and black culture in a rather reductive way. They also considerably underestimate the impact of African Americans and blacks on the literary imaginary of AIDS writing. A reference AIDS writing study, Ross Chambers's *Untimely Interventions: AIDS Writing, Testimonial, and the Rhetoric of Haunting* (2004) is, in this respect, an emblematic example. In his historical genealogy of witnessing writing, Ross Chambers identifies World War I and the Holocaust as the two major traumas that have shaped modern sensibility. Down to contemporary AIDS writing, all testimonial narratives and witnessing writing would be more or less modeled after the pieces written in and about these periods. Chambers pursues his preface by explaining that haunting is a key feature of witnessing writing. The unjustly slain returns as a ghost in the world of the living to draw attention to his ill-fated lot and awaken their consciousness. Though Chambers's study concentrates on European and Australian authors, one may nonetheless wonder why he does not situate Paul Monette and other American authors he analyzes or mentions at the backdrop of the African American experience. In his paradigm of testimonial writing, bounded by World War I and the Holocaust, the conspicuous absence of African American culture and literature is problematic—unless one considers that they did not shape the American sensibility.

Yet one may argue that from Equiano to Dixon, African American literature is nothing but a wide set of testimonial narratives intended to raise consciousness in both black and white readers. Moreover, the theme of haunting, with the return of the dead calling to have his/her unjust death acknowledged, is also a central *topos* in African American literature, rooted in its own cultural tradition and immortalized by Morrison's *Beloved*. Instead, if Chambers acknowledges that for historical reasons black culture has "tended to develop traditions of lamentations and resources for testimonial" (xvi), his focus is more particularly on performance arts, notably Marlon T. Riggs's video *Tongues Untied* and Bill T. Jones's choreography *Still/Here*, the latter still being referred to, a few pages later, within the frame of the two modern traumas of World War I and the Holocaust. Chambers also argues that the ethical teaching of AIDS writing as witnessing literature is to suggest that such an atrocity can happen all over again. In this respect as well, AIDS writing inscribes itself in the lineage of World War I and the Holocaust, the ethical scope from which African American literature is also *a priori* excluded.

In Chambers's theoretical and programmatic prelude, the genealogical and ethical triangulation gathering the witnessing texts of World War I, the Holocaust, and the AIDS epidemic not only casts out black suffering from the pantheon of universal pain but postulates this absence as the norm. Ironically, this critical lack is a reversed *mise en abyme* of the acknowledgment sought by AIDS witnessing that, when written by whites, tends to show similar limitations. Indeed, few authors draw the explicit parallel between the hecatomb of gays in the 1980s and the 1990s, furthered by the carelessness of the administration and health services, and the legalized mass murder of African Americans during slavery, segregation, and after. It is also true that white American authors, such as Paul Monette, are more prone to identify their condition with the Holocaust or World War I than with the African American experience. Haunting and the consciousness awakening that the return of the dead causes may signify the transgression of fundamental boundaries between life and death, here and there, materiality and immateriality, past and present, but one frontier—a trench in consciousness—remains impassable: the color line that obfuscates an American consciousness still lying in the dream of its whiteness. To be lost to AIDS is more than falling into blackness; it is to become black, and that should not be publicly witnessed. This gives another meaning to "indexicality," Chambers's other key concept in his study of AIDS writing:

> The cultural function of the witnessing texts themselves is indexical, in that their characteristic form of "aboutness" is indicative, "pointing" to an X that the culture's conventional means of representation are powerless, or at least inadequate, to reference, precisely because it lies at a point of supposedly distant extremity with respect to what culture regards as its normal, and thus central, concerns. Such indexicality, I propose, as a pointing-towards that has an object, but an object by definition obscure, dubious, hard to envisage or realize, is inevitably experienced by its audience . . . The apprehension thus produced—I mean it in the double sense of the word: something that is *feared* is simultaneously *grasped*—is, in my opinion, the characteristic cultural effect of witnessing practices, an effect that can be reinterpreted as the uncanny mimeticism, the transportation into the other scene. (xv)

If the indexicality of AIDS witnessing texts is to point at the human tragedy society is unwilling to acknowledge, one may contend that this "pointing-toward" relies on, and is in fact conditioned by, the exclusion of black subjectivities with subsequently their reduction to metaphors of objectification. Conforming to the intricacy of American culture's sexual and racial taboos, white AIDS writing implicitly posits that in order to arouse sympathy or compassion and give rise to acknowledgment, gay men, in the grip of death, should not fall in a sub-humanity metaphorized by blackness. In other words, there is a limitation to "the uncanny mimeticism, the transportation into the other scene" that, as a disease, AIDS engenders in patients and, as text, generates in readers. For being such, the other scene needs an absolute point of difference, a radical otherness that does not even belong to the scene. The uncanny quality of mimeticism between the patient and AIDS, or between the witnessing text and the reader, can only be perceived in contrast to a third element that spatializes the production and circulation of meaning through unambiguously discriminated identification and differentiation. This third element, this absolute point of difference is race, a blackness that never blossoms into central characterization and whose metaphors bear another indexicality, in Chambers's sense of the word: becoming black—that which should be feared and *not* grasped, always deferred or displaced into another "other scene." This "other scene," which is not witnessed or acknowledged, is the American scene of miscegenation and interraciality, and it stands in parallel to the American terror of homosexuality dissected by white AIDS writing. It is the ultimate disjunction of race and sex pointed at to preserve whiteness. In other words, in desire and in the disease, the recognition sought for is white.

This phenomenon is overwhelmingly present in Paul Monette's works. In *Borrowed Time*, the autobiographical account of the decline and death of Roger Horwitcz, his lover and life-long companion, African Americans and Latinos are mainly confined to the peripheral roles of the caregivers—nurses and health assistants—and never cross the boundaries of the narrator and his lover's intimacy, reflecting the ethno-racial segregation of the upper middle-class neighborhood where they live in San Francisco. From the outset, it is the narrator's race and class consciousness that are brought to the fore. HIV/AIDS represents a threat for whites' social privileges, a status that African Americans and Latinos are already deprived of. Cynically, the disaster in these communities seems to be therefore less unfair:

> Perhaps the work is especially important because AIDS is striking so many of us just as we're hitting our stride at work. I mean of course the American AIDS of the first half-decade, before it began to burgeon in the black and brown communities. Most of the fallen in our years were urban gay men, and most of these were hard at their work when the symptoms started multiplying and nothing would go away. (1988a: 28)

To defuse racism in what appears, after all, as a mere contextualization, the use of "of course" in the gloss of the first sentence shifts the separation between "us" and "them" from the frame of class stereotypical distinctions to one of temporal partition. But the "us"/"them" divide is later reinforced by exoticification and primitivism: "To the gay men around us, admitting the shadow had fallen on Roger was to unleash a wild surmise naked as the pandemic across the belly of Africa" (Monette, 1988a: 63); "*When is enough,* I kept thinking, as if every tragedy mounting up would finally satisfy some savage god" (70). Thus compared to an indeterminate and malevolent deity, the sheer prospect of HIV infection is inconceivable, beyond reason, in the remote distance of the uncivilized Africa that, with savageness and indecency, personifies the loss of rationality. Falling on Roger, the black shadow of HIV starts a few pages later its mighty work. Under an external attack of black otherness, the closed space of Roger's body now betrays the alteration entailed by what David Wojnarowicz calls in *Close to the Knives* "this tiny, invisible-to-the-eye virus" (1991/1992: 165). It is now the racist imagery of miscegenation that is conjured up to metaphorize the panic-stricken fear of surrendering to the othering process of HIV infection. Like other symptoms, the minor spots on forearms are being scrutinized. They foreshadow the infection that the blood results confirm, leaving one in the dismaying contemplation of an irreversible identity change whose paradigmatic figures, in American literature and Hollywood movies, are the "tragic mulattoes," bound to discover that under their light skin runs an infectious black blood that blackens the whole self. In both cases, the moment of *anagnorisis* propels them into the sub-human category of monsters. Though allegorical, and at the backdrop of the American racialized culture, the parallel between HIV/AIDS and race is obvious. When Monette's narrator avows that "so many monsters have haunted the darkness of AIDS" (1988a: 86), one easily figures out that, in the writing, it is the haunting of blackness that manifests itself—the return of blacks, the culturally dead, into white American consciousness.

If race seems to be such a powerful metaphor of AIDS, it is not only because the two of them are inextricably linked to sex but also because the skin socially functions as the signifier of one's belonging to a racially, ethnically, or medically based group. As Suzanne Yang argues in "Speaking of the Surface: The Texts of Kaposi's Sarcoma," "the skin is often a factor in one's acceptance or disapproval, real or imagined, by others . . . [Dermatological problems] are visible indicators of a disease that remains severely stigmatizing and that is still associated with socially marginalized groups" (Dean and Lane: 324). As the surface separating the body and the world, the skin betrays the stigmas of a penetration from outside that alters the inside to a point of indifferentiation between one and the other. This phantasmagoria of AIDS is the replica of the fantasies underlying race relations and miscegenation—to whiten or blacken the other race. Baldwin has given voice to the two points of view—the white one in "Going to Meet the Man," where the sheriff Jesse howls at a black boy, "You lucky we *pump* some white blood into you every once in a while—your women!" (938), and the black one in *Another Country* (1962), where Rufus has violent sexual relations with his white lover, Leona: "A moan and a curse tore through him while he beat her with all the strength he had and felt the venom shoot out of him, enough for a hundred black-white babies" (384).

The skin therefore operates as a porous frontier separating races, persons with AIDS (PWAs) and persons without, all categories being enclosed in segregated spaces that can nevertheless be bridged through miscegenation or infection. Significantly, Yang states that AIDS "is a disease of boundaries, of the relation between self and environment, and of vulnerability both specific and diffuse to the challenges posed from within and outside the body. These challenges reveal the persistent struggle and overcoming that the immune system ordinarily accomplishes in silence" (323). But in Monette, these spaces, boundaries, and expressions of otherness take on a more and more precise racial dimension. Race is the phantasmatic virus that engulfs persons with AIDS. The syndrome burgeons at the surface of the text. The rational discourse is no longer hermetically closed, and stock images of the African American experience, like the passing or the underground railroad, now pass the border of consciousness:

> We were about to join a community of the stricken who would not lie down and die . . . Some have sat in medical libraries wading through the arcana of immunology. Others pass back and forth over the border, bringing vanloads of drugs the law hasn't got around yet. This network has the feel of an underground railway. It could be argued that we're out there mainly for ourselves, of course, and the ones we cannot live without. But on the way we have also become traders and explorers, passing the world till hope is kindled in places so dark you can't see your hand in front of your eyes. (Monette, 1988a: 103)

The identity change is achieved but only to be despised. Without being desirable, darkness and blackness are incorporated since "whistling in the dark is whistling still" (103). This is confirmed by the concluding lines of Monette's poem "Current Status 1/22/87," published in *Love Alone: Eighteen Elegies for Rog*, which, as in *Borrowed Time*, overlaps in identity change race/ethnicity, medical status, and geography: "I'm learning how to hold a sword / but there is no telling what I will do / when I get there stay at my side will you / so I don't do anything vain or cease to honor / you and all our brothers below the Equator" (1988b: 36).

The shiny sublimity of this brotherhood in arms is darkened by the scatological overtones of both the identity change and the haunting. The bargain Monette strikes with time gives him a mastery over space. For the time stolen from his life, his retaliation will consist of returning into the world of the living as he has been expelled from it—like a stinking and pervasive shit one cannot get rid of. While examining the inside of his bowels, "like an oracle poking entrails," the persona of "Current Status 1/22/87" also specifies that "if you flush / a toilet five feet south of the Equator / the spiral flows clockwise five feet north / flows counterclock" (1988b: 34). Monette again uses this centripetal image of "spiraling down" in *Borrowed Time* when he depicts Rog's ultimate moment of life "as [he] spiral[s] down." The fall is also closely associated with "imprisonment," "exile," "claustrophobia," and "stonewalling" (1988a: 337–39). The only way not to be eternally boxed-in and exiled is to achieve this excremental transubstantiation. One might be forced to join "our brothers below the Equator," as in the flushing of a toilet, but one will come back and haunt the North, the world of the living and the healthy. The North and the South are not only the volumes of life and death, enclosing the wealthy and the wretched; they are also asymmetrical because the return of the dead as shit necessarily identifies sub-equatorial people as "shitty." In this phantasmatic identification where the equator is the anus of the world—the world skin hole opening on the infection and the transformation of one's current status—racism is bordering on homophobic self-hatred since it is also through the anal penetration of the North that one returns as shit.

Retaliation is here symptomatic of Paul Monette's *jouissance* that transforms a source of displeasure into pleasure and that is, as Žižek remarks (1998: 156), captured exactly by the poetic form of the elegy. It is also in this perspective, and with the backdrop of his upbringing on the puritanical East Coast, that one can read Monette and his racial metaphors. Monette's literary pleasure lies in his return to a society that excludes him. The failed identification with white American society and the source of masochistic pleasure are metaphorized by racial expressions of blackness. Meanwhile the indexicality of the spectacle of pain represented in the texts shifts its focus. The masochistic pleasure felt in the process of becoming an Other, sadistically defined as sub-human, disappears behind the textual spectacle of the pain of the Other-as-Self. Dying from AIDS is thus performed as the tragedy of becoming black. Unlike Dixon, for whom AIDS metaphorizes race relations, blackness in Monette's work is the cultural ghost invoked to consolidate whiteness beyond desire and the disease. This is how the pleasurable h(a)unting of blackness rewrites AIDS as white America.

Chapter Seven

The Word's Image

Self-Portrait as a Conscious Lie

From where I am sitting—at my Moroccan table in my Parisian studio flat back from Corsica, the isle of France to depart from and go back to, in the summertime transition, between family and friends, cousins and neighbors, anonymous night lovers and the parts of the self to hold to, books unread, half-read, to be read, shamelessly spread on the table and by the bed, Bill Readings's *Dans les ruines de l'université*, Lawrence P. Jackson's *The Indignant Generation*, Jane Anna Gordon's *Creolizing Political Theory*, and, on the right, slightly further, on the extra-bed shifting tangent of beloved bodies curled in silence from the muffled noisy streets of the capital city, neatly framed by turquoise and pink cushions that my mother disturbs when she visits, alone, not read yet, Foucault's *Subjectivité et vérité*. They suspend the gaze trajectory, the unfolding room. The syncopating walls behind which I know they lie and hide, Jean-Noel Pancrazi's *Indétectable*, Paul Gilroy's *Black Britain*, Fatou Diome's *Celles qui attendent*—read—Emmanuel Carrère's *L'Adversaire* and *La Classe de neige*—no, they're back on the bookshelves but I've read them (there is no room)—Marguerite Duras's *Ecrire*—re-read—Dany Laferrière's *L'Enigme du retour*—unread—the French translation of John Ashbery's *The Vermont Notebook*—half read, half understood (which half?)—possibly not understood at all, but salvaged, still. For "forsythia." The remanent "forsythia": the whistling tree that grows on page 69 and in my home garden, back in Corsica, and whose song sings alike in both tongues—French and English. Wondering how it sounds in Corsican. I don't know my own tongue. My father's tongue and mine rolling around men's long devouring kisses of meat and spit. Fleshing words before they can be mouthed. In the garden, in Corsica, our home, my father calling its name. Forsythia. The real forsythia. In French. Not his mother tongue. *Forsythia* (even more beautiful in italics and whistling still).

From where I look—the perspective narrowing like a camera focus, through the in-between space left by the wall, maimed or unfinished, of the split room—at a short distance, almost at hand and arranged aesthetically, I thought (it's not aesthetics, it's room), I see them. Blue and red. Oblong shapes of tense muscles—the fantasy to come of arching bodies and faces distorted with pleasure and pain—repeating the same to and fro movement. Down the road in the neighborhood swimming-pool, the blue waters of the bathhouse, red towels covering naked men's waists circling—I too am a stranger—the white hollow, the lighted curve between the walls of soon emptied cabins. I see it. The vanishing opening fissure that has no name. It stares at me.

The pictures hang on the wall and I can see five of them. The other two are invisible but felt and remembered enough to be written about. A journey and a pause. This is what they stand for and what it is all about. Trajectory. I keep those unseen for the end.

Génération is for my mother and her family.[1] After Toni Morrison. The story not to pass on, *Beloved*'s sixty million and more flowing through my sleepless English nights, as I awakened in the dead emptying myself like a fucking meteor. I made it in one night in a bathtub. The coffee color is real coffee, beans and liquid. In the febrile emergency of those who know they are dying (there is no time) and with what I had at hand. Coffee, teabags, paper, cardboard, my schoolboy pastels. Bare feet in the bathtub spilling coffee over everyone and the teabags, now absorbed in the board fabric, like disoriented arrows in search of meaning slipping through the continents, slaving for Europe and America's wealth and paradigms of signification, watching, impatient, my impatient watching, what would come out of my memory cooking. From the black blood ocean I midwifed in the bathtub. There are two centers, none of which is truer than the other. She is the mother. He is the elder brother. Both are centers, depending on where one looks, shifting the gaze or not, reinventing space or not, for oneself or not, all considered. The organizing center of the perpendicular frame, the transforming circle—my cosmogony and revolutionary womb—the reversed triangle—hers, the Jewish half-star pointing south and the rising fingers-made vaginas of worldwide marching women, birthing polysemy—there she stands. Next to her, looking straight at the photographer, at me through decades and countless miles, is her brother. Years later, both of us grown-up men, as he drove me back home after the last-but-one visit to my grandfather on his deathbed, he would have that same look, straight on, his pianist hands tight on the wheel balancing his bending head, whispering, as if to himself, the healing words that make loss real. Hardly audible and that I cannot remember. Not looking at me. He is at the center of the photograph—a photocopy not to waste my mother's family album and my legacy—Waster of Remains—and chosen over many others, including that of my grandmother (not the classic Harcourt Studio one of their regained Parisian bourgeois life that would come later, no, not that one—the identity papers one), her beautiful Creole-fashion figure, the elegant bearing of her head crowned with a crafty bohemian haircut, the defying look in her Arawak's slanting eyes. Barred, all barred from the identification second-half reading "Colony of Guadeloupe" (I translate). I would not have known what to do with that anyway. The chosen one is when they all stand together in front of the plane, wings spread, on the tarmac of the airport, ready to fly away again and for good, from Cameroon, where, in the late 1940s, my grandfather had been sent as a French army officer (not the high ranks—barred to blacks), leaving the Caribbean behind, taking his wife and six children with him and the nanny commissioned to raise them through their transatlantic new life, leaving behind—the nanny—what was her name?—her own children.

Guadeloupeans in Cameroon, Corsicans in Indochina. Forefronting the empire. Colonized turned into colonizing sub-agents working through taught domination, inward and outward, steadily, in concentric circles. No flux or sea-change yet, perception shifting up to a point. Shifting still. When my grandfather slapped her—the white woman sending him back with slurs to the black queue of the army base supply shed where he belonged, she said— the circular trajectory started again, revealing the collage central reversed triangle—the photograph immersed in coffee in the bathtub, re-membering and replacing the old structure of feeling and consciousness—from the Americas to Africa to Europe. To Europe to France to Bordeaux. His slap in the face and the state retaliation and the master's lesson. Sent back to Bordeaux, the wine and slave country. Such a sense of history and irony France has. And the empire, the fixed center, Paris, knew well the art of discipline and shifted directions—when, where and how to strike back, delineate spaces, distribute values, and assign positions. Puppeteering syntax as if syntax was life. He tried the state for a decade and won while serving the Antillese community in Paris with the legal knowledge he acquired, and died. They did not grow up destitute or wretched in Bordeaux and the ruptured life was his. His slap on the face, for them and us—my generation— like a comma, the remembered punctuation-mark of world crossings.

On the right side of the collage, further down, below the overlapping triangle and circle, there is a text that reads

il y a
au lieu
le regard
une troncature
de
trait d'union

une place
à prendre
et prise,
à
lacher

It is about (dis)location, (dis)connection, (dis)embodiment. Reading gazes. I wonder if my nephew who studies law in Bordeaux knows that family bio-mythography.

Next to *Génération* is another text. Let me read it to you.

Il me suffisait
d'être là
sans rien dire
ni faire.
De la matière
muette et absorbante,
sûrement
compatissante
aussi.
Prête
à l'emploi
puisque là.
Et leur boîte
à mémoire
s'ouvrait:
C'était un flot
une hémorragie
qui purge et
qui soulage.
Ca suffisait
A jouer
le déclencheur.

The italics are in the original text which can be translated as "I just had to stand there, without saying nor doing anything. Some mute and absorbing matter (like kitchen paper roll, you know), certainly compassionate too. Ready to use since standing there. Then their memory box opened—a flow, a hemorrhage, purging and relieving. It was enough to play the trigger" (not sure about that one; I'll check it later in the dictionary).

That is why the collage is called *Le déclencheur*. Like camera triggers preventing shaking. Cut photographs of Corsica—the sky (blue), burned landscapes (brown), the port (brown and blue). The graying and blackening ones are X-rays because I thought it was fun to tour Parisian clinics and collect unknown people's X-rays meant to be destroyed anyway. I have X-rays in most of my collages. Cutting to look inside. At the time I saw something different. It was the contrast, the conflict, between how I looked and the language I spoke. Side by side, parodying each other, the text and my photograph. 15 or 16. Like you now. 15. It captures the repeated scene of people meeting me, face to face—my being black in Corsica, their phenomenology gone astray, oblivious of the poems and songs of my famed poet and cultural militant of a father that, with my brother and sister, we sang throughout the country and beyond, in Paris, the center to defeat, the unsatisfied beast of exile and sorrow, the tongue twister—your name, oh Paris!—they sang, voicing the freedom that was to be ours. Facing me, the evidence of my being Corsican unseen. Until I started to speak the language history had deprived them of. Then, invariably, the wound would open and unleash tales of aborted attempts to connect with—their past split over the colonizing forefathers, the indigenous warmth and me, in timelessness, triggering the monstrous community. I took it all and like a man (smile)—the man I was becoming, smiling and decentered, not looking at the poster fragment of the 1931 Paris Colonial Exposition, on the top left—the Asian, the African and the North African, the four of us framed by Corsica's scorched earth whose sepia color recalled from the family photographs album—my memory— Algeria, where I was born. Known to me only through Augustine, Fanon, and Ferrari. And my parents, the young and beautiful who, teachers of French, had left the metropolis behind to re-create their lives as Algerians were inventing theirs. This birthplace is a blank page, the white in the picture from which nothing emerges but my nanny's smiling face on the photograph where she holds me up, a naked and laughing baby. We are both center-staged, and I remember that her name was Zorah.

The straight vertical cutting through the collage, between the photograph of me and the responding text, is a chosen motif recurring with variations in *Pervers au jeu ne jouit pas* or *Envi*. Progressively, the bar has become the symbol of moderation as the accepted condition of self-reflexivity. But it has also stood for limitations—socially determined, possibly self-inflicted, certainly fantasized—materialized forcefully as if to compensate the liminality of disconnections. Barred accesses, foreclosed spaces, split subjects— hyphens raised into oblique lines, slashing punctuation, i.e., black/European. Identities *per se* do not matter. What matters is the space where they lie and the narrative they unfold. I am saying this now, now as I peer into the collages—my peers—on par—now that six years and almost a half have passed, re-membering and birthing myself, stretching bars apart to ease writing and desire inside again. Now. After my being barred from French professorship—the written report, sent to my home, prolonging the two lines of reasoning firmly straightening the colonialist twists that Césaire analyzed decades ago—intellectual inferiority and moral corruption, my slap on the face, in my home—the referee's oral confession on the phone, a reported speech and his master's voice through him, yelling how much he hated my work, my theorizing and writing that cost him long and painful hours to take in—dear me, poor him, penetration does not seem as easy as in porn movies;

colon-ization—it's not you, it's your work, carefully read the report when you get it—you know what you're doing, don't you? That's your dexterity, long and painful years of apprenticeship, your ghostwriting expertise—I read it. Carefully. And I saw, emerging from Twain, Faulkner, Melville, and Ashbery, their tortured pages now torturing, jingly bells tightened on a stretching neck, the trained monkey with a collar—his, a minstrelsy, was all gesticulation and imitation—of my childhood dreams, singing with a voice breaking to be heard, on the prow of a slave ship renamed galley, tears drying in the cutting wind. How did he know? Reading sufficed. It was all written in the application portfolio. Perversion—Not mine—Abjection fathering abjection, learned and incarnate, in men and women feasting at the family welcome table—fake, false, a forgery and a fraud—all absorbing and mute, accomplices infatuated with themselves and the shiny sameness of the books they have read at the schools they have been to, stiffening at the same impulse, drive and displaced comma, fucking politely—spit and shit are for others—forcing themselves between tight thighs—the young they once were—to shoot through, rhetorically, the forlorn dream of their deserted empire. Fathering—unreadably blank wide open eyes and no voice heard— the wasteland of their knowledge. Knowledge as chirality. Fucking chirality. And, again, three years later, in a job interview—not at home—the question whose answer is to be found in James Baldwin's "A Lover's Question"— frustration rationalized into ideology—In your black scholarship, is there room for . . . ?—whiteness as suspension of reason. On that same day, across the capital city's blinding lights, in the National Assembly, the home secretary—ventriloquizing the president who, after Hegel, took the African out of history, planned in vain to move Césaire's remains to the Pantheon and who would sign the decree that instituted my becoming a professor, civilly serving France—was launching, in the name of egalitarian republicanist universalism, a timely war against the so-called "*communautarisme.*" Liberals and conservatives hand in hand, huddled in the preservation of their space. Their abstracted France and Europe—not mine—abstracting people. No wonder the university is in ruins and the country in flames. *Bleu, blanc, rouge.*

This was my primal scene of Knowledge whose deferred montage is featured in *Envi*. Deferred and shifted since *Envi*, which came first, actually sketches the primal scene of Consciousness, then abstracted in the untranslatable *Pervers au jeu ne jouit pas*. The red in *Envi* is burning desire, consumed interraciality. After Baldwin and before Dixon. Barred on every side, the text is unreadable except for a few words, originally in French, such as transfiguring, shame, ridicule, and selfishness. Written some twenty years ago, the text is titled "La question." The collage splits the question in two parts, one showing, the other hidden, both about wanting to love and the in-between disconnection that the two verbs, when combined, inhere. The black man's face looking left, piercing through the bars of papers and words, is Frantz

Fanon's as impersonated by black British actor Colin Salmon. The white man raising his eyes performs a fellatio which does not show. He is an unknown sex-worker acting in gay porn movies whose screenshots are reproduced in U.S. magazines. In between the two men, enmeshed within the circumvolutions of what is meant to stand for an enigma are other men gazing, dancing, holding their heads, and masturbating—it does not show—their cohort duplicated, further to the right, in a silver chain, both a metaphor and a metonymy. They signify the inescapable historical and social racialization of desire that pervades everyone and everywhere, leaving as yet untouched its very question and the answer to be permanently reshuffled, provided there is space to connect. Race as imagined desire. Such a conundrum has pursued me since I was a child, only to be solved as I read Baldwin's "Nobody Knows My Name," whose narrated Southern landscape was displacing my nightmare—my father buying my mother on the auction block—onto another scene. The scene of my desire, my subjectivizing fantasy to be lived and written out. Imagined and worded from the lack the old had lain in the new. *Envi* is filled in with such a productive lack, starting with a missing letter—the final "e" of "*Envie* [Envy]," which, purloined, reappears in the framing chain of red signifiers "*envienvienvienvie.*" The incantational embroidery turns the defying invitation to play—"*envi,*" which is to be found only in the modern French phrase "*à l'envi*" meaning over and over again, etymologically points to invitation and challenge—into jealousy and hatred. "*Envie,*" envy, or perversion as an erotic form of hatred. *Pervers au jeu ne jouit pas* represents that mesmerized face of a limitless *jouissance*, when lack and desire do not invite but command, in such an anticipation of the answer that the space for transformation, of difference, shrinks into nothingness. Barring "to love" from "wanting," leaving behind, in the waste, the promise of transformation as sheer surplus. Untranslatable. *Joui-sens. J'ouis-sens.* Not to bar oneself from the pleasurable possibility of seeing and hearing words differently, from a shifted perspective, in a shifting and resignifying perception. *Envi(e)* is also "*en vie.*" Alive. Survival as transforming space.

Envi's rewritten "e" turned into *Génération*. The collage's overlapping triangle and circle reshape the missing "e," whose absence, flying straight from *Envi*, is also materialized by the small papercut at the last point of the triangle, the geographical Bordeaux. It reads "*pensables v"rités,*" or "thinkable truths" in English (the typo—the inverted commas replacing the "e"—is in the original text). It is cut from one of those innumerable letters that my grandfather, a man of archives, wrote on my grandmother's Progress typewriter that today tips the column of my dictionaries and notebooks by my Moroccan table in Paris. I saved some of these letters from my mother and my aunt's furious pain at my grandfather's death, which, besides triggering the memory of their father's selfishness, revived the sorrow of their mother's short life. These were now mine. In one of them, addressed to my mother's elder brother, my grandfather announced that he disowned him for not obeying the order not to marry a white woman. A father's curse, the crushing list of the son's debts stopped mid-way, jolting on unthinkable truths—d' *"impensables v"rités"*—my grandfather's pound of flesh which even his son's bleeding heart could not pay back—two sullying centuries of slavery embedded in a marriage against history. Fathers—biological or adoptive, elicited or self-proclaimed—do not like their sons to disobey. It is an insult to their immortality, intimated and safeguarded. The marriage did take place and my grandfather's last years of life, almost up to his last breath, were spent with a white woman at his side, of course. When, at his death, my uncle drove me back home, his head bent over the wheel, not looking at me, I looked at him and imagined that his inaudible words were eventually speaking his truths and his father's.

My model for desired dialogues never taking place was Baldwin's "Notes of a Native Son," the monologue mourning the death of the father and the son's early childhood, at a time when I was still under my father's partial banishment—not at home—for being gay. Him being a public figure, he explained, erect before the Corsican sky and sea merging together their last nuances of blue, could not have his son return home with a male lover. "*Did he love her?*" Baldwin obsessively asked. I, perplexed, sidestepping from the sunlight into the interlacing shadow of the cherry-tree and the forsythia, could not fathom what he meant, my mind still blurred by the drugs I had been given at the psychiatric hospital in Paris. Who was he, this man who, twenty years ago, in the early 1970s, had left Algeria with a black wife, two black children, and a black newborn, to go back to his then self-identifying white country—who was he?—the militant and poet, reader of Fanon and Memmi, Césaire and Hugo, who celebrated emancipation and freedom and carefree swallows flying away—and who did he think I was and was to be? It took me years to untangle home from Corsica and Corsica from the world. For reinventing space for myself, both sunlit and shadowy. Though, with loving patience, my mother repeated, "It takes time." Though, time passing by, my father eventually welcomed me back home accompanied. Though I had for long understood that Baldwin's love question had to be read through a grammatical transgenderism—"Did he love *me*?" Understood but not felt enough. Revolutions take time, though time is too short for revolutionaries.

With, on the forefront, its double metronome pacing the reading of an open notebook, *La Chute* represents my early twenties, spent in psychiatric facilities. It pieces together copies of a photographic portrait taken by Dominique Cros-Pophillat whom I met at the Lycée Henri IV, the preparatory school drilling into French youths' soft skulls the maddening oxymoron of elitist humanities. While the poison was filtering through, and as the history teacher droned on about the French Revolution, I had my eyes irresistibly shift from Frantz Fanon's *Peau noire, masques blancs*—my father's gift on leaving Corsica—and, not far from me, bent over his book, the intriguing slim figure of his grandson. Years later, when struck by the naked spine of *Giovanni's Room* cover photograph—blond American David, self-exiled in the South of France, blind to the blackness falling down through the window-pane and, before him, to African shores looming afar—I would remember that reflecting image. A multiplying convex mirror made of photographs, X-rays, and paper, *La Chute*, along colored curves and lines, tries to encapsulate harmony, moderation, and control. Narcissus above the water, drowning to save his mind through scribbled foreign words reappropriated. Down in the water and spreadeagled in the warm mud. *Je signe le texte d'un autre.* To fail to save our minds was our constant fear and bond and the essence of our community. The mental health clinic for the young had three pavilions on the wealthy outskirts of Paris, all named after famed French psychiatrists or hygienists, one of which—Clairambault—catalyzed the running anxiety to have one's free movements even more strictly regulated if sent there. Between us, the Honnorat dwellers, rumor had it that patients had to stand behind a white line not to be crossed when talking to nurses and doctors. A bad omen, Clairambault also prosaically implied that neither the treatment nor the therapy worked. We thus watched one another, our strange habits—counting trees in the park, closing one's door over and over again, sniffing cocaine, strolling down the aisle with a funny hat on and Robert Desnos in one's hand, blowing one's brains out like Randall Kenan's Horace—minutely scrutinized, in search of any sign betraying the fall to come. Institutional discipline as much as communal preservation internalized to the bone. Successfully passed on. Several failed and, falling, finally passed, leaving behind the clinic white walls, the silencing white lines and the face of broken youth, haunting. When, some twenty years later, I protested against the institutionalized racism committed to make me tumble down again and send me back to the same field as French football players of African descent getting bananas in their faces—that of desubjectivizing slurs and disciplining brutish force—the first image coming back to my mind—to have it saved—would be that one. The return of my dead and nation, shifting the legacy of keeping faith in knowledge to the determination not to let its use be perverted. And from now on, as for me and my house, the community to preserve would inexorably be tied to the memory of my early twenties and to that of, young and daring, the indignant generations before me.

The Paris "Black France" Conference, in June 2008, was the first academic occasion to operate such as a shift. To the suggestion of having a common name subsuming France's various communities of African descent, I replied that we should rather change, at the outset of the constitution, the definition of the French Republic, by interpolating the clause "*espace de la diversité* [space of diversity]," after "France" and before "*une et indivisible* [one and indivisible]." This would thus make diversity, unity, and indivisibil-

ity complements and not antonyms as, faithful to my experience and memory, I believed that words could transform space and reality. I was responding
to Christiane Taubira, back then already the deputy who had had the slave
trade recognized as a crime against humanity but not yet the minister initiat-
ing the legalization of gay marriage. Immersed in the still tormenting turns
and twists of my personal resistance, I thought my idea was a good and
original one—especially syntactically and symbolically speaking—ignoring
the fact that other countries, including Lampedusa's Italy, had equivalent
wordings in their constitutions. As I passed it on to the deputy, she said,
"But, young man, it takes years to shift a comma in the constitution," laughing. I smiled back at her—a smile that meant "So be it."

This I remembered and thought while watching in turn *La Chute, Pervers
au jeu ne jouit pas, Envi, Le déclencheur* and *Générations* and, unfolding
from where I sat, ethereal, tentative and temporary, the space in-between. I'm
now running out of time to write about the last two pictures. There was not
enough room anyway and they'll have to remain in the portfolio, unframed
and left for the untold, perhaps some day to be told.

Besides, I need to pack. Tomorrow I fly to Corsica—where the world's
forsythias grow too—soon to become a godfather. The witness. God knows
what it may ever mean. But the child's laughter is such a song.

Paris—Loretu-di-Casinca (Corsica)
July 23–August 12, 2014

MOTION, PERCEPTION AND (SELF-)TRANSFORMATION — A POSTDATED NOTE

*I have recently been the witness of a beautifully intriguing scene in a walk I
took by the Seine—an encounter and a small place in itself. I was walking so
fast on the cobblestones that the joints of my feet and legs hurt. But I wanted
my body in pain to split the bitter Parisian cold and open up a vista for
myself—to be stretched in grayness. I had been led to the river instinctive-
ly—its counterflow—counter because in the opposite direction to my walking—was taking me back to the running stream between my house and my
small village nested in Corsican mountains—both a separation and a junc-
tion that, as a child, I perused as the awaited promise of secrets to be
revealed in my to and fro daily travels. Walking fast and attuned to the beat
of techno and pop music blasting in my earphones through the blinding and
numbing cold of the City of Lights now turned itself—and as occurring
repeatedly in the past weeks—into a phenomenological and sensorial experience of re-connection to the world by virtue of which awoke—though unex-
plainable rationally—the acute consciousness of a transformation, the work-*

ing through that affected concomitantly both the self and mundane reality. As if I could see *and* feel *that I was changing with a world peopled of others changing with me—all clustered in the transformative momentum of a performance where we would be in turn mutually determining actors and witnesses. An exhilarating experience whose force is akin to sexual orgasm inasmuch as the communion and commonality it triggers and spreads cannot be dogmatically postulated—only to be enacted in accord with its profound political nature.*

My encounter on the Seine that day took the form of sportsmen in a training session—the choreography of sculpted young male bodies swimming back and forth between the boat and the bank, each reaching out to the other in the linking water, under the benevolent gaze of an instructor monitoring the exercise. I stopped walking to look. The beauty and erotic power of the scene conjured up, in a rush and jostling, James Baldwin's vision of desire—men watching men watching them—and its spatial metaphorizations later explored by Melvin Dixon; nineteenth-century photographer and painter Thomas Eakins's The Swimming Hole *(1885); Slovenian-born researcher in aesthetics Evguen Bavcar's becoming blind and how he had to re-create the world from images seen and recollected, as he confides in the French writer and photographer Hervé Guibert's* L'Autre Journal *(2015); and Euzhan Palcy's documentary film* Aimé Césaire: une voix pour l'histoire *(1994), in which Césaire's intimate friend from Croatia Petar Guberina recalls the poet's bewilderment in discovering that, framed by the window of their Dalmatian summer holiday dwelling, the isle not that far away that he is looking at bears the name of "Martinsca"—Martinique in French—a coincidence worth an epiphany and that triggered the writing of* Cahier d'un retour au pays natal *(1939).*

After a while I resumed walking and headed back home, my 32 square-meters studio flat where, in-between travels to and from Corsica and Martinique, I had initiated and completed my two most recent works, "The Word's Image; Self-Portrait as a Conscious Lie" (2015)—a psychoanalytical and auto-ethnographic essay theorizing the connection between my artistic production as a collagist and my academic research on identity—and Ce qui compte *(2016)—an electronic monograph turning this very theorization into a new work of art investigating the conundrum of such a repetition-with-difference: What was being lost and transformed between the two works and will inevitably be again with the next? And as I immersed myself in the Seine and its mental associations I thought:*

What do I see? What does the world say to me in the performance of its being? And what should I respond from the small place of my/self, a desiring black subject, a subject in search of desiring modes of being black?

As I re-read, write, and look back, I like to think that this work has not only ambitioned to theorize phenomena, events, or bodies of texts and concepts but has rather stimulated the critical examination, through the small places of literature and theory, of a series of experiences that may renew vistas, reshuffle reflections, trigger creation and (self-)transformation. The point here has also been to consider *the Self as a small place* never to be fully discovered or mastered and that the relation to others and the connection to the world maintains in constant motion, potentially expanding the limits of its internal space—be it bodily and physical or immaterial and fantasized—through the touch of hand or that of the mind's eye. When allowed by sociopolitical conditions containing external over-determinations and permitting the relation, the benefit of such an experience is to enrich the small place of the Self with difference. The pitfall is to lose the Self from sight—overflown or led to shrink to the even smaller scale of non-entity. The risk in between—inherent to both benefit and pitfall, a thin ridge line to ride—is both phenomenological and political: What if the experience does not make sense? If perception and self-perception become unintelligible? If the experience itself bars measure and measurement, (re)taking the small place of the Self to the no-place of abstraction, alienation, and subjugation?

This is what a desiring mode of being black ultimately embodies and the reason why it requires a specific frame of reading where unreasonable experiences of perception—distort-ed/-ing, irrational, and hallucinative—are restored in the legitimacy of their creative force and explained for what they are, as Frantz Fanon endeavored to do in his early writings, recently collected in *Ecrits sur l'aliénation et la liberté* (2015): Not the sheer reversal of viewpoints but the safeguard and defense of the possibility of multiplying viewpoints and to have them connecting—be they originating in individuals or collectives, territories or constituted structures, in themselves and between—such as, in a New Bandung of some sort, a worldwide confederation of islands joining, only to name a few, the Caribbean, the Mediterranean, and Southeast Asia, could perhaps proffer one day. Drawing from Sándor Ferenczi's psychoanalytical exploration of transference and introjection, which sketches the fortunes and misfortunes punctuating the Self/Other relation, this materialized polycentrality in texts and contexts would be in vain should it refrain from fully confronting the underlying emotional and affective dimension of the phenomenological and political risk of (not) making sense of the relation—*the fear of loss*. Confront and pass it on so that the knowledge that allows (self-)transformation is being shared, the solidarity that helps to overcome melancholy attachments, including historical ones, is implemented, the disjunctive knot of desiring and being unraveled, both in the linking chain of small places as rooms for change.

Notes

INTRODUCTION

1. See Rocchi (2007b: 56–57).
2. Since *L'Objet identité: épistémologie et transversalité* [The Object Identity: Epistemology and Cross-Disciplinary Perspectives], edited by Jean-Paul Rocchi, in which the first version of this chapter was published in 2006, and the publication in 2008 of its companion volume *Dissidence et identités plurielles* [Dissent and Multiple Identity], edited by Jean-Paul Rocchi, the perspective crossing race, gender, and sexualities has been refined and developed in a transdisciplinary and intersectional book series bringing together four other collective works: *Understanding Blackness through Performance: Contemporary Arts and the Representation of Identity*, edited by Anne Crémieux, Xavier Lemoine, and Jean-Paul Rocchi (2013); *Black Intersectionalities: A Critique for the 21st Century*, edited by Monica Michlin and Jean-Paul Rocchi (2014); *Black Europe: Subjects, Struggles, and Shifting Perceptions*, edited by Jean-Paul Rocchi and Frédéric Sylvanise (2015); and *Black and Sexual Geographies of Community-Building*, edited by Guillaume Marche and Jean-Paul Rocchi (forthcoming).

1. THE OTHER BITES THE DUST

1. Translated from the French: "*pourquoi c'est toujours les immeubles de Noirs qui brûlent?*" (*Libération*, August 27–28, 2005).
2. Translated from the French: "*le nègre n'est pas. Pas plus que le Blanc*" (Fanon, 1952: 187).
3. Criticizing the abusive usage among French psychoanalysts of the notion of the Unconscious, Alain de Mijolla reports in *Préhistoires de famille* [Family Prehistories] (2004) that he "set off an outcry, or nearly, by asserting that "Your Unconscious does not exist" before colleagues who . . . were describing its so-called activities as if they were talking about 'Mister Unconscious.'" Translated from the French: "*J'avais déclenché des huées, ou presque, en affirmant à une tribune 'Votre Inconscient n'existe pas' face à des collègues qui . . . en décrivaient les soi-disant agissements, comme s'il s'agissait de 'Monsieur Inconscient'*" (2).
4. For a critique of heteronormativity in African American studies, see Roderick A. Ferguson's "African American Studies," in Marc Stein, ed., *Encyclopedia of Lesbian, Gay, Bisexual, and Transgendered History in America* (2004). Ferguson also addresses this problem in works

more specifically dedicated to sociology, notably in "The Nightmares of the Heteronormative" (*Cultural Values*, vol. 4, no. 4, October 2000) and in *Aberrations in Black: Toward a Queer of Color Critique* (2003). For an approach to this issue in the field of African American and/or black literary studies, see Charles I. Nero's article, "Toward a Black Gay Aesthetic: Signifying in Contemporary Black Gay Literature," in Essex Hemphill, ed., *Brother to Brother: New Writings by Black Gay Men* (1991); the collection of articles *Critical Essays: Gay and Lesbian Writers of Color* (1993) edited by Emmanuel S. Nelson; *Becoming Black* by Michelle M. Wright (2004); *Manning the Race, Reforming Black Men in the Jim Crow Era* (2004) by Marlon B. Ross; and *Black Queer Studies: A Critical Anthology* (2005) edited by Patrick E. Johnson.

5. Translated from the French: "*la question éthique [dans les sciences de l'Homme] procède d'abord de ce qu'on étudie des êtres humains dotés d'une certaine autonomie, d'une certaine liberté, et d'une responsabilité, et que ceux qui les étudient doivent être eux aussi sous cet angle de l'autonomie, de la responsabilité, de la liberté*" (Supiot, 2001: 100).

6. Borrowed from Emily Miller Budick, *Blacks and Jews in Literary Conversation* (1998), 203.

7. Anthony K. Appiah studied in *In My Father's House: Africa in the Philosophy of Culture* (1992) the essentialism of the concept of race in the works of W. E. B. Du Bois. Judith Butler analyzes the essentialism that founded the definition of sexualities and gender identities in Freud (Butler, 1995: 24–26). These two critical approaches are put into perspective in my article "Baldwin ou les spores perdues de l'Amérique: conscience de l'origine et origine de la conscience" (2001).

8. For an example of this conservative position held among certain French psychoanalysts, see Simone Korff-Sausse's defense in the rubric "Débats" of the newspaper, *Libération* (July 7, 1999). A similar discourse prevails in the works of sociologists like Irène Théry and notably in "Le CUS en question" (Notes de la Fondation Saint Simon) written in October 1997 (cited by Eric Lamien, "Anti-PACS: l'homophobie plurielle. Entretien avec Daniel Borillo," *Ex æquo*, no. 27, April 1999).

9. Translated from the French: "*les chercheurs qui n'embrassent pas les conclusions les plus extrêmes des disciples de Derrida ne sont pas tous victimes de l'illusion objectiviste et disciplinaire: ils sont conscients de construire leur objet, d'être eux-mêmes porteurs, lorsqu'ils établissent une problématique et organisent une démonstration, de valeurs et de préjugés, d'être enfin des individus subjectifs*" (20).

10. Translated from the French: "*[la race] ne tombe pas sous la catégorie d'objet. Quoi que je veuille ou fasse,* l'idée en demeure indélébile dans ma conscience même. *Elle a laissé sur moi inoubliablement sa trace, lors même que je ne sais pas trop où la localiser. Et dût-elle échapper définitivement à ma prise, elle me somme d'avouer d'où je viens. Plus encore, elle me pousse* en avant *dans une direction que je ne sais pas davantage déchiffrer. Bref, c'est elle qui ne cesse d'exiger de moi du dedans mon acquiescement actif, ou cette reconnaissance consciente, dont mon intelligence voudrait bien écarter l'urgence, en la refoulant hors de moi, parmi tous les processus extérieurs, au rang de tous les déterminismes du monde*" (275).

11. Translated from the French: "*[le] défi [que pose] la pensée occidentale à la philosophie comme discours et tradition.*"

12. Translated from the French: "*[C]omment ce qui se donne comme objet de savoir articulé sur la maîtrise de la* tekhnê, *comment cela peut-il être en même temps le lieu où se manifeste, où s'éprouve et difficilement s'accomplit la vérité du sujet que nous sommes? Comment le monde, qui se donne comme objet de connaissance à partir de la maîtrise de la* tekhnê, *peut-il être en même temps le lieu où se manifeste et où s'éprouve le 'soi-même' comme sujet éthique de la vérité? Et si c'est bien cela le problème de la philosophie occidentale—comment le monde peut-il être objet de connaissance et en même temps lieu d'épreuve pour le sujet; comment peut-il y avoir un sujet de connaissance qui se donne le monde comme objet à travers une* tekhnê, *et un sujet d'expérience de soi, qui se donne ce même monde, sous la forme radicalement différente du lieu d'épreuve?*" (487).

13. Translated from the French: "*Il est peut-être essentiel à la nature même de la race qu'elle ne puisse être vue* de face, *mais seulement dans une relation de* latéralité. *On aboutirait alors à ce résultat important que la race n'est pas une chose, un bloc, un principe, une essence,*

mais un rapport*: car ce n'est pas nier une réalité que de faire de cette réalité une 'réalité relationnelle.' Et à ce compte aussi la race redeviendrait donc 'pensable'"* (Varet, 1973: 282).

14. The French academic system is rather keen on honoring blacks that it did not educate. While the African American philosopher Cornel West was given an honorary doctorate by the Université Paris 8 in 2005, Frantz Fanon, though celebrated everywhere for his radical ideas, never received such institutional recognition in France. He remains confined to the margins by conservative universities but also by more progressive institutions that teach and host research on Sartre, Foucault, or Derrida. Today, Edouard Glissant and Maryse Condé, for their part, teach in the United States, and there is no French equivalent of the British scholars Paul Gilroy and Stuart Hall. Moreover, as is often the case in Europe, when asked "Why are there no black directors of such and such university or research organization?" one responds laconically, "We didn't find any." Which leads us to pose, among other questions and beyond just the anecdotal, questions about access to higher education, to the *Grandes Ecoles* about the conformity of courses when faced with the requirements of recruitment and, prior to that, about the academic failure of populations issuing from immigration or those that are visibly different, as underscored by the recent report of the *Cour des Comptes* on the politics of immigration in France (see *L'accueil des immigrants et l'intégration des populations issues de l'immigration: rapport au Président de la République suivi des réponses des administrations et des organismes intéressés*, Paris, Direction des journaux officiels, 2004; this report is available on the internet site of *La documentation française*: www.ladocumentationfrançaise.fr).

15. See my paper *"Widening the Quest*: African [American/*European*] Research: Toward a Queer Triangulation of Black Heterogeneity" presented at the conference "African American and Diasporic Research in Europe: Comparative and Interdisciplinary Approaches," organized in honor of Michel Fabre and Geneviève Fabre by the W. E. B. Du Bois Institute for African and African American Research, Harvard University and the *Cercle d'Etudes Afro-Américaines*, Sorbonne Nouvelle-Paris III, December 15–18, 2004.

16. A euphemistic formula that appeared on the front page of the February 22, 2005, edition of *Libération*.

17. This optimistic reading should be nuanced regarding France. With Article 4 of the law of February 23, 2005, on repatriated French citizens, the *Assemblée Nationale* recommends emphasizing in scholarly programs the "positive role" of the French colonial presence overseas, particularly in North Africa—a legal disposition that incited vivid protests among historians who saw in this an attempt to establish an "official history" of colonization. Or, more anecdotal but just as symbolic, another example is that of the politician and historian Max Gallo, declaring during the December 4, 2004, afternoon televised news on *France 3* that he did not know if the reestablishment of slavery by Napoleon Bonaparte was indeed a crime against humanity. Later going back on his words, Max Gallo presented his excuses to the *Collectif des Antillais, Guyanais, Réunionais*.

Moreover, it should be underscored that certain buried memories tend to emerge better than others, resonating more strongly in the public and the media according to the political and economic logic that are certainly not necessarily those of historiographical research. Thus issues 58 and 82 of *Manière de voir, Le Monde diplomatique*, respectively titled "Polémiques sur l'histoire coloniale" (July–August 2001) and "Pages d'histoire occultes" (August–September 2005), are scarcely interested in French regions (Antilles, Guyane, Corsica, Kanaky, and so on) that, when it is critical of a centralist perspective, remain marginal, including at the scientific level, to a national ranking (on this subject and concerning the epistemological and methodological stakes posed by research on a non-existant historiographical object, see Ghisoni, ed. (1989)). Another example of occultation, that of homosexual memory, as testified to by the difficulty of establishing the Center of Homosexual Archives and Documentation in Paris, is also criticized for its unbalanced representation of lesbian memory.

18. Public confession or expiation, notably concerning crimes such as slavery, is a recurrent theme in American letters, as Emily Miller Budick emphasizes a propos Hawthorne's *The House of the Seven Gables* or Styron's *Sophie's Choice* and *The Confessions of Nat Turner* (see *Blacks and Jews in Literary Conversation*: 204).

19. Translated from the French: "*le savoir a rapport au désir, et aussi au dévoilement de la cause de ce désir. Mais dans la maîtrise du savoir, tout comme dans la maîtrise du désir, une*

part échappe au sujet. Cette part renvoie à ce qui, dans le désir de savoir, peut surgir comme interdit de savoir . . . Elle correspond aussi à l'impossibilité de rendre compte de ce qui nous habite, ce qui révèle la position de l'impossible constituant, chez tout être, sa limite. Le sujet ne peut donc se soutenir comme désirant du savoir qu'en transgressant un savoir de maîtrise, soit en s'engageant dans une quête infinie d'un non-su . . . Dans son rapport à l'Autre, le désir du sujet est donc un contre-dire permanent" (34).

20. Translated from the French: "*spécialiste, c'est-à-dire quelqu'un qui se place au service d'un savoir impersonnel*" (42).

21. Translated from the French: "*la théorie peut aussi devenir un pur instrument de connaissance, une sorte de faire-valoir, qui dispense le sujet de tout remaniement au niveau de l'être*" (37).

22. Translated from the French: "*Ainsi, de Kierkegaard à Ricœur en passant par Heidegger et Lévinas, la philosophie du même est contestée pour laisser place à la philosophie de l'Autre qui n'est pas essentiellement l'autre homme mais l'Altérité comme Etre et Infini . . . Parce que le seul fondement possible du sens et de la valeur, le sujet humain, a été récusé en fait par ces doctrines pour laisser la place à ce qu'elles appellent l'être, elles se sont toutes mises dans la situation paradoxale de philosophies travaillant à leur propre destruction par le recours à un être inconnaissable qui est pourtant censé les fonder et les justifier. Dans ce naufrage volontaire de la philosophie, c'est le sujet lui-même qui risque d'être englouti*" (348–49).

23. Translated from the French: "*rendre compte de cette unité fondamentale et intégrée: seule une conscience qui est un désir est en mesure de se constituer comme sujet et de comprendre cet acte de constitution qui est simultanément existentiel et gnoséologique, éthique et réflexif*" (204).

24. Translated from the French: "*les contenus qualitatifs à l'activité fondatrice et à l'identité personnelle*" (204).

25. Translated from the French: "*dans une description intégrale du désir, le triple rapport de l'affectivité à la liberté, à la conscience, et à l'autre*" (212).

26. This "un" or "without" of the consciousness, which is manifested by denial, lack of responsibility, and, among other affects, guilt, is particular to the white consciousness that Rozena Maart conceptualized as "White Consciousness" (Maart, 1993, 2005) and the representations of which, moreover, Sabine Broeck analyzed in the works of Jamaica Kincaid (Broeck, 2002).

27. Translated from the French: "*pendant toute cette période qu'on appelle l'Antiquité, et selon des modalités qui ont été bien différentes, la question philosophique du 'comment avoir accès à la vérité' et la pratique de la spiritualité (les transformations nécessaires dans l'être même du sujet qui vont permettre l'accès à la vérité), eh bien ces deux questions, ces deux thèmes n'ont jamais été séparés . . . Eh bien maintenant, si nous faisons un saut de plusieurs siècles, on peut dire qu'on est entré dans l'âge moderne (je veux dire, l'histoire, de la vérité est entrée dans sa période moderne) le jour où on a admis que ce qui donne accès à la vérité, c'est la connaissance, et la connaissance seulement*" (Foucault, 2001: 18–19).

28. Translated from the French: "*se forme et ne peut se former que dans une référence à l'Autre*" (59).

29. Translated from the French: "*[cet] autre qui est le maître*" (58).

30. Translated from the French: "*avant d'être le penseur du sujet de la connaissance*" (108).

31. On the fragilization of the interface research-teaching, the pragmatic and economic logic in French university policies, see chapter 3, "La mise en crise de l'ethos academique," and notably pages 43–55, in *Enquête exploratoire sur le travail des enseignants-chercheurs* (Rapport d'enquête, juin 2005) by Sylvia Faure and Charles Soulié (www.specif.org/actualite/faure.soulie.pdf).

32. Spelled "*trans(e)*-disciplinarité" in the original version in French. The French word "*transe*" means "trance."

33. Translated from the French: "*les rapports de la pensée et de la formalisation . . . les modes d'être de la vie, du travail et du langage*" (359).

34. Translated from the French: "*fi de la nécessaire prise en considération de la pertinence de l'outil à l'objet, de la labilité sémantique des termes auxquels on a recours, de la variété et de la différence des regards . . . dissoudre les notions qui sont opérationnelles [dans la*

discipline que le chercheur sollicite], de leur enlever toute efficace par rapt ou par import, réimplantation sur un terrain peu favorable" (11).

35. Translated from the French: "*l'étendue de son a priori*" (7).

3. DYING METAPHORS AND DEADLY FANTASIES

1. I am indebted to Rozena Maart, who was the first to call my attention to the homoerotic content of this biblical passage, which was later confirmed by the reading of Baldwin works such as *Go Tell It on the Mountain, The Fire Next Time*, and *Going to Meet the Man*, all of which articulate homoeroticism and the racialization of Ham's curse.

2. "Fanon offers his own approach to psychoanalysis through the introduction of a discourse on failures. Here he is being phenomenological, psychoanalytical, and dialectical. The phenomenological point pertains to the study of human beings, which he says in the second chapter of *Black Skin, White Masks* is not identical to botany and mathematics—namely, natural science and analytical or deductive systems. It is psychoanalytical because it raises questions of what is repressed by the declaration of failure . . . Nothing intrinsically fails. It simply is. That failure is a function of the human world means that it must be connected to notions of meaning and purpose. Fanon's point is that we should not simply dismiss failures but try to understand them; we should try and learn both about what failure signifies and what it means to us who interpret it as such. And finally, it is dialectical because it involves examining contradictions, wherein learning constitutes the forward movement or consequence of such an engagement" (Gordon, 2008: 85).

3. See especially "Endangered/Endangering: Schematic Racism and White Paranoia" (1993: 15–22). See also "Violence, Non-Violence: Sartre on Fanon" (2008).

4. See especially the chapter "The Part for the (W)Hole: Baldwin, Homophobia, and the Fantasmatics of Race."

5. Fanon, 1952: 183. My translation.

6. Ibid., 109. My translation.

7. Bayard, 2004: 43. My translation.

4. DESIRE AS "E MAG E NATION"

1. "No Rosa, No District Six" was first published in *Fireweed: Feminist Journal* (Spring 1991), then in *Journey Prize Anthology 4* (1992), before once again being published in the short story collection *Rosa's District 6* (Toronto: TSAR Publications, 2004). The present chapter uses the version published in *Journey Prize Anthology 4*, whose typography conforms more closely with the original version and with the author's intentions. All references to the stories other than "No Rosa, No District Six" come from the collection published by TSAR in 2004. Rozena Maart offers a meta-reading of "No Rosa, No District Six" and of the politics of consciousness writing in the chapter "Writing and the Relation: From Textual Coloniality to South African Black Consciousness" (Michlin and Rocchi).

2. Even before its alteration by the deportation of the black and mixed-race population of District Six, the ethnic and religious mix of the neighborhood was nevertheless limited by racial, spatial, and social borders. The "uppersiders," whose sufficiently light skin allowed them to pretend to many of the same privileges as whites, lived on the upperside of DeVilliers Street, at the edge of the more working-class District Six. As the narrator of the short story "The Bracelet" states, and contrary to the racist ideology of apartheid, it is not one's skin pigmentation that is a sign of belonging to District Six, but rather one's posture, manners, and speech (164). This strict association between speech and body language is inspired by Fanon: it

places the body at the center of a process of developing consciousness and makes black consciousness an affair of positioning rather than of a determinism in which skin color is prescriptive of identity. This conception of black consciousness as positioning, choice, and mental attitude is also shared by the intellectual and militant South African Steve Biko, who, in *I Write What I Like*, writes, "Being black is not a matter of skin pigmentation—being black is a reflection of mental attitude" (48, cited by Maart [1992] 1993: 134).

3. The criticism of masculinism in South African nationalism operates also through the fact that Maria de la Quelerie, dominated in her position as a woman, is also in a dominating position in her role as a white colonizer. She also penetrates and colonizes South Africa by the small opening of the Cape. Thus feminized, the patriarchal appanage of penetration—of the colonial and/or sexual variety—loses its self-sufficiency and, with it, the myth of nationalist rhetoric that makes liberation and the entrance in postcoloniality into the masculine response to an offense made to men, thus justifying the subordination of women and persons of LGBTQ orientation in this fight. Rozena Maart responded to this in her poem "Women's Oppression, The Struggle *Still* Continues," published in *Talk About It! From District Six to Lavender Hill* ([1991] 2000: 48–49).

4. In the story "The Bracelet," Rosa reappropriates Maria de la Quelerie, a historical figure held in disdain, by dressing up as her (*Rosa's District 6*: 172). By parading herself in fancy-dress in the middle of Cape Town and outside the institutional or conventional dramaturgical space, the little girl not only offers a presentification of a global history detached from the artifices and the ideological orientations of her unique commemoration but also constructs her own subjectivity. As an actor in the theater, Rosa's performance inverses the norm-dissidence relationship at the historiographical level. As a social actor, this same performance and her dissident or marginal posture makes the norm lose its naturalizing character and reveal itself as the political construction that the subject has resolved herself against. Another example of this double movement can be found in the same story, through the character of Nathaniel's lover, whose publicly flaunted femininity in Cape Town (206–7) extracts him from a history of genders based on the separation of men-women and also makes this division appear as an eminently political and relative social hypocrisy. As is the case in *Peau noire, masques blancs*, where Frantz Fanon affirms being able to "take up his past, valorize it or condemn it by his choices" (184–85; translated from the French), this is not a break with but a re-signification of historical determinism—on the colonial, gender, and sexual fronts—by means of worldly action that also allows the subject to influence the social space in which he lives.

5. On the relationship "mummy-baby" among the women of Lesotho, see Gay (1985; cited by Spurlin: 192).

6. The time frame of this analysis is not that of South African post-apartheid culture, where anti-LGBTQ violence is intense and widespread. The diegesis of the short stories is situated in the 1970s. Referring to the relative fluidity of the sexual expression is therefore accurate only for a specific time period and a specific place—the Cape Town of the 1970s. The theorization on post-identity that opens this chapter is precisely fueled by this experience. It is meant to proffer a counterpoint to the present-day situation and a post-apartheid culture characterized by gender polorization and a reinforced heteronormativity corollary to the rise of nationalism and the advent of a so-called African essentialism. For more on anti-LGBTQ violence in contemporary and post-apartheid South Africa, see Henriette Gunkel's chapter "'What Do We See When We Look at Ourselves': Visual Dissidence towards (Post)Colonial Sex/Gender Organizations within Post-Apartheid South African Culture" (2008) and Antje Schuhmann's chapter "Postcolonial Backlashes: Transgender in the Public Eye" (Michlin and Rocchi).

7. Maart's political writing is avant-garde in more than one way. On the one hand, her Derridian approach to deconstruction, combined with the South African experience of black consciousness as defined by Steve Biko and Frantz Fanon, allow her to cross identities, to reveal the political dynamics informing their construction, such as the importance of the empire on the concept of the South Africa of postcoloniality and white and Western colonialism, which are always used in the study of genders, sexuality, and their sociopolitical dynamics. On the other hand, the texts united in the collection *Rosa's District 6* testify to the fact that the resistance to the categorization of identities in a monolithic system and organized hierarchically by the apartheid regime did not wait for the post-apartheid era to organize itself, to be effective,

and to remain an essential element of social and political transformation. This writing is a feminist and queer foothold in the black male South African nationalism of the new South Africa and in the mythification of the postcolonial moment as a radical break belonging to only ostensibly heterosexual South Africans—a re-reading of history favored, moreover, by the constant marginalization of queer South African literature, relegated to a subalternate position in anthologies and critical studies (on this point, see Spurlin: 191–92).

7. THE WORD'S IMAGE

1. *Génération* and the other collages to which this chapter refers are reproduced in *Black Europe: Subjects, Struggles, and Shifting Perceptions*, edited by Jean-Paul Rocchi and Frédéric Sylvanise, *Palimpsest: A Journal on Women, Gender, and the Black International* 4, 2:225–34.

Bibliography

Abelove, Henry. 1993. "Freud, Male Homosexuality, and the Americans." In *The Lesbian and Gay Studies Reader*, edited by Henry Abelove, Michèle Aina Barale, and David M. Halperin. New York: Routledge.

Ahmed, Sara. 2004. *The Cultural Politics of Emotion*. New York: Routledge.

———. 2006. *Queer Phenomenology: Orientations, Objects, Others*. Durham, NC: Duke University Press.

Ambroise, Jason R., and Sabine Broeck, eds. 2015. *Black Knowledges/Black Struggles: Essays in Critical Epistemology*. Liverpool, UK: Liverpool University Press.

André, Serge. 1993. *L'Imposture perverse*. Paris: Éditions du Seuil.

Apel, Dora. 2017. "Strange Fruit: L'Héritage des lynchages." In *The Color Line: Les Artistes africains-américains et la ségrégation 1865–2016*, edited by Daniel Soutif. Paris: Flammarion/Musée du Quai Branly Jacques Chirac, 230–53.

Appiah, K. Anthony. 1992. *In My Father's House: Africa in the Philosophy of Culture*. New York: Oxford University Press.

———. 2005. *The Ethics of Identity*. Princeton, NJ: Princeton University Press.

Assoun, Paul-Laurent. 1997. *Psychanalyse*. Paris: Presses Universitaires de France.

Avena, Thomas. 1994. *Life Sentences: Writers, Artists and AIDS*. San Francisco: Mercury House.

Baker, Houston A., Jr. 1985. "Caliban Triple's Play." In *"Race," Writing, and Difference*, edited by Henry Louis Gates Jr. Chicago: University of Chicago Press.

———. 1987. *Modernism and the Harlem Renaissance*. Chicago: University of Chicago Press.

Baldwin, James. 1949. "Preservation of Innocence." *Zero*.

———. 1951/1965. "The Outing," *Going to Meet the Man*. London: Penguin Books.

———. 1965. "The Rockpile," *Going to Meet the Man*. London: Penguin Books.

———. 1965. "Going to Meet the Man," *Going to Meet the Man*. London: Penguin Books.

———. 1985. *The Evidence of Things Not Seen*. New York: Henry Holt.

Baldwin, James. 1998. *Baldwin, Collected Essays*, edited by Toni Morrison. New York: Library of America.

———. 1950. "Encounter on the Seine: Black Meets Brown," 85–90.

———. 1951. "Many Thousands Gone," 19–34.

———. 1955. "Notes of a Native Son," 63–84.

———. 1959. "Nobody Knows My Name," 197–208.

———. 1963. *The Fire Next Time*, 291–348.

———. 1985. "Freaks and the American Ideal of Manhood" ("Here Be Dragons"), 814–29.

Baldwin, James. 1998. *Baldwin, Early Novels and Stories*, edited by Toni Morrison. New York: Library of America.

———. 1953. *Go Tell It on the Mountain*, 1–216.

———. 1955. *Giovanni's Room*, 217–360.

———. 1962. *Another Country*, 361–756.

———. 1965. "Going to Meet the Man," 933–50.

Baldwin, James, and Margaret Mead. 1971/1992. *A Rap on Race*. New York: Laurel, Dell Publishing.

Baldwin, James, and Sol Stein. 2004/2005. *Native Sons*. New York: One World.

Bayard, Pierre. 2004. *Peut-on appliquer la littérature à la psychanalyse?* Paris: Éditions de Minuit.

Beam, Joseph, ed. 1986. *In the Life: A Black Gay Anthology*. Boston, MA: Alyson Publications.

Bearden, Romare. 1934. "The Negro Artist and Modern Art." *Chicken Bones: A Journal for Literary & Artistic African-American Themes.* www.nathanielturner.com/negroartistandmodernart.htm.

Bersani, Leo. 1986. *The Freudian Body, Psychoanalysis and Art*. New York: Columbia University Press.

———. 1998. *Homos, repenser l'identité*, translated by Christian Marouby. Paris: Odile Jacob.

Bhabha, Homi K. 1992. "The Other Question: The Stereotype and Colonial Discourse." In *The Sexual Subject: A Screen Reader in Sexuality*, edited by Mandy Merck. New York: Routledge, 312–31.

Biko, Steve. 1978. *I Write What I Like*. San Francisco: Harper and Row.

Boggs, Nicholas. 2000. "Queer Black Studies: An Annotated Bibliography, 1994–1998," *Callaloo* 23, no. 1:479–94.

Boyarin, Daniel. 1998. "What Does a Jew Want? Or, the Political Meaning of the Phallus." In *The Psychoanalysis of Race*, edited by C. Lane. New York: Columbia University Press, 211–40.

Broeck, Sabine. 2002. "When Light Becomes White: Reading Enlightenment through Jamaica Kincaid's Writing," *Callaloo* 25, no. 3:821–43.

Broeck, Sabine, and Carsten Junker, eds. 2014. *Postcoloniality-Decoloniality-Black: Joints and Fissures*. Frankfurt: Campus Verlag.

Budick Miller, Emily. 1998. *Blacks and Jews in Literary Conversation*. Cambridge: Cambridge University Press.

Butler, Judith. 1990. *Gender Trouble: Feminism and the Subversion of Identity*. New York: Routledge.

———. 1993a. *Bodies That Matter: On the Discursive Limits of "Sex."* New York: Routledge.

———. 1993b. "Endangered/Endangering: Schematic Racism and White Paranoia." In *Reading Rodney King/Reading Urban Uprising*, edited by R. Gooding-Williams. New York: Routledge, 15–22.

———. 1995. "Melancholy Gender/Refused Identification." In *Constructing Masculinity*, edited by Maurice Berger et al. New York: Routledge, 21–36.

———. 1997. *Excitable Speech*. New York: Routledge.

———. 1997. *The Psychic Life of Power: Theories in Subjection*. Palo Alto, CA: Stanford University Press.

———. 2004. *Precarious Life: The Power of Mourning and Violence*. New York: Verso.

———. 2008. "Violence, Non-violence: Sartre on Fanon." In *Race after Sartre*, edited by J. Judaken. Albany: State University of New York Press.

Campbell, James. 1991. *Talking at the Gates, A Life of James Baldwin*. London: Faber and Faber.

Cannon, Steve. 2001. "The Art of Romare Bearden: A Retrospective by Geoffrey Jacques." National Gallery of Art, Washington. www.tribes.org/web/2001/07/02/the-art-of-romare-bearden-a-retrospective-by-geoffrey-jacques.

Carbado, Devon W., Dwight A. McBride, and Donald Weise, eds. 2002. *Black Like Us: A Century of Lesbian, Gay and Bisexual African American Fiction*. San Francisco: Cleis Press.

Ceccatty, René de. 1994. *L'Accompagnement*. Paris: Gallimard.

Certeau, Michel de. 1987. *Histoire et psychanalyse entre science et fiction*. Paris: Gallimard.

Chambers, Leigh Ross. 1998. *Facing It: AIDS Diaries and the Death of the Author*. Ann Arbor: University of Michigan Press.

———. 2004. *Untimely Interventions: AIDS Writing, Testimonial, and the Rhetoric of Haunting*. Ann Arbor: University of Michigan Press.

Chénetier, Marc. 1989. *Au-delà du soupçon: la nouvelle fiction américaine de 1960 à nos jours*. Paris: Edition du Seuil.

———. 2005. "'Following strangers': Remarques sur la notion de 'recherche' en littérature contemporaine." In *Etats-Unis: Formes récentes de l'imagination littéraire (II)/"Recent American Letters,"* edited by Marc Chénetier, *Les Cahiers Charles V*, no. 38:5–19.

Cohen, Cathy J. 1999. *The Boundaries of Blackness: AIDS and the Breakdown of Black Politics*. Chicago: University of Chicago Press.

Constantine-Simms, Deloy, ed. 2001. *The Greatest Taboo: Homosexuality in Black Communities*. Los Angeles: Alyson Books.

Cooper, David. 1978. *The Language of Madness*. Harmondsworth, UK: Pelican Books.

Crimp, Douglas. 2004. *Melancholia and Moralism: Essays on AIDS and Queer Politics*. Cambridge, MA: MIT Press.

Cullen, Countee. 1929. *The Black Christ & Other Poems*. New York: Harper & Brothers.

Curry, Tommy J. 2017. *The Man-Not, Race Class, Genre, and the Dilemmas of Black Manhood*. Philadelphia, PA: Temple University Press.

Dagerman, Stig. 1952/1981. *Notre besoin de consolation est impossible à rassasier*. Arles, France: Actes Sud.

Dean, Tim, and Christopher Lane, eds. 2001. *Homosexuality and Psychoanalysis*. Chicago: University of Chicago Press.

Deleuze, Gilles. 1969. *Logique du sens*. Paris: Éditions de Minuit.

Depardieu, Benoît. 2003. "L''Interdit' or the 'Other' text in James Baldwin's 'Going to Meet the Man,'" *Journal of the Short Story in English* 40:109–20.

Derrida, Jacques. 1967/1998. *La Voix et le phénomène*. Paris: Presses Universitaires de France.

Dixon, Melvin. 1983. *Change of Territory*. Lexington: University of Kentucky Press.

———. 1987. *Ride Out the Wilderness: Geography and Identity in Afro-American Literature*. Urbana: University of Illinois Press.

———. 1991. *Vanishing Rooms*. New York: Plume.

———. 1995. *Love's Instruments*. Chicago: University of Chicago Press.

Douglass, Frederick. 1845/1967. *Narrative of the Life of Frederick Douglass, an American Slave, Written by Himself*. Cambridge, MA: Belknap Press of Harvard University.

———. 1895/1950. "Why Is the Negro Lynched." Philip Foner, ed. *Life and Writings of Frederick Douglass*, vol. 1. New York: International Publishers, 491–523.

Du Bois, W. E. B. 1903/1986. *The Souls of Black Folk*. In *Du Bois, Writings*, edited by N. Huggins. New York: Library of America, 347–57.

Duras, Marguerite. 1995. *Ecrire*. Paris: Gallimard.

Edelman, Lee. 1994. *Homographesis: Essays in Gay Literary and Cultural Theory*. New York: Routledge.

Ellison, Ralph. 1952. *Invisible Man*. New York: Penguin.

Fabre, Geneviève, and Robert O'Meally, eds. 1994. *History and Memory in African American Culture*. New York: Oxford University Press.

Fanon, Frantz. 1952. *Peau noire, masques blancs*. Paris: Éditions du Seuil.

———. 1961. *Les Damnés de la terre*. Paris: Maspero.

———. 2015. *Frantz Fanon: écrits sur l'aliénation et la liberté*, edited by Jean Khalfa and Robert Young. Paris: La Découverte.

Fassin, Didier, and Richard Rechtman. 2007. *L'Empire du traumatisme: enquête sur la condition de victime*. Paris: Flammarion.

Faulkner, William. 1931/1981. "Dry September." In V. S. Pritchett, ed. *The Oxford Book of Short Stories*. Oxford: Oxford University Press, 336–37.

———. *Light in August*. 1932/2011. New York: Knopf Doubleday.

Ferenczi, Sandor. 2006. *Le Traumatisme*. Paris: Petite Bibliothèque Payot.

Ferguson, Roderick. 2003. *Aberrations in Black: Toward a Queer of Color Critique*. Minneapolis: University of Minnesota Press.

Foucault, Michel. 1966. *Les Mots et les choses*. Paris: Gallimard.

———. 1976. *Histoire de la sexualité*, vol. 1, *La Volonté de savoir*. Paris: Gallimard.

———. 2001. *L'Herméneutique du sujet, Cours au Collège de France (1981–1982)*. Paris: Seuil/Gallimard.

Freud, Sigmund. 1899/1967. *L'Interprétation des rêves*, translated by I. Meyerson. Paris: Presses Universitaires de France.

———. 1905. *Three Essays on the Theory of Sexuality*, vol. 7, *The Standard Edition of the Complete Psychological Works of Sigmund Freud*, 77–145. London: Hogarth.

———. 1909. *Analysis of a Phobia in a Five-Year-Old Boy (Little Hans)*, vol. 10, *The Standard Edition of the Complete Psychological Works of Sigmund Freud*, 3–149. London: Hogarth.

———. 1914/1918. "From the History of an Infantile Neurosis," vol. 17, *The Standard Edition of the Complete Psychological Works of Sigmund Freud*, 3–124. London: Hogarth.

———. 1915. "Instincts and Their Vicissitudes," vol. 14, *The Standard Edition of the Complete Psychological Works of Sigmund Freud*, 109–40. London: Hogarth.

———. 1915. "The Unconscious," vol. 14, *The Standard Edition of the Complete Psychological Works of Sigmund Freud*, 159–215. London: Hogarth.

———. 1915/1968. *Métapsychologie*. Paris: Gallimard Folio Essais.

———. 1919. "The Uncanny," vol. 17, *The Standard Edition of the Complete Psychological Works of Sigmund Freud*, 217–56. London: Hogarth.

———. 1919/1933. "On bat un enfant," translated by Henri Hoesli. *Revue Française de Psychanalyse* VI, nos. 3–4:274–97.

———. 1920. "The Psychogenesis of a Case of Homosexuality in a Woman," vol. 18, *The Standard Edition of the Complete Psychological Works of Sigmund Freud*, 145–72. London: Hogarth.

———. 1930. *Civilization and Its Discontents*, vol. 21, *The Standard Edition of the Complete Psychological Works of Sigmund Freud*, 59–145. London: Hogarth.

———. 1953–1974. *The Standard Edition of the Complete Psychological Works of Sigmund Freud*, edited by James Strachey. 24 vols. London: Hogarth.

Freud, Sigmund, Sandor Ferenczi, and Karl Abraham. 1965. *Sur les névroses de guerre*, translated by Olivier Mannoni, Ilse Barande, Judith Dupont and Myriam Viliker. Paris: Petite Bibliothèque Payot.

Fuss, Diana. 1993. "Freud's Fallen Women: Identification, Desire, and 'A Case of Homosexuality in a Woman.'" In *Fear of a Queer Planet. Queer Politics and Social Theory*, edited by Michael Warner. Minneapolis: University of Minnesota Press.

Gambone, Philip. 1999. *Something Inside: Conversations with Gay Fiction Writers*. Madison: University of Wisconsin Press.

Garber, Linda. 2001. *Identity Poetics: Race, Class, and the Lesbian-feminists Roots of Queer Theory*. New York: Columbia University Press.

Gates, Henry Louis, Jr., ed. 1985. *"Race," Writing and Difference*. Chicago: University Press of Chicago.

———. 1986. "Talking That Talk," *Critical Inquiry* 13, no. 1:203–10.

———. 1987. *Figures in Black: Words, Signs and the "Racial" Self*. New York: Oxford University Press.

———. 1988. *The Signifying Monkey: A Theory of African-American Literary Criticism*. New York: Oxford University Press.

Gay, Judith. 1985. "'Mummies and Babies' and Friends and Lovers in Lesotho," *Journal of Homosexuality* 11, nos. 3–4:97–116.

Gevisser, Mark, and Edwin Cameron, eds. 1995. *Defiant Desire: Gay and Lesbian Lives in South Africa*. New York: Routledge.

Ghisoni, Dominique, ed. 1989. *Le bicentenaire et ces îles que l'on dit françaises*. Bastia/Paris: Scritti & Syllepse.

Gilman, Sander L. 1985. *Difference and Pathology: Stereotypes of Sexuality, Race and Madness*. Ithaca, NY: Cornell University Press.

———. 1993. *Freud, Race, and Gender*. Princeton, NJ: Princeton University Press.

Gilroy, Paul. 1993. *The Black Atlantic: Modernity and Double Consciousness*. Cambridge, MA: Harvard University Press.

Glave, Thomas. 2000. "(Re-)Recalling Essex Hemphill: Words to Our Now." *Callaloo* 23, no. 1:151–67.

Glissant, Edouard. 1990. *La Poétique de la relation*. Paris: Gallimard.

Gordon, Jane. 2014. *Creolizing Political Theory: Reading Rousseau through Fanon*. New York: Fordham University Press.

Gordon, Lewis R. 1995a. *Bad Faith and Antiblack Racism*. Atlantic Highlands, NJ: Humanities Press International.

———. 1995b. *Fanon and the Crisis of European Man: An Essay on Philosophy and the Human Sciences*. New York: Routledge.

———. 1997. *Her Majesty's Other Children: Sketches of Racism from a Neocolonial Age*. London: Rowman & Littlefield International.

———. 1999. "Douglass as an Existentialist." In *Frederick Douglass: A Critical Reader*, edited by Bill E. Lawson and Frank M. Kirkland. Malden, MA: Blackwell Publishers, 207–26.

———. 2006a. "African-American Philosophy, Race, and the Geography of Reason." In *Not Only the Master's Tools: African-American Studies in Theory and Practice*, edited by Lewis R. Gordon and Jane Anna Gordon. Boulder, CO: Paradigm Publishers, 3–50.

———. 2006b. *Disciplinary Decadence: Living Thought in Trying Times*. Boulder CO: Paradigm Publishers.

———. 2008. *An Introduction to Africana Philosophy*. Cambridge: Cambridge University Press.

———. 2015. *What Fanon Said. A Philosophical Introduction to His Life and Thought*. New York: Fordham University Press.

Gordon, Lewis R., and Jane Anna Gordon. 2006. *Not Only the Master's Tools: African-American Studies in Theory and Practice*, Boulder, CO: Paradigm Publishers.

Greenberg, David F. 1998. *The Construction of Homosexuality*. Chicago: University of Chicago Press.

Greene, Caroll. 1971. "Introductory essay to 'Romare Bearden: The Prevalence of Ritual.'" Museum of Modern Art, New York.

Griffith, Paul. 2002. "James Baldwin's Confrontation with Racist Terror in the American South: Sexual Mythology and Psychoneurosis in 'Going to Meet the Man,'" *Journal of Black Studies* 5, no. 32:506–27.

Gunkel, Henriette. 2008. "'What Do We See When We Look at Ourselves': Visual Dissidence towards (Post)Colonial Sex/Gender Organizations within Post-Apartheid South African Culture." In *Dissidence et identités plurielles*, edited by Jean-Paul Rocchi. Nancy, France: Presses Universitaires de Nancy, 160–85.

Hakutani, Yoshinobu. 2006. *Cross-cultural Visions in African American Modernism: From Spatial Narrative to Jazz Haiku*. Columbus: Ohio State University Press.

Harris, Lynn E, ed. 2005. *Freedom in this Village: Twenty-Five Years of Black Gay Men's Writing, 1979 to the Present*. New York: Carroll and Graf.

Harrison, Lori. 2000. "Melancholy Race: AIDS, Black Writing and the Pain of Grief," *Thymaris* 7.

Hartman, Saidiya V. 1997. *Scenes of Subjection: Terror, Slavery and Self-Making in 19th Century America*. New York: Oxford University Press.

Hemphill, Essex, ed. 1991. *Brother to Brother: New Writings by Black Gay Men*. Boston, MA: Alyson Publications.

———. 1992. *Ceremonies, Prose and Poetry*. New York: Plume.

———. 1995. "'In Living Color': Toms, Coons, Mammies, Faggots, and Bucks." In *Out in Culture: Gay, Lesbian and Queer Essays on Popular Culture*, edited by Corey K. Creekmur and Alexander Doty. Durham, NC: Duke University Press, 32–40.

Henning, Kristin. 2017. "The Role of Policing in the Socialization of Black Boys." In *Policing the Black Man*, edited by Angela J. Davis. New York: Pantheon Books, 57–94.

Henry, Paget. 2000. *Caliban's Reason*. New York: Routledge.

hooks, bell. 1991. *Yearning: Race, Gender, and Cultural Politics*. Boston, MA: South End Press.

———. 1992. *Black Looks, Race and Representation*. Boston, MA: South End Press.

Horsman, Reginald. 1981. *Race and Manifest Destiny: The Origin of Racial Anglo-Saxonism*. Cambridge, MA: Harvard University Press.

Horton, Randall, M. L. Hunter, and Becky Thompson. 2007. *Fingernails Across the Chalkboard: Poetry and Prose on HIV/AIDS from the Black Diaspora*. Chicago: Third World Press.

Hughes, Langston. 1949. "Silhouette." *One-Way Ticket*. New York: Alfred A. Knopf.

Johnson, Clarence Sholé. 2005. "(Re)Conceptualizing Blackness and Making Race Obsolescent." In *White on White, Black on Black*, edited by George Yancy. London: Rowman & Littlefield International, 173–202.

Johnson, Patrick E. 2005. *Black Queer Studies: A Critical Anthology*. Durham, NC: Duke University Press.

Johnson-Rouille, Cyraina. 1999. "(An)Other Modernism: James Baldwin, *Giovanni's Room*, and the Rhetoric of Flight," *MSF Modern Fiction Studies* 45, no. 4:932–56.

Jones, LeRoi. 1964. *Dutchman and the Slave*. New York: William Morrow.

Jones, Therese, ed. 1994. *Sharing the Delirium: Second Generation AIDS Plays and Performances*. Portsmouth, NH: Heinemann.

Joyce, Justin A., and Dwight A. McBride. 2006. *A Melvin Dixon Critical Reader*. Jackson: University Press of Mississippi.

Keller, Pascal-H. 2003. "A propos de quelques analogies du texte freudien." In *Homosexualités*, edited by Michèle Bertrand and Klio Bournova. *Revue Française de Psychanalyse*, vol. 67. Paris: Presses Universitaires de France, 287–97.

Kester, Norman G. 2000. *From Here to District Six: A South African Memoir with New Poetry, Prose and Other Writings*. Toronto: District Six Press.

———. 2002. *Liquid Love and Other Longings: Selected Poems*. Toronto: District Six Press.

Kincaid, Jamaica. 1997. *My Brother*. New York: Noonday Press.

Klein, Michael, ed. 1992. *Poets for Life: Seventy-Six Poets Respond to AIDS*. New York: George Braziller.

Korff-Sausse, Simone. 2006. "Préface." Sandor Ferenczi. *Le Traumatisme*. Paris: Petite Bibliothèque Payot.

Kristeva, Julia. "Un père est battu à mort." "The Dead Father: A Two-Day International Symposium, April 29–30, 2006, Low Library Rotunda Columbia University New York, NY." www.kristeva.fr/pere.html.

Krouse, Matthew, ed. 1993. *The Invisible Ghetto: Lesbian and Gay Writing from South Africa*. Johannesburg: Congress of South African Writers (COSAW).

Kruger, Steven F. 1996. *AIDS Narratives: Gender and Sexuality, Fiction and Science*. New York: Garland.

Kushner, Tony. 1989/2003. *Angels in America, Parts I and II*. New York: Theatre Communications Group.

Lane, Christopher, ed. 1998. *The Psychoanalysis of Race*. New York: Columbia University Press.

Leavy, Barbara Fass. 1992. *To Blight with Plague: Studies in a Literary Theme*. New York: New York University Press.

Le Cour Grandmaison, Olivier. 2009. *La République impériale: politique et racisme d'État*. Paris: Fayard.

Leeming, David. 1998. *Amazing Grace: A Life of Beauford Delaney*. New York: Oxford University Press.

Lejeune, Philippe. 1975. *Le Pacte autobiographique*. Paris: Éditions du Seuil.

Levine, Lawrence W. 1977. *Black Culture and Black Consciousness*. New York: Oxford University Press.

Long, Thomas L. 2005. *AIDS and American Apocalypticism: The Cultural Semiotics of an Epidemic*. Albany: State University of New York Press.

Maart, Rozena. 1991. "No Rosa, No District Six." *Fireweed: Feminist Journal*. Republished in *Journey Prize Anthology* 4 (1992). Toronto: McClelland & Stewart.

———. 1991. *Talk About It! From District Six to Lavender Hill.* Toronto: Awomandla! Publishers.

———. 1992/1993. "Consciousness, Knowledge and Morality: The Absence of the Knowledge of White Consciousness in Contemporary Feminist Theory." In *A Reader in Feminist Ethics,* edited by Debra Shogan. Toronto: Canadian Scholars Press, 129–68.

———. 2004. "No Rosa, No District Six." *Rosa's District 6.* Toronto: TSAR Publications, 1–14.

———. 2005. *The Politics of Consciousness: The Consciousness of Politics, When Black Consciousness Meets White Consciousness,* vol. 1, *The Interrogation of Writing.* Toronto: Awomandla! Publishers.

———. 2005. *The Politics of Consciousness: The Consciousness of Politics, When Black Consciousness Meets White Consciousness,* vol. 2, *The Interrogation of Speech and the Imagination.* Toronto: Awomandla! Publishers.

———. 2013. "Writing and the Relation: From Textual Coloniality to South African Black Consciousness." In *Black Intersectionalities: A Critique for the 21st Century,* edited by Monica Michlin and Jean-Paul Rocchi. Liverpool, UK: Liverpool University Press, 21–33.

Mannoni, Maud. 1979. *La Théorie comme fiction.* Paris: Éditions du Seuil.

May, Vivian M. 2000. "Reading Melvin Dixon's *Vanishing Rooms*: Experiencing 'The Ordinary Rope That Can Change in a Second to a Lyncher's Noose or a Rescue Line,'" *Callaloo* 23, no. 1:366–81.

McBride, Dwight A., and Jennifer DeVere Brody. 2000. "*Plum Nelly: New Essays in Black Queer Studies:* Introduction," *Callaloo* 23, no. 1:285–88.

Meyer, Richard. 2002. *Outlaw Representation: Censorship and Homosexuality in Twentieth-Century American Art.* Boston, MA: Beacon Press.

Michlin, Monica, and Jean-Paul Rocchi, eds. 2014. *Black Intersectionalities: A Critique for the 21st Century.* Liverpool, UK: Liverpool University Press.

Mijolla, Alain de. 2002. *Dictionnaire international de psychanalyse,* Paris: Calmann-Levy.

———. 2004. *Préhistoires de famille.* Paris: Presses Universitaires de France.

Misrahi, Robert. 1991. *La Problématique du sujet aujourd'hui.* Paris: Encre marine.

Mitchell, Koritha. 2013. "Love in Action: Noting Similarities between Lynching Then and Anti-LGBT Violence Now," *Callaloo* 36, no. 3:688–717.

Monette, Paul. 1988a. *Borrowed Time: An AIDS Memoir.* Orlando, FL: Harvest Books.

———. 1988b. *Love Alone: 18 Elegies for Rog.* New York: St. Martin Press.

Moore, Patrick. 2004. *Beyond Shame: Reclaiming the Abandoned History of Radical Gay Sexuality.* Boston, MA: Beacon Press.

Morrison, Toni. 1970. *The Bluest Eye.* London: Picador.

———. 1987. *Beloved.* London: Pan Books.

———. 1992. *Playing in the Dark: Whiteness and the Literary Imagination.* Cambridge, MA: Harvard University Press.

Murphy, Timothy F., and Poirier, Suzanne, eds. 1993. *Writing AIDS: Gay Literature, Language and Analysis.* New York: Columbia University Press.

Nelson, Emmanuel S., ed. 1992. *AIDS: The Literary Response.* New York: Twayne Publishers.

———. 1993. *Critical Essays: Gay and Lesbian Writers of Color.* New York: Harrington Park Press.

Nero, Charles I. 1991. "Toward a Black Gay Aesthetic: Signifying in Contemporary Black Gay Literature." In *Brother to Brother: New Writings by Black Gay Men,* edited by Essex Hemphill. Boston, MA: Alyson Publications.

North, Michael. 1994. *The Dialect of Modernism. Race, Language, and Twentieth-Century Literature.* New York: Oxford University Press.

Pastore, Judith Laurence, ed. 1993. *Confronting AIDS through Literature: The Responsibilities of Representation.* Urbana: University of Illinois Press.

Pavlic, Edward Michael. 2002. *Crossroads Modernism: Descent and Emergence in African-American Literary Culture.* Minneapolis: University of Minnesota Press.

Powell, Richard J. 1997. *Black Art and Culture in the 20th Century.* New York: Thames and Hudson.

Raynaud, Claudine, ed. 2013. *La Renaissance de Harlem et l'art nègre*. Paris: Michel Houdiard.

Reed, Paul. 1984. *Facing It*. San Francisco: Gay Sunshine Press.

Reid-Pharr, Robert. 2001. *Black Gay Man*. New York: New York University Press.

Ricœur, Paul. 2004. *Parcours de la reconnaissance: trois études*. Paris: Éditions Stock.

Roberts, Frank Leon, and Marvin K. White, eds. 2006. *If We Have to Take Tomorrow: HIV, Black Men and Same Sex Desire*. Los Angeles: Institute for Gay Men's Health.

Rocchi, Jean-Paul. 1999. "'*In the darkening gleam of the window-pane*': la parole homosexuelle face au signe noir dans *Giovanni's Room* de James Baldwin." *AFRAM Revue/Review*, no. 49:4–9.

———. 2001a. "James Baldwin: écriture et identité." Doctoral thesis. Université Paris IV-Sorbonne.

———. 2001b. "'That kaleidoscopic word, a man': enjeux et stratégies de la représentation d'une masculinité noire et gay chez James Baldwin." In *Self Portraits/Images de soi*, edited by Frédéric Ogée, *INTERFACES/Word and Image*, no. 18:119–34.

———. 2001c. "Baldwin ou les spores perdues de l'Amérique: conscience de l'origine et origine de la conscience." In *Écritures et représentations des diasporas*, edited by Bénédicte Alliot and Geneviève Fabre, *Cahiers Charles V*, no. 31:141–60.

———. 2003. "Psychanalyse." In *Dictionnaire des cultures gays et lesbiennes*, edited by Didier Eribon. Paris: Larousse, 385–87.

———. 2004a. "'Whose little boy are you?' l'anti-essentialisme de James Baldwin et le nationalisme noir-américain." In *Nationalismes, régionalismes: survivances du romantisme?* edited by Michel Feith. Nantes, France: Université de Nantes-CRINI, 186–98.

———. 2004b. "Baldwin, *l'homotextualité* et les identités plurielles: une rencontre à l'avant-garde," *La Revue LISA/LISA e-journal*, http://www.unicaen.fr/mrsh/anglais/lisa.

———. 2004c. "Le 'sang-mêlé,' le fantasme et l'homosexualité: étude d'une analogie freudienne à trois termes." In *Sang impur*, edited by Michel Prum. Paris: L'Harmattan, 203–31.

———. 2005. "Landmarks for a Study on Violence, Madness and the Cultural Trope of American Interracial Sadomasochism." In *Tuer l'Autre*, edited by Michel Prum et al. Paris: L'Harmattan, 159–68.

———. 2006a. "'*Walls as Words as Weapons as Womb as Woooooow*'; Fente murale, fente t/sex(u)[elle], fondu identitaire: Jouir/écrire ou la post-identité dans 'No Rosa, No District Six' de Rozena Maart." In *Images de soi dans les sociétés postcoloniales. Actes du colloque de l'Université des Antilles et de la Guyane*, edited by Patricia Donatien-Yssa. Paris: Éditions Le Manuscrit, 179–215. Translated by Joelle Theubet and published as "Intersecting Identities and Epistemologies in Rozena Maart's 'No Rosa, No District Six,'" in *Postcoloniality-Decoloniality-Black Critique: Joints and Fissures*, edited by Sabine Broeck and Carsten Junker. Frankfurt: Campus Verlag (2014): 369–88.

———. 2006b. "'*The Evidence of Things Not Seen, The Substance of Things Hoped For*': *Vanishing Rooms* de Melvin Dixon ou le racisme intimement." In *L'Objet identité: épistémologie et transversalité*, edited by Jean-Paul Rocchi, *Cahiers Charles V*, no. 40:291–308.

———. 2006c. "'The Other Bites the Dust.' La mort de l'Autre: vers une épistémologie de l'identité." In *L'Objet identité: épistémologie et transversalité*, edited by Jean-Paul Rocchi, *Cahiers Charles V*, no. 40:9–46.

———. 2007a. "'*Preservation of Ignorance*'; The Lack and the Absence: Self-Reflexivity and the Queering of African American and Diasporic Research." In *Blackness and Sexualities*, edited by Antje Schuhmann and Michelle M. Wright. Berlin: LitVerlag, 15–27.

———. 2007b. "Littérature africaine américaine et *dés*-écriture de l'identité." Document de synthèse de l'Habilitation à Diriger des Recherches, Université Paris-Diderot.

———. 2008a. "Littérature et métapsychanalyse de la race (Après et avec Fanon)." In *Vers une pensée politique postcoloniale. A partir de Frantz Fanon*, edited by Sonia Dayan-Herzbrun, *Tumultes*, no. 31:125–44. Translated by Joelle Theubet and published as "Literature and the Meta-Psychoanalysis of Race (After and With Fanon)," in *Palimpsest, A Journal on Women, Gender, and the Black International* 1, no. 1 (2012):52–67.

———. 2008b. "'Writing as I Lay Dying'; AIDS Literature and the Death of Identity." In *Genre(s)* edited by Frédéric Regard, *Etudes Anglaises*. Paris: Klincksieck/Didier Érudition 61, no. 2:350–58.

———. 2008c. "Sur la dissidence et la pluralité: une introduction." In *Dissidence et identités plurielles*, edited by Jean-Paul Rocchi. Nancy, France: Presses Universitaires de Nancy, 7–23.

———. 2009. "Dying Metaphors and Deadly Fantasies: Freud, Baldwin and Race as Intimacy." In *Historicizing Anti-Semitism*, edited by Lewis R. Gordon, Ramon Grosfoguel, and Eric Mielants, *Human Architecture. Journal of the Sociology of Self-Knowledge* VII, no. 2:159–78.

———. 2012. "'*Native Sons, Creative Friends, and Lovers*'; Le James Baldwin de Sol Stein ou les *dé-liaisons* dangereuses: une enquête épistolaire, éditoriale et psychanalytique." In *Lettres noires*, edited by Claudine Raynaud. Montpellier, France: Presses Universitaires de la Méditerranée, 147–57.

———. 2015. "*The Word's Image*—Self-Portrait as a Conscious Lie." In *Black Europe*: *Subjects, Struggles, and Shifting Perceptions*, edited by Jean-Paul Rocchi and Frédéric Sylvanise, *Palimpsest: A Journal on Women, Gender, and the Black International* 4, 2:225–34.

———, ed. 2016. *L'art de la discipline: disciples, disciplines, transdisciplinarité*, *Quaderna* 3, www.quaderna.org.

———. 2016. *Ce qui compte*. In *On Contemplation*, edited by Myron M. Beasley, *Liminalities, A Journal of Performance Studies* 12, no, 2. http://liminalities.net/12-2/cequicompte.html.

Rocchi, Jean-Paul, Anne Crémieux, and Xavier Lemoine, eds. 2013. *Understanding Blackness through Performance: Contemporary Arts and the Representation of Identity*. New York: Palgrave Macmillan.

Rocchi, Jean-Paul, and Frédéric Sylvanise, eds. 2015. *Black Europe: Subjects, Struggles, and Shifting Perceptions. Palimpsest, A Journal on Women, Gender, and the Black International* 4, no. 2.

Romanet, Jerome de, and Melvin Dixon. 2000. "A Conversation with Melvin Dixon," *Callaloo* 23, no. 1:84–109.

Ross, Marlon B. 2004. *Manning the Race: Reforming Black Men in the Jim Crow Era*. New York: New York University Press.

———. 2013. "'What's Love but a Second-Hand Emotion,' Man-on-Man Passion in the Contemporary Black Gay Romance Novel," *Callaloo* 36, no. 3:669–87.

Rossignol, Marie-Jeanne. 2000. "Quelle(s) discipline(s) pour la civilisation." In *Civilisation américaine: problématiques et questionnements*, edited by Marianne Debouzy, Pierre Gervais, Hubert Perrier. *Revue Française d'Etudes Américaines*, no. 83.

Roudinesco, Elisabeth, and Michel Plon. 1997. *Dictionnaire de la psychanalyse*. Paris: Fayard.

Saint, Assotto. 1992. *Here to Dare: 10 Gay Black Poets*. New York: Galiens Press.

———. 1996. *Spells of a Voodoo Doll*. New York: Richard Kasak Book Edition.

Savran, David. 1988. *Taking It Like a Man: White Masculinity, Masochism and Contemporary American Culture*. Princeton, NJ: Princeton University Press.

Scarry, Elaine. 1985. *The Body in Pain: The Making and Unmaking of the World*. New York: Oxford University Press.

Schuhmann, Antje. 2013. "Postcolonial Backlashes: Transgender in the Public Eye." In *Black Intersectionalities: A Critique for the 21st Century*, edited by Monica Michlin and Jean-Paul Rocchi. Liverpool, UK: Liverpool University Press, 36–50.

Searles, Harold. 1977. *L'Effort pour rendre l'autre fou*, translated by Brigitte Bost. Paris: Gallimard.

Secretan, Philippe. 1984. *L'Analogie*. Paris: Presses Universitaires de France.

Sedgewick, Eve Kosofsky, ed. 1997. *Novel Gazing: Queer Readings in Fiction*. Durham, NC: Duke University Press.

Seshadri-Crooks, Kalpana. 1998. "The Comedy of Domination: Psychoanalysis and the Conceit of Whiteness." In *The Psychoanalysis of Race*, edited by Christopher Lane. New York: Columbia University Press, 353–79.

Sibony, Daniel. 1991. *Entre-deux: l'origine en partage*. Paris: Éditions du Seuil.

Sollors, Werner. 1997. *Neither Black Nor White Yet Both: Thematic Explorations of Interracial Literature*. Cambridge, MA: Harvard University Press.

Somerville, Siobhan. 2000. *Queering the Color Line: Race and the Invention of Homosexuality in American Culture*. Durham, NC: Duke University Press.

Sontag, Susan. 1989. *AIDS and Its Metaphors*. New York: Farrar, Straus and Giroux.

———. 2003/2004. *Regarding the Pain of Others*. New York: Picador.

Soutif, Daniel. 2017. "La marche des artistes: Romare Bearden, Elizabeth Catlett, Norman Lewis, Reginald A. Gammon Jr., Alma Thomas." In *The Color Line: Les Artistes africains-américains et la ségrégation 1865–2016*, edited by Daniel Soutif. Paris: Flammarion/Musée du Quai Branly Jacques Chirac, 282–95.

Spillers, Hortense J. 1996. "'All the Things You Could Be by Now If Sigmund Freud's Wife Was Your Mother': Psychoanalysis and Race," *Critical Inquiry* 23, no. 4:710–34.

———. 2003. *Black, White and in Color: Essays on American Literature and Culture*. Chicago: University of Chicago Press.

Spurlin, William J. 2001. "Broadening Postcolonial Studies/Decolonizing Queer Studies: Emerging 'Queer' Identities and Cultures in Southern Africa." In *Post-Colonial, Queer. Theoretical Intersections*, edited by John C. Hawley. Albany: State University of New York Press, 185–206.

Stein, Marc, ed. 2004. *Encyclopedia of Lesbian, Gay, Bisexual, and Transgendered History in America*. New York: Charles Scribner's Sons.

Stevenson, Bryan. 2017. "A Presumption of Guilt: The Legacy of America's History of Racial Injustice." In *Policing the Black Man*, edited by Angela J. Davis. New York: Pantheon Books.

Steward, Douglas. 1999. "Saint's Progeny: Assotto Saint, Gay Black Poets, and Poetic Agency in the Field of the Queer Symbolic," *African American Review* 33, no. 3:507–18.

Stockton, Kathryn Bond. 2006. *Beautiful Bottom, Beautiful Shame: Where "Black" Meets "Queer."* Durham, NC: Duke University Press.

Stoller, Robert J. 1975/1978. *La Perversion: forme érotique de la haine*, translated by Hélène Couturier. Paris: Petite Bibliothèque Payot.

Sundquist, Eric J. 1993. *To Wake the Nations: Race in the Making of American Literature*. Cambridge, MA: Belknap Press of Harvard University.

Supiot, Alain, et al. 2001. *Pour une politique des sciences de l'Homme et de la société. Recueil des travaux (1998–2000) du Conseil national du développement des sciences humaines et sociales*. Paris: Presses Universitaires de France.

Todorov, Tzvetan. 1985. "'Race,' Writing, and Culture." In *"Race," Writing and Difference*, edited by Henry Louis Gates Jr. Chicago: University of Chicago Press, 370–80.

Toomer, Jean. 1923/1988. *Cane*. New York: Norton.

Varet, Gilles. 1973. *Racisme et philosophie*. Paris: Denoël.

Wallace, Maurice. 2002. *Constructing the Black Masculine: Identity and Ideality in African American Men's Literature and Culture*. Durham, NC: Duke University Press.

Weeks, Jeffrey. 1995. *Invented Moralities: Sexual Values in an Age of Uncertainty*. New York: Columbia University Press.

Weinberg, Jonathan. 2004. *Male Desire: The Homoerotic in American Art*. New York: Harry N. Abrams.

Weldon Johnson, James. 1924. *Lynching: America's National Disgrace*. New York: NAACP.

Wells, Ida B. 1893/1999. "Lynch Law." In Ida B. Wells and Frederick Douglass, Irvine Garland Penn, and Ferdinand Barnett, *The Reason Why the Colored American Is Not in the World's Columbian Exposition: The Afro-American Contribution to Columbian Literature*, edited by Robert W. Rydell. Urbana: University of Illinois Press, 29–43.

West, Cornel. 1993a. *Keeping Faith: Philosophy and Race in America*. New York: Routledge.

———. 1993b. *Race Matters*. New York: Vintage Books.

Whitmore, George. 1989. *Someone Was Here: Profiles in the AIDS Epidemic*. New York: Plume.

Wojnarowicz, David. 1991. *Tongues of Flames*, edited by Barry Blinderman. Normal: University Galleries Illinois State University/New York: Distributed Art Publishers.

———. 1991/1992. *Close to the Knives: A Memoir of Disintegration*. London: Serpent's Tail.

————. 1998a. *In the Shadow of the American Dream: The Diaries of David Wojnarowicz*. New York: Grove Press.

————. 1998b. *Fever: The Art of David Wojnarowicz*. New York: Rizzoli International Publications.

Woubshet, Dagmawi. 2015. *The Calendar of Loss: Race, Sexuality, and Mourning in the Early Era of AIDS*. Baltimore, MD: Johns Hopkins University Press.

Wright, Michelle M. 2004. *Becoming Black*. Durham, NC: Duke University Press.

Wright, Richard. 1940/1993. *Native Son*. New York: Harper Perennial.

————. 1944. "The Man Who Lived Underground." In *Richard Wright Reader*, edited by Ellen Wright and Michel Fabre. New York: Harper.

————. 1945/2000. *Black Boy*. London: Vintage.

Yancy, George, ed. 1998. *African-American Philosophers, 17 Conversations*. New York: Routledge.

Yang, Suzanne. 1998. "A Question of Accent: Ethnicity and Transference." In *The Psychoanalysis of Race*, edited by Christopher Lane. New York: Columbia University Press, 139–53.

————. 2001. "Speaking of the Surface: The Texts of Kaposi's Sarcoma." In *Homosexuality and Psychoanalysis*, edited by Tim Dean and Christopher Lane. Chicago: University of Chicago Press, 322–48.

Young, Robert J. C. 1995. *Colonial Desire: Hybridity in Theory, Culture and Race*. New York: Routledge.

Žižek, Slavoj. 1998. "Love Thy Neighbor? No, Thanks!" In *The Psychoanalysis of Race*, edited by Christopher Lane. New York: Columbia University Press, 154–75.

Index

Africa, 15, 27, 74, 91, 101, 134, 137, 138, 143, 149
African(s), 68, 69, 73–74
African American(s), 1, 12, 18, 23, 52, 121, 135, 136, 137
African American/black studies, 12, 33, 34, 40
African American literature, xi, 4–7, 8–9, 10, 12–19, 113–114, 115, 116, 123, 135; feminist, 3; modernist, 49–61
Ahmed, Sara, 44, 45
AIDS (Acquired Immune Deficiency Syndrome), 5–7, 18–21, 107–108, 109, 110, 119–140
Algeria, 145, 148
Apel, Dora, 52
Appiah, K. Anthony, 15, 154n7
auto-ethnography, 8, 151

Baker, Houston, Jr., 25, 28, 35, 42, 50, 59, 60
Baldwin, James, ix, x, 1, 2, 5, 7, 9, 23–24, 32, 49–61, 63, 66–67, 73–79, 84, 87–88, 89, 91, 109, 113, 114, 116, 117, 121, 133, 134, 138, 146, 147, 148, 151, 157n1; on black, 73–77, 81; and castration, 75–76; on femininity and masculinity, 14; on race and sexuality, 11–12, 17, 32, 43, 77–78; on sadomasochistic trope of interracial relations, 110; un-writing identity of,

10–21; white male characters of, 81
Bayard, Pierre, 17, 83–84, 89
Beam, Joseph, 92, 113, 120, 122, 125
Bearden, Romare, 52, 56
Bersani, Leo, 42, 80, 85, 86
Biko, Steve, 87–88, 157n2, 158n7
black(s), x, 2, 4–5, 6–7, 8, 11, 13, 14, 17, 23, 27, 34–35, 38, 44–46, 73–77, 78–80, 107, 132–133, 134, 135–140, 143, 155n14
black consciousness, 2, 7, 11, 17, 19, 21, 37, 44, 87–89, 91–105, 121, 132, 157n2, 158n7
Black Panther Party, 14
body, 9, 16, 44, 52, 88, 103, 110, 118, 119–120, 129, 130, 138, 139, 157n2
Boyarin, Daniel, 65–66, 68, 71, 87
Broeck, Sabine, 156n26
Budick Miller, Emily, 154n6, 155n18
Butler, Judith, 70, 71, 79, 85, 86, 122, 154n7

Cameron, Edwin, 101
Cameroon, 8, 143
Campbell, James, 49, 55
Cannon, Steve, 56
Caribbean, xi, 46, 143, 152
Caribbean Philosophical Association, ix, 43
castration, xi, 4, 50, 51, 52, 53, 57, 58, 68, 69–70, 71, 72, 75–77, 78, 80, 92

queer, 13, 17, 45, 46, 101, 158n7;
  criticism, 20, 84–85, 86–87; critics, 8,
  16, 70; literature, 67, 93, 107, 108,
  120–121; studies, 2, 3, 12, 83; theory,
  18, 44, 86, 87, 88

racism, 4–5, 6–7, 21, 27, 44, 65, 71, 81–82,
  84, 88, 96, 107–118, 137, 140; among
  white gay men and lesbians, 107–108,
  109; anthropological, 15; anti-, 46;
  antiblack, 13, 45, 68, 79–80, 125;
  biological, 15, 32, 72; experience of,
  31, 39, 42, 49; imagined parallel world
  of, 13; "institutionalized," 34, 149;
  internalized, 125; as "limitation of
  thought," 32; logic of, 79–80;
  sadomasochistic, 115; sexual
  dimensions of, 125; as social pathology,
  11–12; transnational, 31; visibly
  indulging, 71
rape, 7, 53, 54, 56, 57, 73, 75, 76, 79, 110,
  111, 130, 131
Rechtman, Richard, 59
Reed, Paul, 127, 131
Ricœur, Paul, 38, 156n22
Riggs, Marlon T., 113, 135
Rimbaud, Arthur, 128–129
Rocchi, Jean-Paul, ix–xi, 51, 53, 85, 87
Rossignol, Marie-Jeanne, 31
Roudinesco, Elisabeth, 55, 59

Sade, Marquis de, 5
sadomasochism, 77–83, 107–109, 116
Saint, Assotto, 13, 18, 19, 92, 107, 109,
  122, 124–125, 126–127
Salmon, Colin, 147
Scarry, Elaine, 80, 119
Searles, Harold, 36
Senghor, Leopold Sedar, 14
Seshadri-Crooks, Kalpana, 65
Shelley, Mary, x
slavery, 13, 15, 28, 29, 35, 51, 52, 71–72,
  75, 79, 92, 108, 109, 136, 143, 148,
  150, 155n17
sociogeny, 44
Sollors, Werner, 27–29, 39

Sontag, Susan, 20
South Africa, 16, 91–105, 108, 157n2,
  158n3, 158n6–158n7
Soutif, Daniel, 52, 56
Spurlin, William J., 102
Stevenson, Bryan, 52
Stoller, Robert J., 52
subjectivity, 1, 4, 8, 10, 11, 12, 18, 19,
  34–35, 37, 40, 41, 43, 49, 61, 63–64,
  65, 70, 71, 87, 88, 92, 109, 135, 158n4;
  black, 67; inter-, x, 16, 50, 59–60, 81;
  non-, 3
Sundquist, Eric J., 28
Supiot, Alain, 25–26, 154n5

Todorov, Tzvetan, 26–27, 29
Toomer, Jean, 29
transdisciplinarity, 10, 42, 44, 45

vagina, 104, 142
Varet, Gilles, 32, 39, 154n13
violence, 5, 9, 20, 25, 45, 49, 50, 51–56,
  75–76, 77–78, 79, 80, 81, 95, 96, 108,
  114–115, 118, 125, 158n6

Weeks, Jeffrey, 119
Weldon Johnson, James, 52
Wells, Ida B., 52
West, Cornel, 110, 155n14
white consciousness, 11, 16, 73, 81, 87, 88,
  156n26
"white Negro," 134
Whitmore, George, 18, 122–123, 127, 132
Wilde, Oscar, 1
Wojnarowicz, David, 7, 18, 20–21, 120,
  121, 122, 123–124, 125–126, 127–129,
  130, 131, 133–134, 138
Wright, Richard, x, 14, 110, 114, 117, 118

X, Malcolm, 29

Yancy, George, 16
Yang, Suzanne, 138, 139

Žižek, Slavoj, 71, 78, 82, 140

CPSIA information can be obtained
at www.ICGtesting.com
Printed in the USA
LVHW041322020622
720250LV00004B/74